Praise for *Coaching for Breakthrough Success*

"Canfield and Chee have crafted the standard for anyone wanting to be an effective coach. Their actionable and timeless wisdom shows up through principles, questions, quotes, cases, and tools that will enable any aspiring coach to achieve their aspirations. Anyone being coached should make sure that their coach knows and follows these standards."

—Dave Ulrich,
professor, Ross School of Management, University of Michigan,
author of *Leadership Sustainability*

"*Coaching for Breakthrough Success* masterfully shares extremely powerful questions, the heart of professional coaching approaches. The Situational Coaching Model combined with the wonderfully long, and comprehensive list in many chapters will dramatically inform your coaching and empower your clients. This is a 'must have' for any professional coach who wants to take their clients to new heights of understanding and transform their effectiveness. Extremely well done!"

—Thomas G. Crane,
author of *The Heart of Coaching: Using Transformational Coaching to Create a High Performance Coaching Culture*

"*Coaching for Breakthrough Success* is the most exciting and innovative book on the art of coaching to come along in years. Using their Six Paradigms of Situational Coaching, Canfield and Chee show step by step how anyone, anywhere can assist others in improving performance, and achieving personal satisfaction in life."

—Robert B. Tucker,
innovation expert and author of *Innovation is Everybody's Business*

"This powerful, practical book gives you the tools and strategies you need to be an excellent business and executive coach, to help your clients in every area, and to build your coaching business profitably."

—Brian Tracy,
author of over 58 books in 38 languages

"After years of working as an executive coach, I slowly came to the realization that knowing *the answers* to the tough questions wasn't as important as knowing *the right questions to ask* in the first place. This book provides just such resources. Read it and enter the pantheon of great coaches!"

—Kerry Patterson,
four-time *New York Times* bestselling author of *Crucial Conversations*

"The ability to coach is the very essence of effective leaders. Engaging the heart and inspiring the mind will unlock the utmost potential of people in any organisation. This book puts it all together and provides proven techniques to achieve breakthrough performance. I believe it will have a profound impact on you as it has done for me and my organisation."

—Thomas Soo,
General Manager, Intel Technology

"Coaching is one of those terms that is thrown around on nearly a daily basis in modern management circles. But what does coaching mean? What should people do to make coaching effective? Why is coaching so valuable? These otherwise vague questions are insightfully answered in this outstanding book."

—William J. Rothwell, PhD, SPHR,
professor, The Pennsylvania State University and author of over 80 books

"*Coaching for Breakthrough Success* contains practical techniques to help you engage the hearts and minds of your people and inspire them to realize their fullest potential."

—Christopher Goh Soon Keat,
Director, Global Learning and Leadership Development,
Agilent Technologies Singapore (International) Pte Ltd

"*Coaching for Breakthrough Success* has had a profound effect on me, as well as the people in my workplace. My team has told me that since studying Jack and Peter's book I have become a better listener, communicator and leader. The decisions we now make are *our* decisions, and my staff are taking more ownership of the work they do. My career development has come on leaps and bounds after I applied what I learned from this book."

—Nick Jonsson,
General Director, Sophie Paris

Coaching

for

Breakthrough
Success

Proven Techniques for
Making the
Impossible Dreams Possible

Jack Canfield and Peter Chee

New York   Chicago   San Francisco   Athens   London
Madrid   Mexico City   Milan   New Delhi
Singapore   Sydney   Toronto

1 2 3 4 5 6 7 8 9 0   DOC/DOC   1 9 8 7 6 5 4 3

ISBN: 978-0-07-180463-9
MHID: 0-07-180463-3

e-ISBN: 978-0-07-180464-6
e-MHID: 0-07-180464-1

Library of Congress Cataloging-in-Publication Data

Canfield, Jack.
    Coaching for breakthrough success : proven techniques for making
    impossible dreams possible / by Jack Canfield and Peter Chee.
       p.cm.
    ISBN-13:   978-0-07-180463-9 (hardback)
    ISBN-10:   0-07-180463-3 (hardback)
    1. Personal coaching.   2. Executive coaching.   3. Success.
    4. Success in business.   I. Chee, Peter.   II. Title.
    BF637.P36C36 2012
    658.3'124—dc23   2012032962

This book is dedicated to

Jack Canfield's family:
Inga, Travis, Riley, Christopher, Oran and Kyle

Peter Chee's wife and daughter:
Eunice and Adelina

Peter Chee's parents and siblings:
Thomas, Agnes, Maria, Kathleen and Rita

CONTENTS

PART III
ACHIEVERS COACHING TECHNIQUES (ACT)

ACKNOWLEDGMENTS

The completion of this book marks the realization of another one of our breakthrough goals.

We would like to thank the following teams who have helped in many ways to make this vision a reality:

The passionate team at the Canfield Training World for inspiring and empowering people and organization to live their highest vision in the context of love and joy.

The talented multinational team at ITD World all across Asia for their dedication to excellence from conceptualization to completion of this project.

The impeccable design and development team at McGraw-Hill Education for masterfully executing the publication of this book.

The families of Jack Canfield, Peter Chee, Angelina Cheong, and Serely Alcaraz for their constant love, support and inspiration.

INTRODUCTION

We welcome you to the fulfilling and rewarding world of coaching. You have in your hands a book that will help you make a profound difference in the lives of the people you coach, and in the process of coaching people to achieve breakthrough success, you will also grow tremendously and your life will be deeply enriched.

This book is not for those who want to be ordinary coaches. It is a book devoted to all those who want to become *great* coaches for others and support people in realizing their dreams.

Have you ever shared your dream with others and had people laugh at it or say that it was impossible? We have, but because we believed strongly in our dreams and we had great coaches who worked with us and believed in us, we have been able to achieve much more than we ever could have on our own. We want to share with you our own stories that relate to coaching.

Jack Canfield's Story

Jack grew up in Wheeling, West Virginia, where his father made $8,000 a year working in a florist's shop. His father was a workaholic and his mother was an alcoholic. Jack had to work summers instead of vacationing in order to help his parents make ends meet. He was able to attend college on a scholarship where he earned money to pay for his books, clothes, and dates by serving breakfast in one of the college dorms.

Later during graduate school, when he ran out of money, he ate what he later called his "21 cent dinners": tomato paste, a sprinkle of garlic salt, and an 11 cent bag of spaghetti noodles. His life back then was not what one would call a picture of success. He was more concerned about surviving and getting through the day than with chasing his dreams.

A few years after graduate school, things started to change when he met W. Clement Stone, a self-made multimillionaire who became his coach and mentor. Stone hired Jack to work in his foundation, where he was coached in the fundamental success principles on which he still operates today.

One of Jack's lifelong dreams was to become an accomplished author. When he and his friend Mark Victor Hansen came up with the idea of the *Chicken Soup for the Soul* series of books, people said, "You must be dreaming. This will never work." When the first manuscript was completed, more than 140 publishers turned it down. Most people would have given up, but fortunately Jack and his coauthor continued to coach and encourage each other. As well, they sought out coaching from others; they persisted until 18 months later a publisher decided to take their book. Today there are more than 200 *Chicken Soup for the Soul* books, and the series has sold more than 125 million books in more than 40 languages around the world.

Throughout his career, Jack has benefited tremendously from coaching. He has passed on the gift to the thousands of people whom he and his organization coaches. Through his coaching programs he has witnessed many amazing transformations in people: clients have overcome lifelong phobias, self-destructive habits, and limiting beliefs; people who were once broke have become multimillionaires; people who were lost and depressed have discovered their passions, subsequently positively impacting thousands of lives. Such has been the impact of coaching in Jack Canfield's life.

Dr. Peter Chee's Story

When Peter was 11 years old, Thomas Chee, his father, asked him about his dream for life. That was one of the earliest coaching questions he ever heard, and it came from his father. After several coaching conversations, his father asked if he would like to write down his dreams. He agreed, and on a piece of paper he wrote that he wanted to be a doctor of management; he wanted to train managers and travel to countries all over the world; he wished to be a CEO of a multinational corporation; and he wanted to become well known in the field of learning and development.

At the age of 11, Peter was very mischievous and playful. He was consistently at the bottom of his class. His teachers mentioned that he was a slow learner, careless, and lacked abilities. They said he was embarrassed by his own lack of progress. His friends and teachers felt that he was "building castles in the air," and his dreams appeared impossible to achieve.

Today, when we look at the piece of paper on which he wrote his dreams, we notice that he has fulfilled all of his dreams plus much more. He has become an innovative author and one of the world's best trainers and coaches who has impacted the lives of leaders from more than 80 countries in the world. He lives with his lovely wife Eunice and their adorable daughter Adel in their dream home close by the sea and the hills on a beautiful island. When we study his life, we find that the three most outstanding factors behind his success are unrelenting motivation to succeed, unusual clarity of his goals, and continuously learning from the best in different fields.

When he was growing up he cultivated success habits through coaching and training. He has been truly blessed to have had many people who trained and coached him including his father and some of the world's leading gurus: John Maxwell, Brian Tracy, Anthony Robins, William Rothwell, Robert Tucker, and Jack Canfield.

Peter Chee and Jack Canfield's stories are just two of the many coaching success stories from all over the world that you will read about in this book.

In *Coaching for Breakthrough Success*, we want to share with you the mindset and practices of a great coach. We want to show how by applying these principles you can make a phenomenal difference in adding value to people's lives. Throughout this book, when we use the word "client," we are referring to the person you are coaching, regardless of how you are connected. When you apply coaching not only in the workplace, but also with your customers, friends, and family who are open to being coached, the benefits you will derive are tremendous.

Coaching, in a nutshell, is an empowering process of drawing out solutions from people through effective listening, asking great questions, using feedback, appreciating and continuously supporting people to take ownership, and be accountable for taking action to realize their goals.

Part I of this book deals with The Coaching Principles (TCP), symbolized by the *heart of a coach* model. This forms a solid foundation for life, impacting values, beliefs, and philosophies that permeate successful coaching relationships. When we analyzed existing coaching books, we realized that the core principles of coaching have not been sufficiently elaborated in a coherent manner. *Coaching for Breakthrough Success* is the first book to deliver 30 of the most important coaching principles, comprehensively illuminated in a well-organized manner.

In Part II we share with you the Situational Coaching Model (SCM). This constitutes a contemporary conversational model that is symbolized by the *mind of a coach*. It consists of six crucial coaching paradigms that a coach can use in a flexible manner to navigate a coaching conversation. He does this by shifting smoothly from one paradigm to another so as to best meet the needs of the client and the situation. This is the first book to explain the SCM that underlies the effectiveness and uniqueness of each coaching conversation.

Part III consists of the Achievers Coaching Techniques (ACT), which are symbolized by the *energy of a coach*. This resonates within eight key themes that enable you to deliver great results in coaching. This is the first book to bring together the ACT, which constitute many of the most powerful techniques practiced by the world's top achievers applied specifically in coaching while still adhering to the core principles of coaching.

In the true spirit of thriving on originality and innovativeness, this is the only book that presents an all-encompassing *Meta*

Model (30-6-8) that guides you through the entire book in a holistic way to help you achieve professional mastery in coaching. The full-blown model is presented in the next two pages of this book. The numbers 30-6-8 depict 30 of TCP, the six paradigms of the SCM, and the eight themes of ACT. It would be useful for you to bookmark the page that shows the Meta Model so you can easily refer to it when desired.

The heart of a coach (TCP), the mind of a coach (SCM), and the energy of a coach (ACT) build upon each other and work together to produce the best results in coaching that empower people to achieve breakthrough success and to make their impossible dreams possible. They have worked for us and for the many people that we have coached all over the world. We believe that when you persistently practice these principles, paradigms, and techniques, it won't be very long before you obtain truly extraordinary results in coaching. We know that your coaching journey will be filled with more joy, fulfillment, and realized dreams.

We had a dream of creating a resource that would add great value to the much-needed literature on advanced coaching. We had a dream of equipping people to help others make their impossible dreams possible. We had a dream of enriching lives by enabling coaching greatness. We commemorate the realization of our dream with this book.

Go ahead, turn the pages, and begin your magical journey of bringing out the very best in yourself and in others.

Coaching for Breakthrough Success
Making the Impossible Dream Possible

META MODEL 30-6-8: *The Heart, The Mind & The Energy of a Coach*

PART I
The Coaching Principles (TCP)
—The Heart

1. **The Coaching Spirit**
   1. Believe in Human Potential for Greatness
   2. Fulfillment Flows from Adding Value to Others
   3. Bring Out the Best in People and Let Them Lead
   4. Use Influence Rather than Position
   5. Thrive on Challenges and Flexibility
   6. When We Grow Others, We Grow Ourselves
   7. A Coach Still Needs a Coach

2. **Relationship and Trust**
   8. Maintain Authentic Rapport and Humor
   9. Touch a Heart with Care and Sincerity
   10. Practice Integrity and Build Trust

3. **Asking Questions and Curiosity**
   11. Curiosity Ignites Your Spirit
   12. Ask Questions that Empower and Create Buy-In
   13. Avoid Judgmental and Advice-Oriented Questions
   14. Powerful Questions Release Solutions
   15. Asking Great Questions Requires Practice

4. **Listening and Intuition**
   16. Listen Rather Than Tell
   17. Be Present and Turn Off Your Inner Dialogue
   18. Avoid Jumping to Premature Conclusions
   19. Be Impartial and Non-judgmental
   20. Listen Deeply, Use Observation and Intuition

5. **Feedback and Awareness**
   21. Embrace Feedback to Triumph
   22. Awareness and Acceptance Cultivates Transformation

6. **Suggestions and Simplification**
   23. Get Consent Before Giving Suggestions
   24. Use the Power of Simplicity

7. **Goals and Action Plans**
   25. Establish Goal Ownership and Commitment
   26. Create Strategies and Action Plans for Goals
   27. Keep Score of Goals and Action Steps

8. **Accountability and Accomplishments**
   28. Support Goals Completion Continuously
   29. Accountability Drives Accomplishments
   30. Acknowledge Efforts and Progress

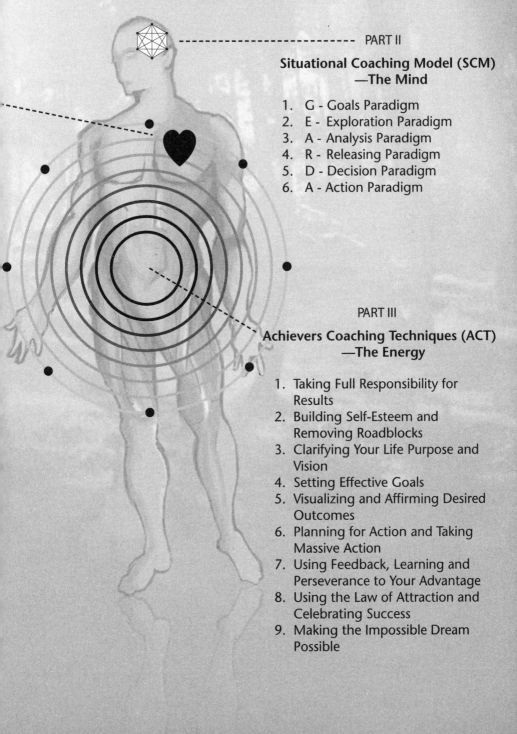

PART II

**Situational Coaching Model (SCM)
—The Mind**

1. G - Goals Paradigm
2. E - Exploration Paradigm
3. A - Analysis Paradigm
4. R - Releasing Paradigm
5. D - Decision Paradigm
6. A - Action Paradigm

PART III

**Achievers Coaching Techniques (ACT)
—The Energy**

1. Taking Full Responsibility for Results
2. Building Self-Esteem and Removing Roadblocks
3. Clarifying Your Life Purpose and Vision
4. Setting Effective Goals
5. Visualizing and Affirming Desired Outcomes
6. Planning for Action and Taking Massive Action
7. Using Feedback, Learning and Perseverance to Your Advantage
8. Using the Law of Attraction and Celebrating Success
9. Making the Impossible Dream Possible

PART I

THE COACHING PRINCIPLES (TCP)

The Heart of a Coach

CHAPTER 1

THE COACHING SPIRIT

1. The Coaching Spirit

8. Accountability & Accomplishments

2. Relationship & Trust

7. Goals & Action Plans

3. Asking Questions & Curiosity

6. Suggestions & Simplification

4. Listening & Intuition

5. Feedback & Awareness

PRINCIPLE 1

Believe in Human Potential for Greatness

Man was designed for accomplishment, engineered for success, and endowed with the seeds of greatness.
—Zig Ziglar

At the heart of a great coach is a firm belief that each person is a uniquely valuable individual with distinct gifts and potential for greatness. A coach knows how to appreciate what is special in others and believes that every person is created to be magnificent in their own way.

Leadership guru John C. Maxwell asserts that talent is never enough. "Belief lifts your talent. Your talent will not be lifted to the highest level unless you also have belief." There are four main ways in which believing in human potential for greatness can be a talent lifter.

- Lift your talent to coach by believing in people's potential for greatness.

3

- Lift the talent of the people you coach by believing in their potential for greatness.

- Lift your talent by believing in your own potential as a great coach.

- Lift the talent of the people you coach when they believe in your potential as a great coach.

As a coach, you gain increased motivation when you are able to see the champion in each person you coach. When you have strong faith and belief in the potential of the people you coach, it lifts their talent and inspires them to accomplish more. When you believe in your own potential as a great coach, you lift your own talent and motivation to coach. When the people whom you coach believe in your potential, it will lift their talent and motivation to be coached.

The net positive effect in believing in one's human potential for greatness is multiplied when it permeates the relationship between the coach and client. Coaching is an unconditionally supportive relationship, and as you coach you want to offer full acceptance and an unbiased belief in the person you are coaching regardless of his or her present performance.

It has been said that belief is more than a thought that a person possesses; it is a thought that possesses the person. A belief in the unlimited human potential for greatness is a habit of the mind in which confidence becomes a virtue to be embraced. In order to be a highly effective coach, you need to make believing in people, yourself, and your mission one of your top priorities. If you want good results, you have to perform good actions. If you want to perform good actions, you must have good expectations. To have good expectations you must first believe your goals are achievable.

The globally acclaimed author of *Fully Human, Fully Alive: A New Life through a New Vision*, John Powell, estimates that an average person taps only 10 percent of his potential, sees only 10 percent of the beauty that is all around him, hears only 10 percent of its music and poetry, smells only 10 percent of its fragrance, and tastes only 10 percent of the deliciousness of being alive. Since most people neither see nor seize the untapped opportunity that constantly surrounds them, there is a vast potential waiting to be unleashed.

You know that people are always capable of much better results than those they are currently getting. This might include better physical fitness, higher job performance, more loving relationships, and so on. As a coach, you will encounter situations where people do not succeed or don't measure up to expectations in the face of huge commitments. During such times, your belief in their potential for greatness is even more important; that belief needs to remain steadfast.

Even at a time when someone is going through great difficulties at work or at home, as a coach you must still be able to see the goodness in them and bring it to the surface. This is easier said than done, but believing in people no matter what must be a conscious choice, a decision you make, and a habit you inculcate with constant practice even when it's challenging. If, as a coach, you covertly believe that your client is not able to succeed in achieving his or her goals, if you feel that she or he is not capable enough, this can undermine your entire coaching process.

If you are coaching someone to become an effective presenter and have seen the person performing poorly, you may have formed a belief that this person is unlikely to become an effective speaker. When this happens, your ability to coach the person will be flawed. When you are pessimistic regarding the outcome, this will undermine your coaching conversations. Your negative expectations could subconsciously affect their confidence and lessen the likelihood of success. This does not mean that if someone sets an unrealistic goal that you should not explore ways to make changes to the goal or work on a different goal. But it *does* mean you should maintain a positive view of the outcome of your coaching.

Sun Tzu wrote in *The Art of War* that when troops prepare for battle, if they lose the fight within their own minds even before the battle begins, their chances of winning are diminished by up to 50 percent. He emphasizes the profound effect that belief has on the ability to win. The certain belief in the great potential that lies within all people, releases the power that drives a successful coaching practice.

CASE STUDY: DAVID'S STORY

David was a general manager of a multinational shipping company based in Long Beach, California, and formerly a captain in the armed forces. His father fought in World War II and while raising his kids had followed a strict military regimen. David was well known in his company as a very tough, no-nonsense boss. His employees feared him since he was good at finding people's faults, though he also fixed them. His command-and-control style meant that employees were not expected to act proactively and creatively in the face of escalating environmental changes. Employee morale was low, and business was declining rapidly. David had to face this crisis on his own without the support of his employees. The prolonged high stress affected David to the point that he had to undergo heart surgery.

One of our professional coaches worked with David. It was very difficult initially, and for the most part his staff believed that he could not and would not change. The coach had confidence in David's greatness and believed that he was capable of notable achievements. When David knew that the coach was fully present for him and would champion his cause without being judgmental, he began to speak what was in his heart. When David fully articulated the tremendous pain in his life and his coach listened empathically, it was as if a massive weight was lifted from his shoulders. David became aware that his leadership approach was not bearing fruit. The awareness and acceptance of how his approach was limiting his achievements became the eureka moment that fueled his transformation. It gave David the motivation to invent his new approach to leadership, which he called "Participative-Appreciative Leadership."

Old habits take time and discipline to change, so David's coach encouraged him to create a way to remind himself to stay with his new approach until the new habit became locked in. One of the many self-created support structures that proved effective for David was this: He instructed all his employees that every time he reverted to his old style of leadership, they were to say to him, "Yes, Captain!" He knew—or suspected—that when they did this he would laugh out loud at himself, interrupting his old military pattern.

As he constantly replaced his old pattern with the new one, he began to reap the rewards of what his coach believed he was capable of achieving. His belief in himself soared, and so did his performance.

Nine months into the coaching relationship, David had created a new work culture that increased staff satisfaction and performance. The change was so profound that he received the "Outstanding Leader of the Year" award from his head office. His wife expressed deep gratitude when she told the coach that David was now a changed man. In his acceptance speech David said, "I am eternally grateful to my coach for believing in me when no one else did. You are the wind beneath my wings. You lifted me up and that changed my life." When he paused to wipe away his tears, you could have heard a pin drop. The song "Wind Beneath My Wings" sung by Bette Midler played in the background, and David's coach and staff were moved to tears.

––––––––––

The mindset of a coach includes the belief that people are inherently good; they want to contribute, and they want to improve. The coach knows people make mistakes but that most people do not make those mistakes intentionally. Remember to take a stand for people's greatness and always start from a belief that people want to succeed in their goals and commitments. Everyone has talents and strengths, and the role of a coach is to bring these out and to help people to use their core genius purposefully. When they do, they will shine magnificently.

The more you believe in people's potential, the more reason they will give you to believe in them. Eventually you will wake up one morning realizing that you have also been transformed, and the way you look at people and life will never be the same.

Imagine when you are searching for that rainbow, faced with an apparently unassailable mountain range in your way, that there is a coach who truly supports you, wholeheartedly believes in you, and knows that you are capable of climbing over those mountains. You will be inspired to grow and become the best person you can be. Such an experience is tremendously uplifting and enriching. That is when you will embody the true spirit of a coach who firmly believes in human potential for greatness.

> *You must understand that seeing is believing,*
> *but also know that believing is seeing.*
> —Denis Waitley

PRINCIPLE 2

Fulfillment Flows from Adding Value to Others

> *Where your talent and the needs of the*
> *world cross, your calling can be found.*
> —Aristotle

Calling, Life Purpose, and Fulfillment

Great coaches realize that coaching is a calling, a clarion command to use your talent to serve something bigger than yourself for a greater good. Answering a calling keeps our life purpose from becoming self-ish, while it addresses our deep desire to use our lives for something significant and worthwhile. Ultimate fulfillment and significance come from a lasting sense of joy and satisfaction, from fully living a life purpose centered on adding value to others. An important part of personal fulfillment is the sense that we are part of something bigger than ourselves, that our work makes a difference for others. As coaches, we know that the world is a better place because of what we have done.

How Coaching Adds Value to People

Coaches add value to people, in five ways. They help people to find satisfaction in (1) achieving goals, (2) overcoming problems, (3) learning and developing, (4) installing new beliefs and habits, and (5) experiencing fulfillment in their work and lives by uplifting others. As we saw in the earlier case study of David, the coaching process made a big difference for David and created lasting fulfillment for the coach. The strong feeling of fulfillment and gratitude that he received touched the coach so deeply that he would remember it for the rest of his life.

What People Appreciate and Remember Most

When world-renowned leadership author Richard Boyatzis asked people who had been the most valuable people to them in their careers, he found that about 80 percent of all people said that it was those who had helped them extend their dreams and reach for new positive experiences in their lives. On the other hand, those people who highlighted people's faults and made others feel small were not valued.

The Absence of Fulfillment

We all know people who pursue money, power, or pleasure as an ultimate end. They are never happy because they can never get enough, and they always want more and more for themselves. These things are temporary and fleeting, and even if their possessions make people feel good for a while, soon enough they run out; yet like an addiction, they keep yearning for more. There are many people in the world who seem to work very hard and achieve success, money, and fame—yet a true sense of lasting fulfillment is still largely absent from their lives because they have not dedicated themselves to serving a greater good. The positive emotions of true fulfillment tend to come most strongly as a result of hard work and sacrifice in the service of an end that is bigger than yourself.

CASE STUDY: JESSICA'S STORY

At the age of 28, Jessica was depressed and devastated. It had been a bed of roses when she was in school in Hong Kong. She won a national interschool speech contest, wrote award winning poems, was very popular and scored straight As. She was in a great school with supportive teachers, counselors, and schoolmates. When she was able to shine, she felt loved and appreciated by the people around her.

After completing her master of banking and finance degree in Sydney, Australia, she took a job as branch operations executive in a bank.

Twenty-four months into this unfulfilling job, she was totally disillusioned about life. She hated her boss and secretly called him a sadist since he seemed to gain pleasure from making people suffer—just because he had gone through a lot of pain himself. At the slightest mistake he would trample on Jessica in front of others. He never seemed to leave the office, and his staff was not supposed to leave before him.

Jessica's parents had high expectations of her, but she felt no love from them when she could not achieve the success they wanted from her. Her boyfriend decided to leave her, sending a note saying that he could not live with a loser. Every night she cried herself to sleep in her lonely apartment.

A friend invited Jessica to a life-changing seminar by Anthony Robbins. During the seminar she raised her hand to say that she needed help and expressed the seriousness of her problems. "Before the end of the seminar," she says, "I was approached by a coach who said he was willing to work with me with no expectations or monetary reward; I decided to give it a try. Since my coach was a very busy person from Malaysia, we did two-hour sessions every two weeks using Skype. My coach knew that the pain in my life was unbearable. He did not talk much, so I did most of the talking. By the third session, I broke down in tears. After I had poured out all my suffering, I suddenly felt empty but much lighter. He then started to ask me about what I loved to do most and what I did well in school."

The coach gave Jessica a template to fill out each week over a period of 12 weeks. She was to write down what she did well and enjoyed doing at work. It was difficult at first but eventually she came to a realization that what she did well and loved to do at school and at work boiled down to similar things. "I loved to express myself in front of many people, socialize with like-minded people and develop and create new things that others could enjoy. My coach asked me how I could embrace my true strengths and passion and that became my revelation. Before that I had totally forgotten about my giftedness. Now I began to engage it."

With encouragement from her coach, Jessica had the courage to visualize what her life would be like if she used her gifts to the fullest. "He even asked if I wanted to create my own affirmation." She fashioned one that sounded like, "I am gratefully and masterfully presenting, creating, and relating with people." She recorded this with her special tune on her smartphone and programmed a reminder to play this six times a day.

"My turning point came when my coach asked me how I could change the circumstances that I was faced with. I thought about it for a whole week, and the answer came when I met the head of training in the bank during a training session. I spilled out my affirmation to him and asked if I could work with him. I was astounded when he called my boss, called my coach, and then called me to say yes."

From then on, Jessica's coach worked with her to hone her passion and strengths to the point that she got a standing ovation from people who attended the training that she created and delivered. She later spoke on national TV about her turnaround story. Jessica continued working with her coach for eight months more until, as she says, "I felt it was time I helped others. One of the final questions from my coach was, 'Why do you think God gave you special talents and what do you think you have been put into this world for?' After several months of soul searching, I believe I found my life purpose which is summarized as 'enriching lives with love and humility through transformational programs.'"

In a long letter to her coach, Jessica wrote, "When there was a dark storm on my horizon, and I didn't think I could get through it, you had unceasing faith in me. You saw the goodness in me and gave me the courage to be what I was really born to be. You gave me hope and inspiration to stay alive when I felt my life was worthless. I will always remember your words, 'The future is in your hands. It's time to come alive, because your moment has arrived.' And true enough you helped me find the answers that lie deep within me, that I alone could not reach. I want to thank you from the bottom of my heart. I made it through the 'hurricane' of my life. The world is a much better place because of a great coach like you. You have inspired me to pass on this gift to others through my life purpose."

A Fulfilling Job

A fulfilling job engages your strengths and talents in contributing to people, the organization, and the community. Such fulfillment is intrinsic and comes from within through acknowledgment, acceptance, and affection rather than from money or material gain, which are extrinsic. You cannot demand fulfillment. Nor can you create an experience of fulfillment in someone else—that must come from within. It is a result of doing the right things, and it flows naturally when you make a meaningful contribution to a cause that positively impacts the lives of others. Coaching can ultimately bring happiness, satisfaction, and meaning to the life of the coach, as well as to the people being coached.

Benefits of Fulfillment for the Coach

To add value as coaches, we need to constantly prepare, grow, and develop ourselves.

- Fulfillment gives the coach more inspiration to be even better at her or his job. It releases a profound sense of happiness that money alone cannot provide.

- Fulfillment creates gratitude and gratitude attracts even more to be grateful for.

- The joy that comes from a sense of meaningful fulfillment directs people toward more fully living their life purposes that make significant contributions to others.

As a coach, it is important to align your vocation with your life purpose. When you do that, you will derive the greatest satisfaction and happiness in your journey through life. Coaching is a skill you can practice long after retirement, and those who continue to coach never really retire. Mother Teresa is a prime example of someone who served till her last breath, and as a result, her impact on the world lives on. You too, can make a lasting contribution to creating a better world through coaching.

Words of Wisdom

Stephen R. Covey, in his book *The Eighth Habit: From Effectiveness to Greatness*, wrote about primary and secondary greatness. He stated that secondary greatness involved position, wealth, talent, and popularity, whereas primary greatness is about service above self, contribution, respect for all people, moral authority, servant leadership, and sacrifice. Covey speaks of the need to live, to learn, to love, and to leave a legacy. The people who have made the greatest difference in the world understand the significance of adding value to others.

Consider Nobel Prize winners such as Nelson Mandela, Albert Schweitzer, and Mother Teresa. These people were less interested in their positions or possessions than in their contributions to others. Study their lives and you will notice that they wanted to make things better for others. A coach who sincerely lives this principle does not see coaching as a task or a job but as a privileged calling. By doing so, he or she makes life really worth living. A coach's fulfillment flows from adding value to others.

> I don't know what your destiny will be, but
> one thing I do know: The ones among you
> who will be really happy are those that
> have sought and found how to serve.
> —Albert Schweitzer

PRINCIPLE 3

Bring Out the Best in People and Let Them Lead

> At the center of your being you have the answer; you
> know who you are, you know what you want and
> you know what you need to do.
> —Lao Tzu

Empowerment and Self-Leadership

To bring out the best in a person, you must first believe that the best is within them and that they are capable of doing much better. This has its roots in Coaching Principle 1, but it takes much more than believing in a person's potential for greatness to bring out the best in them. A coach uses effective listening and asks the right questions (more details in Chapters 3 and 4) to draw out solutions that lie within his or her clients. He lets people lead themselves and make their own decisions rather than providing the answers.

Since leading others begins with self-leadership, one of the best gifts a coach can offer is to help people to lead themselves well. Lao Tzu, a well-known ancient Chinese philosopher, stated, "The leader is best when his work is done, the goals fulfilled, and the people will say: 'We did it ourselves.'" When you stop wanting to control people, *that's* when you begin to empower them to take responsibility for and ownership of the choices they make and the actions they take.

Ken Blanchard, author of *Leading at a Higher Level*, said, "Empowerment is the process of unleashing the power in people, their knowledge, experience, and motivation and focusing on that power to achieve positive outcomes." Empowerment means people have the freedom to decide and to act. It also means they are accountable for their results. The strength of empowerment is self-leadership, the ability and willingness to lead, to take initiative and be proactive—in short, to make things happen. Empowerment, in fact, is what the coach gives to people. Self-leadership is what people exercise in order to make empowerment work.

One of the main causes of a lack of empowerment is the coach's over-management. She feels fully accountable for the outcome of coaching and is reluctant to relinquish control. When a coach keeps managing, controlling, and instructing, the outcome is disempowering. The client feels powerless and lacks autonomy; he becomes dependent on the coach. The sense of ownership is absent and his motivation and creativity are impeded. Soon he begins to lose trust in himself and his capability to lead himself. This problem, if allowed to continue, suppresses the client's development, ultimately preventing him from being the best he can be.

When you push people where they don't want to be pushed, you will face even more resistance. To reduce the resistance for change and action, the coach has to give the power back to the person being coached. As a coach you have to ensure that the client is responsible for the outcomes she creates. You will also realize how liberating that is for you as a coach. If she makes inappropriate decisions, she—and *only* she—is accountable for them and you are not to be blamed for that. If she does something very well, you can rejoice with her, but she gets the reward and acknowledgment.

Sometimes the client is not used to being empowered. Occasionally you'll encounter people who are accustomed to working under highly controlling managers and have developed the habit of waiting to be told what to do. Many people are used to being bossed around and so lack a feeling of personal empowerment; they've forgotten how to take responsibility for leading their own lives. If personal empowerment is a new habit for a client, it will take time to instill it. As a coach, you must emphasize the benefits of empowerment and persist in encouraging and facilitating self-leadership in your clients. Above all, you must not revert to the command-and-control approach, which is not the way to effective coaching.

Directive versus Nondirective Approaches

Here are three different scenarios that demonstrate what a coaching conversation will sound like if, as a coach, you are in control and you are using a directive approach versus using a nondirective approach and allowing the other person to lead:

Scenario 1: Removing Roadblocks

The person you are coaching had a major conflict with a key customer. If you're exerting a directive position then you could say, "The customer is always right; you should apologize and make good with the customer." But if you want to empower the person, to lead them, you might ask a question like, "What could you do to make things better for you and your customer?"

Scenario 2: Establishing the Agenda

The person you are coaching is unsure about which direction to take the conversation. If you want to be in control, you could say,

"I have been thinking about what we should focus on today, and I am convinced that we should deal with your financial goal first." But if you want the person to take the lead, then you might ask, "Where would you like to focus our conversation today so that you can move forward with your important goals?"

Scenario 3: Making Decisions on Next Steps

The person you are coaching is considering moving to another department. If you take charge, you'll say something like, "You have to talk to your boss first before making any rash decision." If the client is in charge, then you'll say, "What action might you take if you feel it is necessary to discuss your intention with others?"

Effective coaches constantly choose to use a nondirective approach to coaching and to empowering people to succeed at leading themselves. They have faith that people are always capable of improving and finding their own solutions. The person with more information, responsibility, and investment in their own future is not the coach. The person being coached has more information about herself or himself, their past, present, future, their environment, and their circumstances. The client has more responsibility, and she or he puts in more time, more resources, and is more affected by the outcome of their actions than the coach. Therefore, it is logical to let the client set the direction and make his or her own decisions on those things that will impact their lives.

Do your best and expect the best from those whom you coach. Remember that coaching is about helping people to realize their *own* inner wisdom and to release the talent and strengths that lie within them. A great coach is someone who helps you look inside yourself so that you eventually find your own internal wisdom and guidance.

The former chairman of IBM, Thomas J. Watson, said, "Nothing so conclusively proves a man's ability to lead others, as what he does from day to day to lead himself." When the people you coach are able to lead themselves well, they will produce better results, and they will earn the right to lead others. As coaches, we make a much bigger difference in people's lives when we allow them to find their own solutions, when we enable them to take ownership and responsibility for their actions, and when we empower them to lead themselves. That is when we bring out the best in people.

> *He who controls others may be powerful, but*
> *he who has mastered himself is mightier still.*
> —Lao Tzu

PRINCIPLE 4

Use Influence Rather than Position

Use positive influence to energize people so that
they collaborate with you because they want to,
not because they have to.
—Jack Canfield and Peter Chee

A wise coach knows that when it comes to determining the coaching agenda, making decisions, and taking action, the person being coached has to be empowered to lead. When it comes to creating a successful coaching relationship and enabling a fruitful coaching conversation, the coach uses relational influence to lead rather than positional authority. To influence is to get someone to make decisions or take action because he or she really wants to as a result of their own free will. According to Laura Whitworth, the coauthor of *Co-Active Coaching*, the role of a coach is not to set the agenda but to *focus the coaching conversation* in line with the client's agenda and move it toward action.

The notion of the boss as the coach or of the coach acting like a boss does not work when the command-and-control approach is being used. When the boss instructs people what to do and uses his authority to get things done, this does not constitute good coaching. As a coach, you will use a very different approach, collaborating with people rather than acting as an autocrat or boss. With positive relational influence from you, the people you coach will do things willingly and wholeheartedly.

CASE STUDY: JOHN'S STORY

John was a sales engineer of a leading equipment supply company who had accumulated a number of customer complaints. At first, a director in his company was told to resolve the issue with John. In the second instance, John chose to work with a professionally trained coach. The outcome of each encounter was very different.

Here is a snapshot of the conversation for the two different encounters:

First Instance

Director: John, let's spend some time today dealing with your problem of having constant misunderstanding with customers.

John: What?

Director: What do you mean by what? You should show some respect to me and take this matter seriously. Otherwise you'll regret it.

John: Whatever you say.

Director: I heard that when customers complain about your service, you just argue with them and do not take any corrective measures. Why do you do that?

John: It's not about my service; it's the company's practices that are not customer friendly.

Director: I don't believe that is the case. You need to change yourself instead of blaming others. What you are doing is causing the company a lot of trouble.

John: What change do you want me to make?

Director: Stop arguing with the customers and give them what they need.

John: They need timely deliveries and lower prices, and that is not in my control.

Director: The company is already doing its best on prices and speed of deliveries.

John: So what can I do?

Director: I don't know. You tell me.

John: I don't know. You should tell me, since you are the one in charge.

Director: This conversation is getting us nowhere.

John: Well, I am just looking to you for direction.

Director: Just do as you are told and stop causing problems with customers.

John: Yes, sir. So sorry, sir. I need to go and pick up my wife now. Could you please excuse me?

Outcome

John felt victimized, frustrated, and confused. He did not know what to do, and things just got worse. This is a conversation gone wrong and violates Coaching Principle 4. The boss is attempting to coerce rather than to influence.

Second Instance

Coach: Hi, John. How are things going with you?

John: I am feeling down. A lot of complaints and problems from customers.

Coach: You know, John, I really appreciate your openness. I would love to be of service to you. Would you like to spend some time talking about this with me?

John: That could be helpful.

Coach: I am really curious; please tell me more.

John: I am faced with a lot of customer conflicts, and this is causing me sleepless nights. They keep complaining about our prices and delayed deliveries.

Coach: I understand how you feel. What do you think can be done to overcome this challenge?

John: I would have to consult the top management and explore some possible solutions.

Coach: John, I believe that you can get on top of this challenge. Imagine if you were in the top management. What would you do?

John: Well, let me think. (Pause for a few seconds.) Okay, I would increase our storage capacity and stock quantity in line with demand, since we found that this is the main cause of delayed deliveries.

Coach: Sounds good. What else could you do?

John: It will make a big difference if we communicate effectively with our customers to show how our product is differentiated and why it's of superior quality and worth paying for.

Coach: That's very interesting. I am glad to hear great ideas coming from you. Is there anything else that you can do personally to make a difference?

John: Thanks for this great question and your constant encouragement. I realize that I should also be more patient. I need to listen to the customers and work on solutions instead of giving excuses and arguing with them.

Coach: This sounds really brilliant. Would you like to come up with an action plan and work with the top management to put the solutions into action?

John: That would be great. I would love to do that.

Coach: When would you like to get started?

John: I will get on with it first thing tomorrow morning.

Coach: How do you feel about today's conversation?

John: I value this very much and thank you. I really appreciate your support.

Coach: You are very welcome. Shall we meet next Friday to work on this further and evaluate your progress?

John: Yes, certainly. I look forward to working on this and to sharing good news with you.

Outcome

John was highly motivated; he made changes and he took action to produce results. This was an effective coaching conversation that clearly demonstrates how a coach uses the positive relational influence of asking questions, listening, and caring, rather than using authority.

Increasing Your Relational Influence

When you practice Coaching Principle 1: Believe in Human Potential for Greatness; 2: Fulfillment Flows from Adding Value to Others; and 3: Bring Out the Best in People and Let Them Lead. Your influence as a coach is already making an impact because you have demonstrated a deep faith in people. You sincerely want to make a positive difference for them, and you are empowering them to lead themselves.

There are many more ways that a coach can heighten his relational influence. Some significant ways include establishing a caring and trusting relationship with the client and championing their agenda (further details in Chapter 2); being a good listener, showing interest in the other person, and asking great questions that are helpful to them (more details in Chapters 3 and 4); providing useful feedback and suggestions to nurture and enrich them (more details in Chapters 5 and 6); providing continuous support and encouragement toward accomplishing goals, acknowledging progress, and showing genuine appreciation (more details in Chapter 8); and helping them discover and focus on their talent and strength (more details in Chapter 12).

Just as a good servant leader has a strong relational influence over followers, a servant coach works with people as a collaborative partner and sets a good example by serving people from the heart. A coach shows the way by being humble and giving up any impulse to be superior over others. People who act as if they are better than others and that they always have the right answers often make poor coaches. They trip over themselves when they make wrong judgments at the expense of others. Thomas G. Crane, author of *The Heart of Coaching*, states, "To become the powerful and magnificent coach I am capable of becoming, I must learn how to detach, to set my ego needs aside, and to listen deeply with my heart."

Coaching does not reside in the domain of therapy. Therefore coaches must give up the need to fix others. Instead, they guide people to find their *own* solutions. When a coach applies positive relational influence, the client becomes more motivated and committed and puts in more effort to achieve results willingly rather than being instructed to do so. That is when you realize the power of coaching by using influence rather than position.

> *Managers who use influence and integrity*
> *to empower people are the ones who become*
> *truly respected coaching leaders.*
> —Jack Canfield and Peter Chee

PRINCIPLE 5
Thrive on Challenges and Flexibility

Problems are to the mind what exercise is to the
muscles, they toughen and make us strong.
—Norman Vincent Peale

Challenges with the People You Coach

When you coach, you will inevitably come face to face with adversity, which can appear in many different and unpredictable forms. Here are just a few examples:

- You entered into a coaching relationship with someone and then come to realize later that deep inside, they are still looking for a consultant to provide them with all the right answers. That is not the role of a coach.

- Someone comes to you for coaching who is totally lost. They don't know what they want and where they are going, and they keep changing their mind during each coaching conversation. Things are going in circles.

- You're working with someone who prefers to think of coaching as a purely social discourse. They vent their frustrations without creating any clear outcomes, assuming their employer provides them a coach as part of their entitlement.

- Someone you coach commits to take action steps after each conversation but keeps coming back with good reasons for not getting things done.

- After several conversations, the person you are coaching sets a resolution to wake up at 5 a.m. so she can find time to finish writing her book. Each time she tries, she fails, and the old habit of waking up late persists.

- You progress through many conversations with a client, setting clear goals. Suddenly the person is faced with a major family crisis and has to switch gears to focus on different problems.

Challenges with What You Do as a Coach

Some of the setbacks that you might face in coaching include:

- You ask too many inappropriate questions, and that causes people to feel interrogated and helpless.

- You make inaccurate assumptions about people, causing them to feel wrongly judged.

- You get carried away in your own thoughts when the person you are coaching is speaking. This causes you to feel lost.

- You give unsolicited advice to the client and as a result, he feels controlled and disempowered.

- You jump to conclusions too quickly, missing out on important implications that affect the person you are coaching.

- You feel emotionally affected by the many problems that you and the client are facing. As a result, you are not able to think objectively.

- After listening to the client talking nonstop for too long, you have an overload of information, and this confuses you.

- You feel frustrated or resentful about the lack of progress with the person you are coaching.

Thriving on Challenges

To thrive on the many coaching challenges that pop up from time to time, you need to approach coaching with the right attitude. Every problem is an opportunity to learn and rise higher. When you look at matters from this viewpoint, you have the internal strength to work persistently and use the various techniques, models, and skills of effective coaching included in this book. Whatever the problem is, one thing separates good coaches from poor ones: their reactions to the challenges they face. John Wooden, a well-known basketball coach and accomplished author said, "Things turn out best for those who make the best of the way things turn out." It is the attitude more than the aptitude that ultimately determines the altitude of a coach.

An important step in weathering setbacks is not to personalize it and to make sure that you understand that *having* a failure does not make *you* a failure. Don't take things personally, and don't let problems drag you down. When that happens, you become an ineffective coach. Focus on learning from your mistakes and appreciate the good side of the difficult situation. Identify solutions and take action to bounce back. The reality of coaching is that the challenges you and your client face are potentially endless; each relationship will be unique. When you embrace the coaching challenge and approach it with optimistic determination, that's where the fun begins.

Flexibility

In the face of inevitable challenges, it is essential to take a flexible approach to coaching. Each situation you face as a coach is unique and cannot be treated with a formula solution. What worked yesterday may not necessarily work today or in the future. Whatever brilliant insight, question, or idea you had in the previous sessions could be irrelevant or inappropriate in subsequent conversations. Coaching is a client-centered relationship, and every person is different. Therefore each coaching assignment presents a new challenge, not to be taken for granted.

The people you coach need flexibility because they are facing the realities of constant changes in their environment. These could change their coaching needs and objectives. Your client may not know what she really needs from the coaching relationship, and she may want to change direction as a result of the practical issues she faces in real life. A coach needs to be spontaneous, even in the middle of a coaching session, adapting to the needs of the client. Each response you receive from your client gives you information about where to go next. A coach constantly senses what is most important and chooses a skill or question that suits the circumstances. The art of sensing and adjusting along the way, the readiness to embrace change and to move in a new direction with agility is what Laura Whitworth, coauthor of *Co-Active Coaching*, calls "dancing in the moment."

Creating the Coaching Challenge

If you feel a lack of challenge in a coaching relationship, both you and the client may just be sailing along on a light breeze, enjoying the conversation but not achieving much. The lack of challenge is never good for a coaching relationship. Coaches need to ensure that their assignments pose strong enough challenges to the clients so as to stretch them to grow. As a coach, you want to bring out the best in your client. In this way, she or he derives far greater benefit, and you also are challenged to become a better coach.

If you pose an obstacle sincerely to a client, you're indicating that as a coach you believe they are capable of achieving more; this actually strengthens them. This is not to say the client has to accept your challenge. It's still their choice, and they might take on the hurdle only partially or come up with another challenge. Of course, they might also fully accept the challenge. Whichever way they decide, they are likely to end up better off with the challenge than without.

We had the experience of coaching a person who wanted to complete a tough research project that was critical for her next promotion. However, she got caught up in too many social activities. We discussed various options with her, and she came to realize that she was procrastinating due to a lack of confidence. This caused her stress to escalate to such a level that she was mentally paralyzed, feeling down, and lost for ideas. We challenged her to eliminate three hours of social time every day in order to complete her research project within 60 days. She freaked out; instead she counter-suggested that she commit to $1^{1}/_{2}$ hours each day and take 10 days from her annual leave to complete the project within 90 days. We continued to coach and challenge her, and she ended up accomplishing her goal within four months. She got her promotion within six months. Later, she mentioned to us that without effective coaching, accountability, and our constantly challenging her, she would not have been able to get through such a tough project on her own. Challenging the people you coach in the right way almost always reaps better results.

CASE STUDY: ZAHARA'S STORY

After Zahara heard about the power of coaching, she attended a training session to get herself prepared to coach. She thought that things would go smoothly after that, but she had no idea that there would be so many obstacles to overcome when she started coaching. One of her first assignments was to coach Mohamed, a manager from another department, and she was shocked to find out that when she tried to coach him, he would not cooperate with her. There was a strong cultural barrier; he was prejudiced against her, and he felt that a female coach did not have the right to tell him what to do.

Whatever skill Zahara used was ineffective, as Mohamed's mind was practically shut. She and Mohamed had very empty conversations; she could tell that he was just going through the motions because his boss had made it compulsory for him to receive coaching.

With much anguish, Zahara expressed her frustrations to the director of learning who recommended that she get coaching support. "From the questions my coach asked," she says, "I realized that I had the solutions and it gave me the courage to speak to Mohamed using direct and respectful communication. I made it very clear to him what real coaching was, and after I clarified that, as a coach, my commitment was to listen to him, to serve him, and to champion his agenda rather that to tell him what to do, he began to open up to coaching." Things improved, and Mohamed started to get benefit from the coaching. However, after two months of making good progress, Zahara encountered a new series of obstacles. Mohamed had serious problems in his working relationship with others; he concluded he was a "victim" of negative politics in the company. Their coaching conversations quickly became an avenue for him to express his displeasure about others. He said he wanted to improve his relationship with his colleagues, but he would not take any action. Every time he felt angry with others, he changed his mind about trying to improve things. To add to the problem, Mohamed felt like he had "lost it all" when the stock market crashed, wiping out his family savings.

Despite her best efforts, Zahara was emotionally affected by his problems. In fact, she was consumed by his problems. During their sessions she got lost in her own thoughts, so her ability to listen and ask good questions became blocked. Her belief in Mohamed and herself became weak, and she began to judge him negatively. "At one point," she says, "I felt that he was wrong in several ways and I forgot about the Coaching Principles, so I tried to advise him what to do. He detested it and started to shut me out again. I felt like a helpless coach. My stress level went out of control, and I just wanted to quit."

At that juncture, Zahara's coach spent a lot of time listening to her, asking her very important questions about her future. The coach continued to have faith in Zahara, even when Zahara had lost faith in herself as a coach. "It was a good thing that I persisted and decided to focus on finding solutions rather than on the problems. I started to learn from my mistakes and looked at it as an opportunity to improve. When I finally accepted that the work of a coach needed great mental and emotional strength, I changed my mindset and began to welcome the challenges that I faced in coaching."

Zahara stepped up and apologized to Mohamed for her shortcomings. She told him that she sincerely cared for him and wanted to continue to offer him supportive coaching in line with his goals. He decided to give her another chance; in the subsequent eight months of coaching, both coach and client continued to face challenges but the difference lay in Zahara's ability to rise to the challenge. She began to believe that "when the coaching gets tough, the tough coach gets going," and she worked on finding ways to become a stronger coach.

When the coaching assignment came to an end, Mohamed had been empowered through the coaching process to find many of his own solutions and was able to turn his life around. "When he expressed his sincere gratitude to me," says Zahara, "he was very pleased to hear from me that because of him, I had become a better coach. Since then, I have coached 35 other managers to achieve higher performance at work. I fully believe in the Coaching Principle, 'Thrive on Challenges and Flexibility' because this is what it really takes to become a great coach. I have also been coaching other coaches, and people in my organization refer to me as a resilient coaching leader. I eventually became the first woman in my company to hold the position of senior vice president."

As Zahara's story demonstrates, the best coaches are those who are resilient in the face of adversity. They know that the path of least resistance is the path of weakness, whereas the path of greatest resistance is the path of strength. Effective coaches know how to fail forward, and how to turn setbacks into stepping stones for success. When clients fail, the coach helps them to learn and to see the bigger picture. Coaching is a process that takes time and persistence; it's not about just giving answers and a quick fix. Coaching people to help them find their own answers and to achieve worthwhile results means rising to triumph in the face of challenges. The bigger the problem and the bigger the goal, the bigger the gain will be when it is conquered.

The beauty of coaching is that when people face high aspirations and tough obstacles, they can learn how to develop themselves to become more masterful. As a coach, you need to be courageous. You will constantly believe in people's greatness and rise to the challenge of any given situation facing the person you are coaching. When faced with challenges and the need to be flexible, you tackle it with faith, confidence, and enthusiasm and work persistently to win. When you are able to thrive on challenges and flexibility, you will be well on your path to coaching greatness.

> *The greatest glory in living lies not in*
> *never failing but in rising every time*
> *we fall.*
> —Nelson Mandela

PRINCIPLE 6

When We Grow Others, We Grow Ourselves

*When we push others down, we can't help but push
ourselves down. When we bring others up, we can't
help but bring ourselves up.*

—Jack Canfield and Peter Chee

There are coaches who coach for a fee and there are coaches who coach for free. If you coach for a fee, you will find that the joy and fulfellment of coaching far surpasses any financial reward you may earn. In his book *Winning with People*, Dr. John C. Maxwell talks about the Boomerang Principle, which says that "when we help others, we help ourselves." Even when there is no direct return of investment on those we have helped, the sense of fulfillment, which comes from helping others, is in itself worth it. People derive a true sense of happiness when they act in the service of others and are involved in charitable works without demanding anything in return. If you coach for free, of course, you will also receive those same benefits.

The Benefits of Coaching People

One of the most valuable outcomes from coaching people is that you also develop yourself in the process of coaching. It is the genuine passion and intention to grow others that spurs us on to transform ourselves. To develop others, we have to first develop ourselves ... and to continuously change others, we can't help but continuously transform ourselves. Before we coach, we learn, we prepare, and we reflect on how we can be an effective coach. During the coaching session, we gain hands-on experience and practice coaching skills and techniques. After coaching, we reflect on what transpired during the dialogue and what went well, what didn't, and how we can do better next time. This cycle of learning returns over and over again throughout the entire coaching relationship. As we coach more people, we inculcate knowledge, skills, and competencies in coaching that will help us in many aspects of our professional and personal lives.

When we constantly apply these coaching competencies into what we do daily, we are enriched and we become better leaders, team players, spouses, parents, and friends. Thomas G. Crane, author of *The Heart of Coaching*, asserts that transformational coaching is applied leadership. In many ways, being a good coach for the people who work with you makes you a better leader because the ability to coach and develop people has come to be accepted as one of the major competencies of a good leader. According to John Whitmore, the author of *Coaching for Performance*, "A manager's job is simple—to get the job done and grow his staff. Time and resource pressures limit the latter. Coaching is one process that accomplishes both."

If you are a leader who effectively coaches others, you grow your people. When that happens, they produce better results; this in turn brings you and your organization to a higher level of success. When you coach a lot of people in your company, and they see the great value that occurs, this motivates them to become coaches too. This creates a multiplier effect that often goes beyond those who report directly to you. It helps create a culture of coaching and leadership excellence throughout the whole organization. This is what Jeff Fettig, the chairman of Whirlpool Corporation, did to grow his organization. He fully committed himself to coaching people and to creating a coaching culture. He firmly believed that when he developed others, he developed himself and when he developed himself and others, he developed his organization. Coaching people is so important to developing leaders that Jack Welch, the legendary former CEO and chairman of GE, decreed that those who did not coach others would not be promoted. Welch knew that when his leaders grew others, they grew themselves and the organization.

As you have seen in the Coaching Principles explained in the earlier part of this book, when you develop as a coach, you learn to believe in people's potential; you learn how to empower people to bring out the best in them and to let them lead; you cultivate the ability of using influence to motivate people from within rather than using authority to command them from without; and you develop resilience and the ability to thrive on adversity and flexibility.

As you delve further into this book, you will discover other principles that when applied in coaching will develop your ability to establish rapport and build good and trusting relationships with people. You'll learn how to become a good listener in order to gain valuable input from others; to use intuition and observation to help you discover solutions and root causes of problems; to ask effective questions to draw out the best from others; to give and receive effective feedback for creating awareness and making improvements; to provide useful suggestions and use the power of simplicity to establish clarity and focus; to set goals and develop action plans that create ownership and commitment; to establish a system to keep track of action steps and progress; to solicit accountability that drives accomplishments; and to provide ongoing encouragement, support, and acknowledgment for the attainment of goals.

When you successfully apply the Achievers Coaching Techniques explained in Chapters 10 to 17, you will become a highly effective coach. When you grow to such a level, you will have acquired the ability to help people transform and develop themselves in the following ways:

- Changing their mindsets and their habits

- Overcoming their limiting beliefs

- Building stronger self-esteem

- Discovering their life purposes and their visions

- Using the power of visualization and affirmations to accelerate the accomplishment of their self-chosen goals

- Coming up with effective strategies and action plans to achieve their goals

- Staying in action to achieve their highly ambitious goals

These same capabilities will also help you become a better team player, spouse, parent, and friend. For example, when you develop better listening skills, your spouse will feel that he or she is important to you and that you understand them better. Your friends will appreciate you more when you give them the gift of attention by listening to them more intently. Your children will feel more understood when you take time to listen to the problems they are facing rather than simply telling them what to do. When you continue to coach people over time, you will discover that it will benefit all areas of your life.

CASE STUDY: KAYASHIMA'S STORY

As a quality manager working in the United States for a multinational Japanese manufacturing company, Kayashima had to learn to adapt himself to work with people from very different cultural backgrounds. His style of dealing with employees was focused on problem solving and controlling processes and people to ensure conformance to the quality standards that were set. By standardizing and controlling the work flow, he was able to ensure quality but his team members were not developing themselves very much and they lacked creativity as things had become fairly routine and predictable. Over time, there was a lack of performance improvement, motivation was low, and people felt "robotic" as they were not really engaged at work. "When I started to learn about the coaching principles," he says, "I noticed that they were quite different from my predominant behavioral style, so I wanted to challenge myself to learn a different way of doing things and to find out for myself how it would impact the results that I achieve.

"I learned and practiced coaching at work by getting involved in coaching sessions every two weeks with my team members. I attended coach training, prepared myself before each coaching session, applied the principles when I coached, and after each session, I would think back about what I learned and how I could be a more effective coach. This went on continuously for six months and then suddenly over dinner one evening, my wife and daughter gave me the most beautiful smile, and guess what they said? 'You are a good husband and father, and we love you always.' It was a very touching moment for me, and a big surprise as I did not remember them saying that to me before. Later they explained to me that over the past months, I had been more patient and understanding and had cared for them more. Little did I know that when I acquired new coaching habits that were beneficial to my team, I had unconsciously adopted them with my loved ones as well, and they just loved it."

Instead of controlling and always telling people what to do, Kayashima practiced effective listening, asking questions that elicited the good side of people.

His other Japanese friends were amazed and asked him how he had managed to overcome his weaknesses and develop the many good habits that got his team members and family to appreciate him more. "The gist of it," he says, "was that through practicing coaching principles and techniques, I had learned how to motivate, support and encourage people from deep within, and they felt important, capable and cared for instead of being manipulated by me. I also now know how to raise people's self-esteem and ask powerful questions that help people create self-awareness coupled with a strong willingness to change their mindsets for better achievements. I believe that this is just the beginning, and I am committed to continue coaching and to learning more coaching techniques because I see worthwhile gains to the people I coach. My experience of becoming a coach has radically changed me for the better and as long as I am still alive, I wish to continue coaching."

———————

From Kayashima's story, it is evident that coaching enabled him to change and grow in many ways. Because he was clearly aware of the phenomenal development he would experience from coaching, he had the passion to continue coaching and to commit himself to it for the rest of his life. We know from our own experience that our involvement in coaching has significantly shaped our lives for the better. Growing others and growing ourselves goes hand in hand.

In the process of giving we are already receiving
—Jack Canfield and Peter Chee

PRINCIPLE 7

A Coach Still Needs a Coach

To be a great coach, you yourself need to be humble
and coachable.
—Jack Canfield and Peter Chee

As you have seen in Coaching Principle 5, the path to coaching greatness can be a very challenging one. It's like scaling a very tall mountain, a journey of a thousand miles that requires you to continuously learn and develop. To become more and more successful, you need to humble yourself and learn from other coaches. You yourself must receive coaching so you can be a shining example of the power of coaching. When you begin your journey as a coach, the learning curve can be very steep. There will be times when you have to travel to a lower point of the mountain before you can conquer new peaks. When you receive coaching, you will accomplish more in life and you will also become a better coach.

The main things that prevent coaches from receiving coaching are pride, complacency, and a lack of commitment. They think they have reached the peak of the mountain ... but they have not. They are content with where they are and do not aim to go higher. Either that or they give up and start descending when they find that climbing to higher levels is too tough and takes too much out of them.

The greatest enemy of learning is thinking that you already know. It keeps you from seeking new information and expanding as much as you can. When pride sets in, people think they already know it all; they close their minds to new ideas and valuable feedback, and they are not willing to admit their mistakes. Such people do not make very effective coaches. Being aware of these barriers helps those who want to become great coaches. They know that in order to overcome such barriers, they must consciously make a choice to constantly build new habits and take action to keep learning and getting coached by others.

From this book, you will gain important knowledge about The Coaching Principles (TCP), the Situational Coaching Model (SCM), and the Achievers Coaching Techniques (ACT). You will notice there is so much to put into practice that to do it alone would be very difficult. To coach without being coached would make a coach incomplete. You need to coach and also to be coached to become a better coach. Just as leaders first need to learn how to be good followers, coaches need to learn how to be coached in order to first appreciate what it's like to receive coaching. Being on the other side of the mountain allows you to enjoy and appreciate a different view so that you become more understanding, empathetic, and helpful toward the people you coach.

Coaches also fail to teach effectively when they don't practice what they preach. When a coach encourages people to be disciplined, it would not reflect well on the coach if the coach is showing a lack of discipline. Coaches teach best by example and not by instructing. When a coach tells people that coaching is good, it is much more compelling when the coach is also undergoing coaching and has gained value from being coached. Living the life of a coach is like living the kind of life you want for the people you coach. As a coach, you need to model the more effective ways to live and work so that people can observe that you are living a balanced and happy life with good relationships, having your priorities in order, engaging your strengths, and experiencing fulfillment at work.

Coaching is more caught than taught. We catch good coaching by encountering good coaching in action. The best way to master coaching is not by being told what to do but to observe how good coaching is done, to practice coaching, and to constantly gain experience from being coached by a good coach.

CASE STUDY: SHARON'S STORY

After completing her MBA, Sharon started working in an international pharmaceutical firm. She worked very hard to prove herself and was promoted three times over a period of eight years. She was recently promoted to business manager and was given the opportunity to be trained in many areas including leadership, mentoring, and coaching.

Top management had decided to include coaching and developing employees as one of the key performance indicators (KPIs) for managers in the company. Sharon was given the responsibility to coach five people in different departments.

Sharon was a good individual performer before becoming a manager, and after undergoing some training as a coach, she thought that she knew everything. She began to behave as if she was superior to others. With much pride, she began to coach.

She admits, "When the result didn't turn out as well as I expected, I blamed those whom I coached for not being coachable. I was given feedback from my director based on what he had gathered from the people whom I coached. I was told that instead of coaching, I was trying to teach and instruct people to accept my point of view based on my own experience, which they could not accept. I did not take the feedback well, and I argued with my director to prove that I was better than the people I coached. I was furious, and to make things worse, I failed to achieve my KPIs for the first time in my career, and as a result, I felt like resigning from the company."

Sharon turned to her dad's advisor, who was a trusted mentor. The family friend advised Sharon to pursue a legitimate coaching certification program and to receive professional coaching. "Over a four-month period," Sharon says, "I had to deliver results from playing two major roles—both successfully giving and receiving professional coaching. This assignment humbled me a lot and opened my eyes. I found that I had many of my own self-image and relationship problems to be solved. I was highly stressed and living an imbalanced life like a workaholic aiming for perfection in my career. The coaching I received helped me a lot to resolve the personal problems I had, and at the same time, I learned how to be a great coach.

"It was somewhat miraculous to me that when I experienced for myself the true benefits of coaching, I improved personally and at the same time I became a better coach for others. After I became a fully certified professional coach, I was able to exceed all my work-based KPIs and received several letters of appreciation from the people I coached. I overcame my weaknesses, achieved my goals, and became an effective coach mainly because I got the right coaching. Today I am part of a community of fellow certified coaches and we continue to learn from each other. There is a lot more for me to learn, and I do wish to continue giving and receiving coaching."

Jim Collins, in his book *Good to Great,* stated that leaders of great companies have a unique combination of professional will to achieve outstanding results together with personal humility. Great leaders coach others to achieve excellence rather than instruct and manipulate people. They also *humble themselves* to receive coaching to keep their work and lives on track and to be able to lead *themselves* well. Great leaders know that it can be lonely at the top and that the most difficult person to lead can be themselves. They know why they need coaches to take the journeys with them. They realize that it is difficult to keep seeing themselves when they don't have a mirror in front of them. That's why they need feedback and coaching from others to help keep themselves on track to building great organizations.

As a coach, you are only human; you have your own needs to be fulfilled, problems to be solved and goals to be achieved. When you listen to the many people whom you coach and focus fully on attending to their needs without others listening to and supporting you, it can be tiresome. That is why a coach still needs a coach. One of the great challenges of being a coach is that you are constantly providing for others, accepting, and believing in them. It is difficult to focus attention on the people you coach when you have a lot of your own issues aching inside and yearning for attention.

For anyone facing huge stress, frustrated at work, having conflicts at home, facing troubled relationships, not achieving your goals, and not improving yourself, it is difficult be an effective coach. Deprived people don't make great coaches. They won't have much to give to others; rather, they often try to use others to boost their own egos. Coaching flows from who you are, and who you are is what you have to offer. You need emotional excellence to coach well and it's difficult to give what you don't have. The day that you are convinced how beneficial and life changing coaching can be to all human beings, you would not want to miss out on the opportunity to be coached. That is when you embrace that principle that a coach still needs a coach.

Those who give and receive coaching are at a great advantage compared to those who don't.
—Jack Canfield and Peter Chee

CHAPTER 2

RELATIONSHIP AND TRUST

1. The Coaching Spirit

8. Accountability & Accomplishments

2. **Relationship & Trust**

7. Goals & Action Plans

3. Asking Questions & Curiosity

6. Suggestions & Simplification

4. Listening & Intuition

5. Feedback & Awareness

PRINCIPLE 8

Maintain Authentic Rapport and Humor

All things being equal, people will work with people they like. All things not being equal, they still will.
—John C. Maxwell

The first seven coaching principles you have read so far capture the coaching spirit that lives within great coaches. The next three principles will focus on the foundation upon which coaching conversations are built: relationship and trust.

Can you imagine a coaching session where there is no rapport, connection, or openness? One that is instead filled with antagonism, doubt, or mistrust? That would not seem like a coaching session at all. The coach and the client need to relate well to each other, to feel comfortable with one another's presence, and find common ground on which to build a positive and productive coaching relationship.

Authentic Rapport

The first step in developing this kind of relationship is building rapport. The word *rapport* comes from the French verb *rapporter*, which means *to bring back* or *refer*. If you develop good rapport with your client, you *bring them back* to the "same wavelength," and both of you *refer* to the "same page." Words such as *chemistry, being in sync, similarity, understanding*, and *harmony* have been used to define rapport. You could even visualize it as a dance in which the partners respond to and reflect each other's movements with movements of their own. Their body language complements one another as they engage in a dance of mutual responsiveness and synchronicity.

Think about a time when you first met someone and both of you got along really well. The conversation seemed to flow effortlessly; probably you had some common interests or opinions, or perhaps you identified with something about the person. Before long, the two of you started to naturally reflect each other's physiology—posture, body language, gestures, facial expressions, and eye contact—as well as tone and speed of voice, emotions, and level of enthusiasm. You established a physical, mental, and emotional connection with one another; you were then able to use that relationship to build a climate of mutual trust and respect.

For some coaches, building rapport is something that they do naturally; others may need to learn and practice the skill of building "authentic rapport."

CASE STUDY: ROBERT'S STORY

Take the case of Robert, vice president in a leading development bank in Madrid. He does not smile very often and does not engage in idle chit-chat. He expects only the best from his people, so when they deliver results, he does not compliment or give appreciation. He only talks to his people when there is a problem that needs to be solved, and when he does, he gives them instructions on what to do and what not to do. He once tried to ask questions of his staff and got either blank stares or wrong answers. Now he doesn't bother to ask them anymore.

When he learned about the Coaching Principles and attended a coaching program, Robert realized he had failed to establish rapport with the people around him. He started to smile a bit more and was surprised when people started to smile back at him. He made a conscious effort to remember their names and blocked out time in his schedule to get to know more about them. It was not idle chit-chat anymore; rather it was an opportunity to better understand where his people were coming from. He wanted to appreciate their views, beliefs, preferences, styles and opinions. He took the advice of Dale Carnegie in his classic book *How to Win Friends and Influence People*. Carnegie suggested that to be successful, executives should "become genuinely interested in people" and "make the other person feel important, and do it sincerely."

Robert didn't stop there. He was so inspired by the changes he had seen in his relationship with his team that he wanted to continue building an arsenal of rapport-building tools and techniques, which he could use when faced with challenging team members. He started reading about *Neuro-Linguistic Programming* (NLP) in coaching and learned that unconscious rapport is initially dependent upon how you "pace" and "match" the other person's body posture and rate of speech (physical), words and phrases (mental), as well as mood and feelings (emotional).

NLP rapport building means mirroring the other person but not necessarily acting in exactly the same way. How a person looks, talks, and acts contribute to your impression that the person you're talking to is either like you or different from you. Literally and figuratively, people like people who are most similar to them.

With this in mind, Robert started positioning his body in such a way that he was a near-perfect mirror image of the person to whom he was speaking. After he matched a person for several minutes, he found that if he shifted his posture, the other person also readjusted his or her body position.

Robert also realized that people prefer to listen at the same rate as they speak. Now, if someone he's talking to speaks quickly and urgently, he speeds up his rate of speech. If they speak slowly and deliberately, he slows down as well. He also matches the tone, tempo, volume, and timbre of their voices. Robert also tries to identify whether they have a visual ("it looks good to me"), auditory ("it sounds good to me"), or kinesthetic ("it feels good to me") sensory modality or thinking orientation and matches his words and phrases accordingly.

Pacing and matching effectively is a subtle art, and Robert is careful not to overdo it. He knows that if he tries too hard to mimic every gesture the other person makes and mirror every body movement, he will end up making this person feel even more distant or cause doubt about his actions and intentions. Typically, other people will focus more on what they have to say so that they won't notice these techniques. As Robert continues to improve his rapport-generating skills, he has developed his ability to notice people's reactions to him and his communication, and he's made the necessary adjustments along the way. As a result, Robert has become a much more effective leader.

Like Robert, we too can harness our ability to build and maintain authentic rapport in a coaching relationship. Taking time to establish rapport at the start of the coaching relationship and at the early stages of each coaching conversation is a worthwhile investment. More rapport between the coach and client will typically make the coaching go more smoothly and produce results more naturally. Less rapport, not surprisingly, will make it less effective. As a coach, when you feel a lack of rapport, work on increasing it before you move forward. Less effort up front to create rapport will mean you'll need more effort later to facilitate the client taking the right actions.

It has been said there are three main reasons why people resist change: They don't know it, they don't like it, and they don't like you. You can handle the third reason with relational influence and authentic rapport.

Humor and Likeability

Another way of increasing likeability is the good use of humor. Hugh Sidey, a well-known American journalist, said, "A sense of humor ... is needed armor. Joy in one's heart and some laughter on one's lips is a sign that the person down deep has a pretty good grasp of life." Sidey knew what he was talking about. As coaches, we need this armor. A big smile, shared laughter, and a warm atmosphere can go a long way in breaking the ice and strengthening the bond between you and your client. This bond can prove to be valuable when the coaching relationship is put to the test, when you and the client confront challenging issues, and when difficult decisions need to be made.

This is what William Arthur Ward, author and educator, was referring to, when he said, "A well-developed sense of humor is the pole that adds balance to your steps as you walk the tightrope of life." A well-developed sense of humor can generate hope and optimism, improve overall mood states, and yes, ignite joy and laughter—and it has been said that laughter is the best medicine. Not only has laughter been scientifically proven to be beneficial to a person's health, it has also been known to improve communication, reduce anxiety, relax the muscles, lower the defenses, and bring a sense of connection and shared experience.

The key word in this coaching principle is *authentic*—maintain authentic rapport and humor. As a coach, you're trying to build rapport and use humor, but you must be sincere and acting in the best interest of the client, not driven by self-interest or an urge to patronize. You can't get someone to do something that deep down they don't want to do. If they perceive that you are trying to build a fake rapport or make them laugh to get them to do something they are not ready to do, quite rightly they'll doubt your sincerity. On the other hand, if people understand your true intention is to connect with them and laugh with them, this will reduce their tension, help them relax, and allow them to come up with better and more creative solutions than they would have done without a strong sense of trust and mutual respect.

The famous American comedian Bill Cosby once said, "You can turn painful situations around through laughter. If you can find humor in anything—even poverty—you can survive it." Maintain authentic rapport and humor, and this will help you to reap a bountiful harvest in coaching.

If I had no sense of humor, I would
long ago have committed suicide.
—Mahatma Gandhi

Touch a Heart with Care and Sincerity

Too often, we underestimate the power of a touch,
a smile, a kind word, a listening ear, an honest
compliment, or the smallest act of caring, all of
which have the potential to turn a life around.
—Leo Buscaglia

Now that we have built and maintained authentic rapport and humor, we can further strengthen the relationship with our client by touching his or her heart with care and sincerity. What does this mean?

If we want to engage people and influence them, we must touch their hearts. To touch and embrace their hearts, we must also come from our own heart; *we must care.* When we care, we feel an authentic desire for good will and happiness for another person, a genuine concern for their well-being, and a true feeling of sincerity, openness, and understanding.

In their book *From Chaos to Coherence: The Power to Change Performance*, Doc Childre and Bruce Cryer capture the essence of this coaching principle when they write, "Underlying the application of care in your workplace is sincerity. Without sincerity, caring acts ring hollow. Sincere care is required to achieve a true service attitude with people. When care is mechanical or insincere, it causes resistance and reaction in others, undermining adaptability. Coworkers, family, clients, and superiors can tell the difference between required courtesy and sincere care."

It's true; in a coaching relationship, your client can tell when you're demonstrating "required courtesy" or "sincere care." Although you may be nodding in agreement with what the client is saying or asking a question to clarify his understanding, a client can still sense whether these actions are something mechanical and contrived or something sincere and from the heart.

It has been said that a sense of sincerity is one thing that somehow gets across to others in a very subtle way. People seem to possess some instinct that allows them to sense sincerity. The lesson for you: A coach must truly and sincerely care for his client.

In fact, care and sincerity should be unconditional. A coach sincerely cares even when the client does not deliver or measure up to expectations. During a coaching appointment, you must leave your agenda at the door and focus on the client's agenda and growth. This isn't a time for your frustration either with the client or his lack of action—or, for that matter, with youself. It is in challenging coaching situations such as this when the client most needs a coach who believes in him, who trusts in her, and who sincerely cares for her.

Coaching is an unconditional relationship. It is not a contract with a stipulation that "I will only coach you if ..." or "I will care for you and champion your goals when you. ..." A coach must offer full acceptance and unwavering belief in his clients, independent of their performance. This is what we were referring to in the first Coaching Principle: Believe in Human Potential for Greatness. If you're coaching from this paradigm, you will champion the other person's goals and agenda. At all times you will act in the client's interests. You will touch her heart with care and sincerity.

How else can you show this level of caring? Well, you can establish an open and trusting relationship at the onset, showing interest in the client. You can be a good listener. By asking great questions that are helpful to them; providing useful feedback and suggestions to nurture and enrich them; offering continuous support and encouragement toward accomplishing their goals; and acknowledging progress and showing genuine appreciation; you can help your clients discover and focus on their talents and strengths.

CASE STUDY: EUN HEE'S STORY

This was how Eun Hee increased her relational influence with her clients. Even at the start of the coaching session, she saw them as magnificent—no biases, no prejudices, no partiality. She made her clients feel important by calling them by name, remembering important information and details they shared, and was genuinely concerned about their well-being.

Coach Eun Hee, from Seoul, South Korea, creates a trusting and encouraging environment, listens very openly and intently, and adds value by being there for her clients. She recognizes them for their progress, empathizes with them and encourages them when they have fallen short, and rejoices with them when they have achieved a milestone.

Imagine a relationship with someone who is fully committed to supporting you in achieving what you want in work and in life. Imagine what it's like if someone knows your priorities and vision in life and holds you true to them. Imagine someone who holds the flag at the top of the mountain, motivating you and cheering you on, someone who helps you learn from your failures and celebrates your achievements. Imagine someone being there for you, in good times and in bad. That "someone" is the coach who has touched your heart with care and sincerity.

> *The best and most beautiful things in the world*
> *cannot even be touched. They must be felt with*
> *the heart.*
> —Helen Keller

PRINCIPLE 10

Practice Integrity and Build Trust

The most important persuasion tool you have in your
entire arsenal is integrity
—Zig Ziglar

It has been said that a relationship without integrity and trust is not a worthwhile relationship at all. Trust is the thread with which the fabric of all relationships is woven. It is the glue that binds and the oil that lubricates all relationships. How can a coaching relationship move forward if the coach doesn't trust the client or the client doesn't trust the coach? "Should I share this information with him"? "Does he have another agenda"? "Will he do what he promised to do"? These are the questions and doubts running through one's mind when integrity hasn't been practiced and trust hasn't been built.

As explained earlier in this chapter, maintaining authentic rapport and humor can provide the spark needed to get the coaching relationship started. Touching the heart with care and sincerity paves the way for greater understanding and further strengthens that relationship. Practicing integrity and building trust complements these and brings the relationship to an even higher level, one that will positively impact the success of the coaching experience.

With a foundation of integrity and trust, the client will be more receptive, engaged, and committed. This is what happened to Andrea who had been working with Teresa, her coach, over a period of six months. In the course of their conversations, they were able to develop a coaching relationship built on the pillars of respect, support, truthfulness, honesty, growth, and fulfillment. Andrea can communicate with her coach more openly, enjoy the coaching relationship more, and be more motivated to improve and achieve results from what has been agreed upon during coaching.

Practicing Integrity

According to Dictionary.com, integrity is "adherence to moral and ethical principles; soundness of moral character; honesty." It stems from the Latin adjective *integer*, which means *whole, complete*. In this context, integrity is the inner sense of "wholeness" deriving from qualities such as truthfulness and consistency of character, actions, principles, and values. Men and women who are imbued with integrity stand for something, make and keep commitments to themselves and others, and remain open. They "walk the talk"—their actions are consistent with their words. Time and again, this may require courage and conviction.

Relationships based on integrity are the ones in which we are real and we don't have to pretend to do something or be someone else. When your client puts on a mask or is clearly trying to impress you, it prevents the coaching conversation from being genuine and dealing with the real issues. The same applies, of course, if you're trying to do those things to the client. The power of integrity in coaching is the result of a relationship that is transparent. When the coaching relationship is characterized by honesty, transparency and vulnerability on the part of the coach, it makes it easier for the client to be open, honest, and vulnerable as well.

When we practice this kind of communication with our client, we become a role model for them to do the same. One good exercise in the early stages of a coaching relationship is for you, the coach, to share some of your stories with your client. Make a point to include not only success stories but also your failures, the problems you have faced and the lessons you have learned in overcoming them. This helps set the stage for the client to appreciate the value of openness and deep sharing and to be sincere and honest about the real issues to be confronted and resolved. This also makes it safer for your client to talk about their fears, failures and challenges.

We once worked with a client who was constantly trying to look good and impress us. We quickly realized that and started sharing real stories about the problems and difficulties that we have had to deal with. This set the tone that enabled the client to quickly remove his mask and openly discuss the important issues that he needed to deal with. He realized that the only way we could help was for him to let down his barriers, face his shortcomings, and practice honest, direct, and open communication.

Another factor in building trust is assuring the client that what is discussed in coaching is confidential. You are not going to share what is said with anyone, especially their bosses or supervisors. Honest disclosure from the client is crucial because it leads to the discovery that is necessary for action and without the safety and assurance that confidentiality provides, coaching will not be fully transparent. There would be an undercurrent causing us to wonder what key, necessary information was being withheld by the client. We'd have some questions, if not doubts, about the real story, intention, or motivation behind the client's action; these sorts of confusions could hinder the progress of the coaching session.

Whether working with individual clients or those sponsored by organizations, it is necessary for you to maintain the utmost confidentiality.

This is a key ingredient for a safe and open conversation. It's best if the client is the one to decide what information needs to be revealed about the coaching or if she discloses what is most relevant about the outcome of coaching to others in her organization. At the same time, ask the client to keep you apprised of what information has been revealed to others in order to maintain a good understanding between all the different parties involved, including you.

Building Trust

According to Dictionary.com, trust is defined as: "reliance on the integrity, strength, ability, surety, of a person or thing; confidence." Trust is also "the obligation or responsibility imposed on a person in whom confidence or authority is placed: *a position of trust.*" Both definitions imply that trust is a relationship of reliance: The coach relies on the client, and the client relies on the coach.

As this makes clear, trust goes both ways. You both must be transparent, do what you have agreed to do, and maintain confidentiality. As a coach, you need to trust the client, and the client must also trust you. If that relationship doesn't exist, then it will negatively impact the results of the coaching session. The coach needs to give trust to the client and at the same time also works to gain trust from the client.

Trust operates on two levels: emotional and rational. Emotional trust focuses on: affection, liking, interest, confidence, gratitude, security, acceptance, admiration, respect, appreciation, and contentment. On the other hand, rational, cognitive, and logical trust are grounded in assessments of a party's credibility, which play significant roles in the decision to trust.

According to Steven M. R. Covey in the book *The Speed of Trust: The One Thing That Changes Everything,* this decision about whether or not to trust someone begins with our evaluation of the four Cores of Credibility. These involve:

1. A person's intent or desire to do something

2. A person's integrity, which is the conscious willingness to put in effort to act on the stated intent

3. A person's capability or ability to fulfill an intent

4. The results which are demonstrated from taking action on an intent

How can you gain credibility and earn trust? It begins with working on your character and your competence. The client will then find you credible, and therefore potentially worthy of his trust, if he is comfortable with who you are (character) and what you are capable of doing (competence). When the client believes that your intent is good, and your actions are consistent with that intent, the client determines that you are a person of good character; henceforth he'll be inclined to trust you. Character is the personal minimum requirement for trust, because it is the filter through which your competency will be assessed.

How long will this take? Trust is built over time as both you and the client learn that you can count on each other. The client also learns that this impacts the relationship and the results obtained. For your part, trust is built on small things like being punctual, speaking the truth, and doing what you say you will do. Make commitments wisely, commit to things that you are confident you can meet, record these commitments, and set priorities to ensure their fulfillment. If you won't be able to meet commitments, inform each other well beforehand and agree on a new timeline to fulfill your agreements. Establish clear and honest and realistic expectations. Acknowledge your limitations and know when to get help or refer to others. And finally, don't get into therapy and try to "fix" people ... because that is not coaching.

Truth Shall Set You Free

Clients need to hear the truth from the coach. They are often so engrossed in their situation and habits that they are sometimes not able to see the true facts. Clients rely on the coach to see what is real and true and bring it to their awareness for their benefit. Telling the truth does not have to be confrontational. It can be delivered in an impartial and neutral manner. Don't be attached to the need to be right. If what you perceive as the truth turns out to be not the case, you can just acknowledge it, let go, and move on.

Trust takes time to build, but it can be easily and quickly eroded and difficult to regain when lost. A magnificent building takes a lot of time and effort to erect, but a fire, bomb, or earthquake can destroy it in a second.

How do you rebuild trust if you've done something to lose it? It can be done, but it will take time and effort. Start by acknowledging what went wrong, by apologizing for any "wrongs" that were committed, and by practicing accountability. When you are rebuilding trust, make sure to clarify your expectations to make sure both of you are on the same page. Demonstrate your ability to continue to deliver results and make a commitment to continuously learn and improve. Moving forward, show respect and high regard for your client (and others), create transparency in all your dealings, and fulfill your commitments, no matter how tough or challenging.

When you practice integrity and build trust, you increase the emotional bond between yourself and the client and increase the level of commitment in the coaching relationship. It is easy to say that you are committed, but unless you back up your words with action and competence, it is wishful thinking or self-serving lip service. Action and follow-through demonstrate the level of true commitment in the coaching relationship. When you bestow the gifts of integrity and trust on the people you coach, you will reap the benefits in abundance.

The glue that holds all relationships together—
including the relationship between the leader and the
led is trust, and trust is based on integrity.
—Brian Tracy

CHAPTER 3

ASKING QUESTIONS AND CURIOSITY

1. The Coaching Spirit
8. Accountability & Accomplishments
2. Relationship & Trust
7. Goals & Action Plans
3. Asking Questions & Curiosity
6. Suggestions & Simplification
4. Listening & Intuition
5. Feedback & Awareness

PRINCIPLE 11

Curiosity Ignites Your Spirit

I have no special talents. I am only passionately curious.
—Albert Einstein

Curiosity and Great Achievements

When we look at the lives of famous inventors, we notice a common thread among them: their never-ending journeys of inquiry and exploration, and their quests to create new things that would make a difference for humanity. Thomas Edison was infinitely curious about how to bring light into the world without having to light a fire, and he invented the lightbulb after reportedly making over two thousand attempts. The Wright brothers relentlessly pursued their dream of human flight, and they were the first to make that dream a reality. Albert Einstein, who dropped out of elementary school, failed to get into the Swiss military, and had to work as a Swiss patent clerk, was among the smartest men who ever lived. He professed that it was his passionate curiosity that mattered most.

Alexander Graham Bell was not complacent after the invention of the telephone. His many laboratory archives prove that he was driven by intellectual curiosity and this kept him constantly striving, searching, and wanting to learn and to innovate. Throughout his life, he continued to explore the realms of communication, airplanes, sheep breeding, water distillation, hydrofoils, and artificial respiration. Just before he died, a journalist who interviewed him quoted Bell as saying, "There cannot be mental atrophy in any person who continues to observe, to remember what he observes, and to seek answers for his unceasing curiosity about things."

Releasing Your Curiosity

A Zen master once poured tea into a cup until it started to overflow and spilled onto the mat. His disciple, curious, asked why he did that. The master replied that if a cup is already full then it is not able to contain more tea. By this he meant than when a student's mind is full, it is not ready to receive new knowledge. Curiosity stems *from knowing that you do not know* and wanting to know because you know that something is worth knowing. If you thought you already knew something, you would not be curious about it. On the other hand, if you have a clear purpose of knowing, that makes your curiosity even more intense.

How does all this tie in with coaching? Curiosity nurtures your innate drive to explore and discover better ways of being and acting that lead to more desirable outcomes in your coaching sessions. That benefits both you and your client.

As a coach, you need to first acknowledge that you do not have all the answers the client is seeking. If you enter coaching convinced that you know everything there is to know, you run the risk of putting on the hat of an instructor or consultant and not that of a coach. As a coach, you are expected to ask great questions and be an effective listener in order to draw out the answers that lie within the person you are coaching. But if you're not really interested, your listening will lack depth and the questions you ask will be superficial. Genuine curiosity for a good purpose makes you open to new ideas. You become enthusiastic about learning so you ask a lot of helpful and insightful questions.

Curiosity is something you can develop in yourself. One good way to switch it on is by formulating questions. Start a question with the words, "I am very interested to know," or "I am so curious to find out," followed by the question. By using these phrases during the coaching conversation you will stimulate creative thinking on the part of the client, who is looking for the answer.

Another way to encourage curiosity is to engage in "radiant thinking." This involves focusing on a person or an issue and look- ing at it from many different perspectives in order to discover new in- sights. For example, when someone you coach is considering a new strategic direction for his organization, you can creatively explore his various intentions, plans, and the possible repercussions that might occur together with the strengths, and opportunities he has, as well as the weaknesses and threats that might exist. In this way, your cli- ent can get a lot of valuable input for consideration before rolling out the change.

When you get really curious about how to achieve better and bet- ter outcomes in your coaching, it motivates you to keep thinking and trying new creative approaches. As you ask better questions and lis- ten more deeply, you help people find more ingenious solutions. Your authentic curiosity helps to spark *their* innate curiosity. This will lead them to want to know where their true strengths and passions reside, what gives them true fulfillment and happiness, what is the desired outcome they wish to create, what they need to do to achieve better results, how they can overcome their internal problems and their ex- ternal roadblocks, and what new behaviors they need to commit to.

When both you and your client interact from a position of "I don't know, but let's explore this together and find out," you embark on an exciting journey of discovery.

> *Curiosity stems from knowing that we do not*
> *know and wanting to know because we know that*
> *something is worth knowing.*
> —Jack Canfield and Peter Chee

PRINCIPLE 12

Ask Questions that Empower and Create Buy-In

Successful people ask better questions, and as a
result, they get better answers.
—Anthony Robbins

By asking the right questions, you can establish a strong sense of empowerment and buy-in with the people you coach. Questions that empower are the ones that raise your client's self-esteem by demonstrating your confidence in their capability and potential. When the questions you ask reflect your interest about their strengths and their passions, what they love about themselves, what others appreciate about them, what makes them happy, their achievements, and the reasons that drive them to succeed, you begin to draw out the best from them. This is what truly empowers them.

When people feel a sense of ownership for the solutions and action steps that arise from the coaching conversation, they become more motivated to take those actions. Since the people whom we coach also have much more information about themselves and their circumstances than we do, the plans they come up with themselves tend to yield better results than those we might create for them. People are much more committed and energized to carry out the ideas and plans that they are responsible for having developed. When people are told what to do, if they are not part of that decision, they resist change.

There are other ways you can help your clients develop buy-in on solutions:

- Give them the freedom to make their own decisions.

- Help them to find out what they really want.

- Help them realize what is most important to them.

- Help them realize what brings them the most satisfaction and lasting fulfillment.

To further ascertain the level of buy-in that your clients have developed toward their coaching goals, ask them questions about their personal commitment to take action and the timeline, the amount of effort and sacrifices that they have already made, and what they are willing to put in now. If they seem to be reluctant to commit to action steps and target dates, you will need to ask more questions that generate empowerment and buy-in.

Empowering Questions

You can use the following questions or modify them to fit the specific context in which you are coaching. For example, the first two questions could be rephrased as, "Imagine you have the solutions to having high energy at work. What would it look like?" and, "Assuming all the roadblocks in working with your president have been removed, what would you have done to accomplish that?"

Here are the questions:

1. Imagine you have the solutions to this issue. What would it look like?

2. Assuming all the obstacles have been removed, what would you have done?

3. Putting on the hat of the wisest person that you know, what tactics do you propose?

4. If you have all the resources you need and you can't possibly fail, what would you do?

5. Put yourself in the shoes of your best advisor. What advice would you give yourself?

6. If you reached deep inside yourself for the best answers, what answers would you discover?

7. Consider this to be a defining moment. What is the best thing that you can do?

8. What would really pump you up to win this game?

9. What would it take to fire you up in pursuit of this goal?

10. I am curious—what gives you the greatest motivation to win this race?

11. What do people appreciate most about you?

12. Which of your accomplishments makes you feel very pleased with yourself?

13. What do you love most about yourself?

14. Imagine you are fully engaged in using your natural strengths and pursuing your true passion. What would you be doing right now?

15. When you visualize experiencing fulfillment in your job, what pictures and words come to mind?

16. Knowing that your destiny is in your own hands, what action would you take to become a master of your fate?

17. What would it be like to have the power to make your dreams come true?

18. When you get close to the end of your life's journey in this world, what story would you like to be able to tell about your greatest contribution and achievement?

Imagine if your own coach had asked you some of these questions and you had come up with answers to them. What would that feel like? One powerful question can create deep insights and lead to a new sense of empowerment in the client. At other times, a series of these questions can create a cascade effect that accelerates the speed and power of the coaching process.

Questions that Create Buy-In

When you have asked empowering questions and the client has come up with their answers, you have created a deeper level of buy-in. Here are some more questions that will help you build further buy-in. Again , they can be tailored to meet the specific needs of each coaching scenario.

1. What was the extent of the freedom you had before you decided on this course of action?

2. To what extent were you involved in creating this strategy?

3. How did you engage your creativity in coming up with this solution?

4. To what extent do you feel as if this plan is your own "baby?"

5. Why is this a worthy cause that is worth pursuing?

6. What would most effectively get you to your destination?

7. Why is winning this challenge important to you?

8. In what way will realizing this goal bring you to a desired outcome?

9. On a scale of 1 to 10, how high would you rate each of your goals?

10. Visualize realizing this goal. In what way do you feel a personal sense of fulfillment upon its completion?

11. How would realizing this vision really satisfy you?

12. You've gotten hold of Aladdin's Lamp, and now the genie is waiting to grant you three wishes. What do you wish for?

13. How have you established and engaged your team in pursuing this goal?

14. How committed are you to realizing this goal?

15. On a scale of 1 to 10 how would you rate your level of determination to do whatever it takes to achieve this goal?

16. What sacrifices are you willing to make to accomplish this mission?

17. Relax, take a few slow and deep breaths, and close your eyes. Using all your senses, visualize the attainment of your dream. What do you see happening and how would you describe your feelings?

18. What specific action steps and timeline would you be willing to commit to in order to complete this project?

People often ask coaches to help them make critical decisions, but most of the time they already know what to do. They just need the assurance and confidence to step up and do it. Self-confidence is a key factor in most people's development. Imagine the impact you create for the people you coach when you ask questions that empower them and build buy-in, as opposed to simply advising them what to do. As a coach, when you ask people for their views on things that really matter to them, you are sending them an empowering message that says they are capable of coming up with great ideas and that you have faith in their ability to do that.

When the people you coach answer your questions, you can observe optimism and excitement in the words they use, their voices, the looks on their faces, their postures, body movements, gestures, and so on. By asking empowering questions, you can give people the courage to do what they thought they could not. Imagine a world where people feel enthusiastic about their lives and the work they do. As a coach, you will enjoy asking questions that empower and create buy-in, particularly as you see the results unfold before you.

The answers lie in the questions we ask.
—Jack Canfield and Peter Chee

PRINCIPLE 13

Avoid Judgmental and Advice-Oriented Questions

The wise man doesn't give the right answers,
he poses the right questions.

—Claude Levi-Strauss

When a client shows some signs of despair and says that she is feeling down, you might interject with a question such as, "What was it that you did that made you feel so depressed?" Her response could very well be defensive: "I didn't say I was depressed. What makes you think that I am depressed and that I did something wrong? I am just feeling a bit 'off color' today.'" In such a case, people don't focus on what they want, they focus on what you've said. This also affects the rapport between the coach and the client.

It's *always* better if the words and expression come from the client rather than from the coach. Avoid implying that your client did something that she should not have done or there is something about her that she needs to change. One way to avoid this is called "mirror technique." Use the very same words your clients employ. Rather than asking questions, which might make them feel as if you're judging them, instead ask them to tell you more about their situation. For example, you could say, "I am curious—would you like to paint me a picture of your feeling, the one you say is a bit 'off color' today?" Compare the impact of judgmental questions as opposed to differently formulated questions:

Judgmental Questions	Better Questions
How could you have been so rude to your staff?	In what way would you have wanted to talk to your staff that would have felt better?
Why can't you keep to your agreement and complete the action steps?	What could you do to accomplish those action steps?
Don't you realize that you could destroy this relationship?	In what way would you like to maintain this relationship?

(Continued)

Judgmental Questions	Better Questions
Are you out of your mind? Why did you say that to your daughter?	What could you have said to your daughter to get the desired outcome?
Don't you think you are doing too many things at the same time?	How might you want to focus on what matters to you more?
How could you have fallen for such a scam as this?	How would you like to keep yourself informed so as to avoid such scams?

When people understand that coaching involves listening and asking good questions rather then telling, some coaches try to follow the question-asking mode without realizing that they are still giving people advice and indirectly instructing their clients, albeit in the form of a question. Advice-oriented questions are usually disempowering for people because they still depend on the coach, rather than on the client exercising self-leadership. When the coach is constantly thinking of what solutions to provide, even in the form of a question, they're not really listening to the client.

Instead of trying to solve your clients' problem in your mind and formulating an advice-oriented question, even as you're "listening" to them, leave it to the people you coach to find their *own* answers. Have faith in them and ask effective coaching questions with a curious mind. Here are some examples of advice-oriented questions compared to better questions.

Advice-Oriented Questions	Better Questions
Couldn't you use interviews to gather the data?	In what ways could you gather effective data?
Why don't you send her a necklace and a letter to make it up to her?	What could you do if you want to make it up to her?
How about taking regular exercise for one hour, three times a week?	What could you do to maintain your health and fitness?

Advice-Oriented Questions	Better Questions
Would you have completed this project if you stopped procrastinating?	What could you do to get moving in order to complete this project on target?
Could you ask your manager to help you overcome this bad habit?	Can anyone be of support to you in cultivating your desired habit?
Shouldn't you talk to your team before rushing into this decision?	Who might you like to talk to regarding this decision?
Wouldn't it be better to stop blaming everyone else except yourself?	What would you do if you could take full ownership of this issue?
If you keep focusing on bad thoughts, won't you feel more stressed?	What thoughts could help you feel better and less stressed?

Notice how judgmental and advice-oriented questions make you feel. They tend to make the client feel as if her options are closed. When you give direction and advice you may be disempowering her and preventing her from accessing her own creativity. These advice-oriented questions may also limit your creativity in addressing the situation.

When you revert to asking the better questions, it communicates that you have greater confidence in your client and are genuinely interested in discovering her best answers rather than implying that she did something wrong. The better questions are more open ended and the answers they generate will widen your understanding of the situation. They ultimately give you greater freedom and flexibility to help the client develop a plan more appropriate to her situation.

Eliminating judgmental and advice-oriented questions requires a change of habit and mindset for some coaches. The first step is to become aware of its downside and then consciously make the effort to change. When you find yourself wanting to give unsolicited advice, check your own motives and emotions. Make sure that you are not imposing your beliefs, values, and negative emotions on them, and feeding your ego at the expense of the people you coach. It is deeply wrong to pass a sentence of "guilty" on someone before you have all the facts. If you think you have all the answers to other people's lives, you will be less effective as a coach.

When you get caught up in judgment and giving advice, the power of coaching quickly diminishes. You unwittingly assist in diminishing people's self-esteem and motivation, and their ability to think out of the box is weakened. However, by asking the right questions, you are able to enhance people's confidence, uplift their morale, enable them to be creative and optimistic in finding solutions to move forward, and strengthen their determination to win.

> *Questions provide the key to unlocking*
> *our unlimited potential.*
> —Anthony Robbins

PRINCIPLE 14

Powerful Questions Release Solutions

The right questions evoke self-discovery and
awareness that energize change.
—Jack Canfield and Peter Chee

The Six 'Ws' and One 'H' Formula

To ask powerful questions, you have to be curious and courageous on the client's behalf. You need to believe that the client is able to handle tough, direct questions. The art of asking powerful questions comes from knowing the right direction to take them (*where*), having the right intentions (*why*), using the right questions (*what*) and (*which*), asking them in the right way (*how*), asking them about the right person (*who*), and asking at the right time (*when*).

We call this the six 'Ws' and one 'H' formula of inquiry. It's is a very useful way of helping you to remember the questions that you need to ask others and yourself:

1. "Where we are going?"

2. "Why do we need to ask the question?"

3. "What type of question and what do we ask about?"

4. "Which question do we ask?"

5. "How should we ask?"

6. "Who should we ask?"

7. "When do we ask?"

These are all very important questions that you need to ask so that you can ask effectively and benefit from the power of asking.

The process of asking powerful questions happens naturally and quickly for excellent coaches because their minds have already been trained by lots of practice. With your understanding of six 'Ws' and one 'H' formula as well as experience in how to apply it, you'll instinctively know how to ask powerful questions without hesitation.

Applying the Six 'Ws' and One 'H' Formula

In your coaching conversation, you have been exploring and analyzing various options and decisions regarding a person's goals. Now the conversation needs to move to a series of action steps before concluding. You know clearly that the conversation is moving in this direction (*where*); you want to see if the client is sufficiently motivated to take action (*why*); you choose to ask empowering questions that create buy-in (*what*); you ask two potentially powerful questions because you sense that they are the most appropriate: "What makes you really energized to achieve this goal?" and "What specific action steps are you excited about and willing to commit to for the realization of this goal?"(*which*).

You ask the questions in a smooth flow, speaking clearly in a neutral and impartial manner with a helpful and enthusiastic disposition. You maintain a facial expression and tone of voice that reflect neutrality but with a curious, caring heart (*how*). Before asking the question, you confirm that you're asking the right person (*who*) and you ask the question when the person is ready to receive it, not when they're angry and need to express their frustrations (*when*).

Determining when to ask powerful questions helps you to become aware of the importance of using the right question at the right moment. With experience comes a certain intuition about a good time to ask a particular question. In fact, you can ask the client for the right time to ask certain questions: "Would this be a good time for me to ask you about your accomplishments so far?" "When do you think it would be a good time for me to ask you about your accomplishments?"

You should also be on the lookout for teachable moments to ask direct and powerful questions that energize change. For example, if the person you are coaching has been facing a lot of conflicts at work due to a lack of emotional control, asking direct questions arising from feedback given by coworkers could result in your client pulling back into a defensive position, bristles raised, resisting change. When someone talks about a conflict that he would like to solve, you can choose the right time and ask him what he would like to do to avoid future conflicts.

The "where" aspect of powerful questions is pertinent because you need to be conscious about how the coaching conversation has evolved, where it is at a particular point in time, and what direction it may take. For example, by the conclusion of each coaching conversation, you and the client should agree on action steps. In the subsequent session, you will need to ask appropriate questions to ascertain what the client has accomplished with these steps before you work together to create further steps to take. If you jump straight to further action steps without seeing if the client has completed the actions he committed to earlier, an important link is missing, and the continuity of the conversation will be affected.

In Chapter 9 you will learn about the Situational Coaching Model (SCM), which will serve as a valuable guide, providing you with plenty of exemplary questions to ask in each coaching situation. The SCM will help you ask powerful questions after taking into consideration where the coaching conversation developed from, where it's at during the present moment, and where the conversation is heading.

Concerning "what" questions, an experienced coach uses open-ended queries rather than closed-ended questions. That's because the latter tend to restrict and shut down conversations. People typically respond to closed-ended questions with a yes or no answer and then stop talking; whereas open-ended questions encourage clients to share their ideas and possible solutions more openly.

If you ask open-ended questions and the client still gives short answers, limiting their ideas and options, you can ask a broader question that encourages a wider spectrum of possible answers. The important thing at this stage is to get the client talking.

When you focus on open-ended questions and broader questions, you stimulate "out of the box" thinking and widen people's horizons. However, there are occasions when after spending a lot of the time on such questions, you and your client need to narrow down the options to arrive at particular decisions. In such cases you could use closed-ended questions or options questions like the ones below.

1. Closed-ended questions:

    a. Are you planning to stay with this job?

    b. Are you happy with your job?

    c. Do you think it's time for you to make a career change?

2. Options questions:

    a. What do you think about sticking with this job versus a career change?

    b. Are you happy or unhappy with your job?

    c. On a scale of 1 to 10, with 10 being high, how would you rate your level of happiness with your job?

    d. How would you choose between staying with your job or a career change?

3. Open-ended questions:

   a. How do you view your commitment to staying with this job?

   b. Tell me more about your level of happiness in your current job.

   c. What are your thoughts about your future career plans?

4. Broader questions:

   a. How are things going with your career and your life?

   b. How do you view your level of happiness in your career and your life?

   c. What are all the possible career options that you can think of?

5. Deepening questions:

   a. You mentioned finding a way to engage your passion in your job. Tell me more about that.

   b. You said that creative writing is your passion. Please tell me more about this.

   c. You stated that you could use your creative writing skills as a writer in your company. Can you elaborate further on that?

Powerful Questions Are Clear and Simple

When it comes to creating powerful questions, clarity, simplicity, and direct questions work better. A complex question pushes people to try to make sense of what the question is before they respond; they may get lost trying to figure out what the question is really asking of them. A question is powerful when it is short and simple, easy to understand, and cuts directly to the heart of the issue.

Complex questions:

1. I was wondering about how you felt when you got that promotion and your director said that you are the "star" and the whole department looked at you with admiration, and the CEO invited you to his house. How do you feel about all this? What are you really looking for, or not looking for? What would give you what you want so that you feel valued in this job?

2. If you think about the upcoming conference, the number of people expected, their positions, educational backgrounds, the type of companies people come from, the amount of publicity generated, and the quality of the speakers, do you think you are doing enough? Is there anything that you are missing? Perhaps someone else can help you with all of this. What could you do to make things better?

3. Could you please tell me about the completion of this project. Who is supporting it? Who is not supporting it? Who has excess capacity? If you are overloaded with work, are there other people not involved who might want to help so you can garner their support? Could you ask your vendor to help you get the project done on time?

Clear and Simple Questions:

1. What makes you feel appreciated at work?

2. In what way can you make this conference more successful?

3. What help would you need to complete this project on time?

Silence and Reflection Follows a Powerful Question

Silence from the client after you ask a powerful question indicates that they are thinking and working to find the answers. As a coach, you need to allow for and honor these silences. Don't let silence make you uncomfortable. When you ask a significant question, it is normal for your client to need some time to think about it. It's good to allow that moment of silence before you make other statements or ask further questions.

If the moment of silence seems to go on too long, you can say something to encourage the client to answer the question; alternatively, get consent to ask a different question. You could say something like, "It would be fantastic if you could just 'throw out' whatever comes to mind right now;" or, "Can I go ahead and ask you another question instead?"

A powerful question does not always need immediate answers. In cases where the client really needs more time to reflect on the answer, you can revisit this question later during the conversation or at a later date.

The Value of Powerful Questions

When a person asks you a question, it moves you in a particular direction to look for the answer. Julie Starr, author of *The Coaching Manual,* states that when a question is really a powerful question, "you can almost hear minds crunch into gear. It's as if the human mind cannot resist the challenge of a really great question."

When the mind is searching for answers in the pursuance of a purpose, there is an apparent gap between reality and the intended vision. Psychologists describe this as the creation of "structural tension" in the brain. This increases a person's receptiveness to available resources, helps generate creative solutions, and motivates one to act in order to resolve the tension.

Powerful questions can stimulate deep reflection in search of answers, reflection that goes beyond the time boundary of a single coaching session. People will answer the questions that you ask during the coaching dialogue, but after the session is completed, they may talk to others, take action, and reflect about what was asked and discussed in the session. Though some valuable insights will surface during the coaching session, there may be other important discoveries made before and after each subsequent session. A good practice to facilitate deeper learning is to offer some action steps that involve powerful inquiry questions that the client can work on after the session. You can then explore the answers to those questions during your next session.

Clients are usually much more capable than they imagine. Powerful questions can stimulate people to access their own brilliance and come up with their own solutions.

In some cases, clients need to be encouraged to try their best and answer the questions by articulating their thoughts spontaneously, openly, and honestly. Tell them that their answers do not need to be correct or perfect. When they express themselves and you listen intently with great interest and care, asking more questions and drawing out the wisdom that lies within them, they'll feel validated and gain more confidence. Eventually, the solutions that the client never thought were there emerge from deep within.

Powerful questions have the potential to change lives. They can evoke innovative solutions and self-discovery, inspire us to believe in ourselves, change our mindset, and drive us to take action. Asking questions is one of the most important skills of a coach, so great coaches need to be able to ask great questions. When you master asking powerful questions, you will become a highly valued asset to the people you coach.

A plan in the heart of a man is like deep water,
but a man of understanding draws it out.
—King Solomon

PRINCIPLE 15

Asking Great Questions Requires Practice

He who asks is a fool for five minutes,
but he who does not ask remains a fool forever.
—Chinese Proverb

In the previous coaching principle, we focused on formulating powerful questions, asking them at the right times during coaching, and the value they bring to the coaching relationship. In this coaching principle, we will identify common mistakes to avoid when it comes to asking questions. To become a master at asking great questions takes constant learning and practice. Even seasoned coaches sometimes make mistakes, but with constant practice you can keep your "tools oiled" and develop the skill of asking better questions.

Asking Mistakes

Some of the more common mistakes made when asking questions have already been mentioned in the last three coaching principles. These include asking *judgmental* and *advice-oriented questions,* constantly asking *closed-ended questions* that tend to shut down a conversation, and asking *complex questions* that cause people to get confused. Here are some other common mistakes that coaches make:

Misplaced Questions

When a question does not fit with the situation or is not delivered with the right timing, it can disrupt the conversation, distract the person you are coaching, and affect the smooth flow of dialogue. For example, the coach asks the client about coming to a final decision when they still need to explore more possibilities and do not yet have enough information needed to make that final decision. Or the coach asks questions about sensitive problems when the client wants to talk about her achievements. Take special care to be constantly aware of the following trio:

- Where did we come from?

- Where are we now?

- Where are we going?

These three questions will help guide you to ask the right questions at the right time.

"Why" Questions

If we ask questions to interrogate, to question people's intentions and cast doubts on them, we can cause people to become defensive. They may try to "look good" in front of you, maintaining some image that is important to them, and not reveal the whole truth or totally close themselves up.

A coaching conversation, in which you ask too many "why" questions can be akin to a tension-filled interview during a crime scene investigation in which a detective interrogates a suspect. Imagine a coach asking this series of questions:

- "Why did you get angry at her for nothing?"

- "Why can't you control your emotions?"

- "Why have you become like that?"

- "Why didn't you learn good manners?"

Does this feel like good coaching or a series of accusations?

Instead of asking, "Why did you do this or that?" rephrase the question to, "Tell me more about what you did." Rather than ask, "Why are you so angry?" ask, "What is it about the situation that makes you angry?"

You can insert a statement that you heard the client make earlier and ask them to elaborate on it. For example, "You mentioned that you got angry at her for no apparent reason. Can you elaborate more on that?" You can also change a "why" question into a "what" question. For instance, ask, "What do you think happened here, when you said that you just lost control of your emotions?" rather than "Why did you lose control of your emotions?"

Distracted Questions

When you start thinking of the next question to ask while your client is still speaking, you are distracted from listening effectively. As a result, you miss out on some points that could guide your subsequent questions. Listen attentively; you don't need to think of the next question. There's plenty of time for that. When the other person has finished talking, a short pause in between gives you a chance to come up with the next question, which, if you have been listening and using your curiosity and intuition, should flow naturally. (More on this in the next chapter.)

Repetitive Questions

How many times do you need to ask the same question? How much is enough of asking a question in different ways? If your client is giving you the same or similar answers, it could be they're picking up an indication that you're not satisfied with their answers or that their answers are not good enough. In either case, this can cause people to feel alienated and destroy rapport. Instead of repeating questions, it's better to ask people if they would like to elaborate further or if they have more things to share about the question. If the client asks you to move on with a different question, just proceed with that.

Disruptive Questions

Do your questions interrupt clients who are still talking? This can disrupt their train of thought and give them the impression that what they are saying is not important to you. Make a habit of waiting five to ten seconds to ascertain that people have finished talking or are pausing to wait for your reaction or your next question.

Poorly Expressed Questions

How you use your voice when asking a question affects the way the question comes across to others. An overly loud, fast, and high-pitched voice can be interpreted as you expressing anger; on the other hand an overly soft, slow, and low-pitched voice is perceived as a sign of low energy, depression, and lack of motivation. Be aware of how you use your voice, because it creates a significant impression. Ask others for feedback on how you use your voice to project your intended message. Then adjust accordingly based on the feedback you receive.

Meandering Questions

Some clients may be baffled if your question seems to be beating around the bush or going around in circles. A straightforward approach is almost always best. Ask direct questions with clear thinking and a good flow. It helps to prepare before a coaching session; this will ensure that you enter the session with a clear mind. If something has happened to upset you—a traumatic incident, a quarrel with your partner, and so on—take time to clear your head before beginning the coaching session. It's also a good idea to a take a short five-or ten-minute bathroom and water break halfway through a dialogue, rather than grinding on for an hour or more nonstop. A break will give you a chance to refresh and organize your thoughts.

Bombarding Questions

The speed at which coaches ask questions also affects the tone of the discussion. Asking too many questions too quickly does not allow people the breathing space they need to understand the question properly or to think of the answer. It's good practice to pause for at least ten seconds after asking a question before saying anything further. This also gives you a chance to ask for feedback on whether or not the client is comfortable with your pace and style of questioning. Perhaps they prefer a slower or faster pace.

Delayed Questions

Consider how you time your questions. For example, if you let the client talk for too long a time and neglect to interrupt with any question or comment at all, the client might be confused and begin veering into irrelevant tangents, recounting too many unnecessary details and not achieving the coaching objective they have set. There are times when, for the client's benefit, you need to interject a question to get back on focus. Getting permission to interrupt with another question might sound like this: "You are doing great at expressing yourself. Would it be all right if occasionally I interject some questions to keep us on track with your stated agenda so we make the most of the time we have?"

Mismatched Questions

Think about who should ask different questions so that the right person asks the right questions. For example, "Should you be treated by a psychiatrist?" is a question that should be answered by a specialist not by the client. "What advice would you like me to give you?" might be suitable for people who you are mentoring or consulting rather than someone being coached. Take the trouble to check that you are asking the client a question that they can and should answer.

CASE STUDY: DANIEL'S STORY

As a factory manager in a garment factory in Toronto, Daniel was well trained in giving clear instructions and asking questions as a superior to check if things were going as they should. When he started to learn how to coach, he had no idea that asking the right questions was so important. He thought he was good at asking questions. But he was surprised to find out that the type of questions he was used to asking as a manager did not make him a good coach.

"I want to tell you what happened to me after I practiced coaching extensively and received the right coaching and coach training. I used to ask questions mainly to find out if people were either doing their jobs well or otherwise. If they did well, then they were merely doing what was expected of them. When they did not do well, I would question them further until they admitted all their wrongdoings and I would force them to commit not to repeat it. If they refused to confess their mistakes, then I would ask threatening questions like, 'Do you know that many other people are waiting to get this job?' Since I had a very tight schedule, I asked questions very quickly just to get straight to the answers that I was looking for, and I was not interested in listening or learning from others about how I could help them develop."

This was Daniel's way of communicating and he used this same approach in coaching. He was assigned to coach six staff members in the company but they were reporting to the director of marketing. "The people I was supposed to coach would give excuses that they were busy. Our coaching conversations never went beyond two meetings. I felt bad about this and wanted to do something about it, but I did not know how."

When the company was bought by another group, the new CEO, who had been educated in Malaysia and Australia, told managers that "the future of leaders would depend on their ability to coach and develop other leaders." A companywide survey showed that Daniel was one of the managers who failed to grow other employees. In fact, the staff turnover in his area was the highest in the whole company.

"This was a serious wake-up call for me," Daniel recalls. "I knew I had to force myself to change or I would become extinct in the company. Fortunately, my CEO, who was a well-trained coach, sent me to a good coach training institution. This laid a strong foundation, and the CEO began to coach me himself for a couple of hours every two weeks. I am glad he gave me a chance to improve and cared about my career development and enrichment. I never realized how liberating and empowering coaching could be because I never received such good coaching and training before in my life."

After Daniel experienced the power of coaching, he knew what he had to do for the people who reported to him and the people he coached. When he found out that asking effective questions and listening was the cornerstone of coaching, he began to learn what it took to listen well and to ask good questions. Gradually he overhauled his approach.

"One of the most important lessons I learned," Daniel says, "is not to be complacent and proud. If I think I know everything and I am always right, I am not open to improving myself. Previously I would keep trying to manage and instruct people rather than to develop and empower them with great questions. I still do make occasional mistakes when asking coaching questions, but I become quickly aware of it when they occur. I've learned from my shortcomings and keep working to improve my skill in asking great questions, with regular practice, reflection, and time for feedback from others."

The most recent leadership survey in Daniel's company showed he was ranked among the top three people who made a difference to other leaders by coaching and developing people. Now he has started coaching his two teenage sons instead of shouting at them. "I found that they respond to me with appreciation, and things at home are much happier than ever before."

It can be very challenging indeed when a less experienced coach is faced with the challenge of asking the right questions. With lots of practice over time, you will know better how to ask great questions, questions that evoke self-discovery and release creative and effective solutions.

Some skills such as riding a bicycle stick with us for life. Sadly, that's not the case with asking great questions. If you don't use this skill much, you'll forget how to do it. Maintaining this ability is more like training our muscles: We need to work on them regularly to keep them in shape. When the flame of your curiosity burns brightly, and your question-asking muscles are kept well toned, you can lift more weight off the shoulders of the people you coach and let them stand tall, rejoicing in the discovery of greater achievements.

Millions saw the apple fall, but Newton asked why.
—Bernard Baruch

CHAPTER 4

LISTENING AND INTUITION

1. The Coaching Spirit

8. Accountability & Accomplishments

2. Relationship & Trust

7. Goals & Action Plans

3. Asking Questions & Curiosity

6. Suggestions & Simplification

4. Listening & Intuition

5. Feedback & Awareness

PRINCIPLE 16

Listen Rather Than Tell

Courage is what it takes to stand up and speak;
courage is also what it takes to sit down and listen.
—Winston Churchill

Come here. Sit down. Wash your hands. Eat. Finish your food. Take this. Wait. Hurry up. Call me. Run.

Do these words sound familiar to you? Do you remember them from when you were a kid? Parenting entailed a lot of "telling you what to do" at home by your parents and at school by your teachers. In the workplace, telling others what to do is the command-and-control style of management. On the surface, it seems efficient. Telling is a direct, and, at times, fast way to get things done; however—and this is the point of this chapter—*telling results in compliance rather than commitment from others.*

Too much telling and not enough listening can also short-circuit your effectiveness as a coach. Coaching is not about telling people what to do or providing simple answers or solutions to their questions or problems. Instead, coaching uses the Socratic method of helping people discover the answers for themselves. The assumption of coaching is that clients themselves know best, even if they don't know they know it. Let them do most of the thinking and find their own solutions—that's the essence of good coaching. This unleashes their potential to maximize their own performance, inculcates self-leadership, and empowers them rather than directs them. Moreover, by following this strategy you obtain a much deeper commitment than mere compliance. This approach may be more time-consuming than giving orders, but is also much more satisfying to both the employee and the manager acting as a coach.

For a lot of people, this is very difficult. Over the years, we've been taught to read, speak, and write. But very few of us have been trained to listen. There is no class in school devoted to teaching us to become better listeners. Listening has become the forgotten skill. So, what does listening mean?

Listening and Its Importance

When asked about the meaning of listening, some people would say listening means hearing. However, hearing is a physical act. Listening is an intellectual and emotional act. Hearing acknowledges sounds, whereas listening requires that we understand what was said. If we are really listening intently, we should feel a bit tired after our speaker has finished. After all, effective listening is an active rather than a passive activity.

Abraham Lincoln, a great leader with excellent listening skills, once said, "When I am getting ready to reason with a man, I spend one-third of my time thinking about myself and what I am going to say and two-thirds about him and what he is saying." The key to effective listening is to turn off the focus on ourselves and place it on the other person. We need to listen more and talk less. That is the attitude and the practice that is required of a good coach and leader.

In fact, John Maxwell, in his book *Leadership Gold: Lessons I've Learned from a Lifetime of Leading*, identified Lesson #1 as: "The best leaders are listeners." He says, "Leaders listen, learn, and then lead. For great leaders, there's no such thing as being lonely at the top. Instead of being isolated or withdrawn, they're walking alongside their people, listening to them." Listening is indeed the best way to learn. When we fail to listen, we miss a valuable learning opportunity. We also run the risk of letting small problems escalate into big ones. Leaders who listen can identify prospective trouble spots before they become bigger issues.

Listening positively impacts not only the quality of our work but also the quality of our relationships. It lessens arguments, reduces stress, and shows others that we care. The need to be listened to is a deep social need. We all feel better when we feel listened to and understood. When someone cares enough to listen to what we have to say, we feel appreciated and important. When people do not listen to us, we feel ignored, misunderstood, alone, and insignificant.

Nowhere is this truer than in a coaching relationship. A client once relayed her frustration and hurt feelings with a coach who continually glanced at his watch while supposedly "listening" to her story. Another client shared his disappointment and annoyance when a coach seemed more interested in a magazine article on top of her desk than in what he had to say. Clients know when they haven't been listened to. Their "coaches" did not apply the higher levels of listening needed in a true coaching interaction.

Improve Your Listening Skills

If listening is so important for a great leader such as Abraham Lincoln, how then can you emulate him and become a more effective listener? In his article, "The Power of Active Listening," author and consultant Bill Brooks advises his readers to open their mind, ears, and heart and switch off all negative thoughts and feelings about the person; be receptive to the messages he or she is giving. Listen from the first sentence. In fact, pretend that there is a quiz at the end of the other person's message, so listen intently and block out all interruptions and distractions. Brooks also recommends that we mentally record what the other person is saying, then paraphrase or summarize what we heard them say just to check for understanding. If needed, ask for clarification; offer feedback as appropriate.

Also listen "between-the-lines"—that is, to the words that are left unsaid—and be responsive to the other person. We can repeat back to them what we think they are feeling as well as what they are saying.

Becoming an effective coach requires an extraordinary ability to listen. What prevents most people from moving forward in their lives is a lack of confidence in their own ideas and their ability to express in words what they think and feel. Listening to these people affirms and encourages them to articulate their thoughts and emotions. When they do that, their confidence levels increase and new insights surface. When we verbalize our thoughts to someone else, someone who is listening, we also listen to *ourselves* talking and we think more clearly and confidently than we do alone. When you listen to people rather then tell them what to do, you send a message that tells them that they are important, you believe in them, and they are capable.

Author and speaker Brian Tracy says, "Listening builds trust, the foundation of all lasting relationships." To build a solid coaching relationship, great coaches prefer to listen rather than tell.

It is the province of knowledge to speak and
it is the privilege of wisdom to listen.
—Oliver Wendell Holmes

PRINCIPLE 17

Be Present and Turn Off Your Inner Dialogue

Our presence is a present to the people we coach.
—Peter Chee and Serely Alcaraz

Being Present

One of the greatest gifts you can give to someone is to be present. In fact, referring back to the previous principle, in order to listen to someone, you have to be present. Being present with someone means being on his agenda, available to interact with him, able to let him know you understand his situation, challenges, resistance, and fears. To be present means you fully accept where you are and who you are with in your life. In other words, it means to be in the moment, to enjoy that moment. In a fast-paced world with our busy schedules, people and things can easily interrupt us. People are so multitasked that they do not stop and think for a moment. It is said that in great music, it is the silence between the notes that makes the music. We too need a time to be still, to be silent.

For coach and client to hold one another mutually accountable in a coaching session, the coach must be present not just physically but mentally and emotionally. Your mind cannot be somewhere else while your physical body is present. Being truly present means paying attention and being fully available to the person you are coaching.

In the course of our everyday activities, whether in the office, at home or whenever we are with someone, we have a tendency to drift away from the present moment. Our mind goes wondering about something that happened yesterday, about a report or an assignment to complete for the boss, or about what we have to do tomorrow. This stream of external information and thought is so constant that we barely even notice it.

To be present means using our senses to constantly scan the environment, to be fully aware of the emotional state and facial expressions of others. We have to be in the present and be aware of what's going on in our surroundings. How can we show that we care for someone when we are not giving them our full attention? Quality time is not measured by the amount of time spent with a person, but by the degree to which we focus our attention on their spoken and unspoken words.

As coaches, our clients need us to be in the "here and now," rather than somewhere else. They want our undivided attention. This is true even if your thoughts are related to the coaching experience itself. During the coaching conversation, avoid thinking of what solutions are needed to the client's problem and what question to ask next. When the person has finished, acknowledge him and let the next question come naturally. It's all right to pause for a moment to think about the next question before proceeding. This allows for the breathing space that is needed every now and then by both the coach and the client. So when the client talks, let's listen to him fully and be truly present.

Focus and Remove Distractions

It has been said that the first rule of focus is this: "Wherever you are, be there." If you are in a business meeting, be there. If you are doing paperwork, be there. If you are in a coaching conversation, be there. As coaches, we cannot afford to be there only some of the time. Our clients need us to be there fully with them and for them. According to Barbara De Angelis, a relationship consultant and author, "Only when your consciousness is totally focused on the moment can you receive whatever gift, lesson, or delight that moment has to offer." This is the power of focus.

How can we focus on this "coaching moment"? Prior to the coaching conversation, systematically remove distractions from the environment. These can include:

- Noise

- Other people talking

- E-mails and text messages

- Telephone ringing or vibrating

- Room temperature too hot or too cold

- Room too dark or too bright

Your list of other work may be in front of you, your door may be open with people walking in and out, you might have rushed in to the appointment, or you might be thinking of another task that you need to complete. Before you start to coach, set all these aside.

Are you hungry, thirsty, tired, stressed, or worried? Do take time before each conversation to relax and clear your mind of any other issues not pertaining to the coaching and get ready to fully focus. Maxwell Maltz, author of *Psycho-Cybernetics: A New Way to Get More Living Out of Life,* says, "You can do only one thing at a time. I simply tackle one problem and concentrate all efforts on what I am doing at the moment." When you are listening during the coaching conversation, focus on what the client is saying and not saying. Observe them closely, and use your intuition. Be aware of your thoughts, and if your thoughts have drifted away, bring yourself back to the present. If you were not present, as sometimes unintentionally happens, acknowledge it and gracefully ask the person to recap what they just said so you are back on track with them.

Turn Off Your Inner Dialogue

Another challenge for us is the continuous conversation going on in our heads from the moment we wake up every morning until we finally fall asleep at night. Our internal dialogue is the constant chatter that goes on in our heads. It could be playbacks from the past, judgments about people and situations, comments on what is going on, and plans for the future. "Oh my, she shouldn't have done that," or "That must have cost a lot," or "I think I better consult this person."

This inner dialogue continues throughout the day while we're working, eating our meals, driving to work, and, unfortunately, while we're talking to others. This inner conversation that we have with ourselves can be positive or negative. It can act as a filter on what we are listening to from others and can be biased if it is not checked.

Our emotions are strongly determined by how much we talk to ourselves and how we interpret the events happening around us. A great deal of energy, time, and attention can be wasted on small and insignificant incidents just because they are continually being replayed in our minds. In his online article "The Inner Dialogue," Remez Sasson says: "These inner dialogues bring about a snowball effect. The more we conduct them, the more we become chained to them and unable to stop them. When the emotions are also evoked, more power, energy, and attachment are added. This has an adverse effect on behavior, judgment, and general performance."

Spencer Johnson, in his book *The Present: The Secret to Enjoying Your Work and Life, Now!,* emphasizes that when you are fully engaged in what you are doing, your mind doesn't wander. You enjoy life. And you are happier and more effective. You are intent only on what is happening at that moment. That focus and concentration leads to your success. So let's be present and turn off our inner dialogue. Indeed, our presence is truly a present to the people we coach.

Successful people control their inner dialogues.
—Brian Tracy

PRINCIPLE 18

Avoid Jumping to Premature Conclusions

Jumping to conclusions seldom
leads to happy landings.
—Author Unknown

The Cookie Thief Story

In one of our *Chicken Soup for the Soul* stories, there was a young lady waiting for her flight at the airport. Since she had to wait for several hours to board that flight, she decided to buy a book to pass the time. She also bought a packet of cookies.

She found a place to sit and to read her new book. A man came and sat beside her, opened his magazine and began reading. When she took a cookie from the packet beside her, the man took one also.

She was annoyed, but said nothing. In her mind, she wanted to punch the man for being so daring. As she took another cookie, the man took one too. She was becoming irritated but did not want to cause a scene. Soon there was a competition for eating the cookies. Every time she took one, the man would take one as well. Finally, there was only one cookie left, and she wanted to know what the man would do.

The man took the last cookie, broke it into two halves and offered her one half. What arrogance! That was too much for her to swallow and she angrily stormed off to board her plane. When she sat down in her seat inside the plane, she opened her handbag to get her glasses. To her surprise and mortification, there was her packet of cookies, untouched and unopened.

You can imagine how ashamed and embarrassed she felt. She had forgotten that she had put her cookies in her handbag. The man had been so kind to share his cookies with her and even gave her half of the last cookie. There was no opportunity to explain herself or to apologize. She was the cookie thief herself!

Premature Conclusions

Jumping to premature conclusions means to judge or decide something without having all the facts; to reach unwarranted conclusions. It is very easy to jump to conclusions in our personal and professional lives. Have you ever jumped to a conclusion, or even a solution, without considering all the facts? Have you ever had a visit to a doctor who just gave you a prescription without doing a thorough diagnosis of what was wrong with your health? Have you ever observed another person's actions and assumed that you knew what they were going through?

In the short exercise below, the words are covered so you can only see part of each letter. Try to read them anyway. What do you think they say?

IUMRING TO CONCLUSIONS

If the black bar is removed, you will see the following:

IUMRING TO GONGIUSIONS

In this exercise, you only see part of each letter. Your brain compares this part to its memory of the relevant letters and tries to figure out what the covered-up part might look like. Your brain looks for a pattern. What word could have all these letters? Then your brain fills in the missing pieces. Because your brain tries to make sense of the word, it completes the letters to produce familiar words.

Advice for Coaches

In her article, "How to Avoid the Five Sins of Life Coaching," Julie Melillo identified "Never jump to conclusions" as one of the sins a coach should be beware of committing. She shares the example of a client who says, "I feel stupid that I lost my job." An ineffective coach will not seek to clarify this potentially damaging and confusing statement. Rather, the coach will arrogantly assume that he knows what that means, and move on to the next question. But the statement "I feel stupid" doesn't tell the coach very much. Why does the client feel stupid? What does the word "stupid" mean to him? Does he feel stupid that he's no longer doing the work he was previously employed in? Or does that part not matter and it's only the fact that money isn't coming in that's stupid? Does he feel dumb for reducing his prospects of getting a future job because people will know that he was fired? Or does he feel stupid because his wife said he was stupid when she found out he'd lost his job? If the coach jumps to premature conclusions and doesn't ask, he risks not understanding the client, and the coaching process won't work.

Imagine the impact of "jumping to premature conclusions" during a coaching conversation. When we listen to our client and we think we already know the outcome, our interest to continue listening will be affected. Will we still listen intently to our client? Will we still be present and turn off our inner dialogue? Most likely not. We may find ourselves selectively listening only to the things that we want to listen to in order to back up and confirm our assumptions. This common "sin" in coaching will cause us to make mistakes.

How do we avoid doing this? The first step is to become aware when we are jumping to premature conclusions. Step back and look at what the information really is, not what we are inferring from it. Consider the quality of the information. It is better to clarify than to assume. Find out more information that is relevant to the situation before we say or do anything. Even when the temptation is great, let's not jump to premature conclusions until we have enough information to fully understand what was said or what has taken place.

> *A wise coach keeps an open mind and does not*
> *make assumptions about people.*
> —Jack Canfield and Peter Chee

PRINCIPLE 19

Be Impartial and Nonjudgmental

> *An essential part of true listening is the discipline*
> *of bracketing, the temporary giving up or setting*
> *aside of one's own prejudices, frames of reference*
> *and desires so as to experience as far as possible the*
> *speaker's world from the inside, to step inside his or*
> *her shoes.*
> —M. Scott Peck, MD

BusinessDictionary.com defines coaching as *"impartial* and *non-judgmental* feedback on performance." Coaching expert, Noble Manhattan reaffirms that coaching "provides a confidential, *non-judgmental, impartial* and completely personalized support structure that enables the individual to achieve far more than they ever would 'doing it alone.'" The key words in both these definitions are *impartial* and *nonjudgmental*. When the coach becomes an impartial and nonjudgmental third-party observer, the perspective that he can offer is a clear and unobstructed one. As we've discussed in previous coaching principles, the coach needs to set aside his biases and prejudices and turn off his inner dialogue so he can be fully present. He should resist the temptation to take sides, judge the client's actions, and jump to conclusions. How can he best do this?

One of the ways to be impartial and nonjudgmental is for the coach to listen with empathy. Empathy is the ability to put one's self in another person's position, to enter into the mindset of another person in order to better understand that person's emotions or feelings.

To empathize with another person does not mean agreeing or disagreeing. It is trying to see things from the other person's point of view. Ray Schafer says empathy involves the inner experience of sharing in and comprehending the momentary psychological state of another person. It is listening with the heart in an attempt to understand.

Empathy and sympathy are not synonymous. Sympathy means feeling pity and sorrow for someone's misfortune, like having pity for fire or flood victims. Empathy is the ability to step into another's shoes, identify with and understand his or her situation, feelings, and motives. Simon Baron-Cohen defines empathy as spontaneously and naturally tuning into the other person's thoughts and feelings, whatever these may be.

There are two major elements to empathy.

1. The cognitive component: Understanding the other's feelings and taking their perspective.

2. The affective component: The appropriate emotional response to another person's emotional state.

When you listen with empathy, you let the client know, "I understand your problem and how you feel about it; I am interested in what you are saying, and I am not judging you." You can convey this message through words and nonverbal behaviors, including body language. You can look the client in the eye, nod your head, and respond in a way that lets the other person know that you're "there" and fully present for him. You let the other person dominate the discussion, you're attentive to what is being said, and you're careful not to interrupt the flow of thought. You must be sensitive to the emotions being expressed and able to reflect back to the other person the substance and feelings expressed. Your focus stays on the other person until he completes what he is sharing. When you do all these things, the other person will feel the deep connection and the sense of importance that you have bestowed upon him.

Jonathon Chace, associate director of the U.S. Community Relations Service, recalls a highly charged community race-related conflict he responded to more than 30 years ago when he was a mediator in the agency's mid-Atlantic office. It involved the construction of a highway that would physically divide a community containing a public housing project. When the final negotiation session ended, the leader of the community organization bolted across the floor, clasped the mediator's hand, and thanked him for being "different from the others."

"How was I different?" Chace asked.

"You listened," was the reply. "You were the only one who cared about what we were saying."

People know when we have truly and empathically listened. When we listen only in order to take sides, whether in favor of our client or another party, we lose focus on listening. When we listen and start making judgments about things in our mind, we lose our objectivity. We start looking for evidence to back up our judgment. Then, when we speak or ask questions, this is revealed and the client feels wrongly judged. Questions such as, "How could you have been so gullible?" or "Don't you think you have been unfair to your staff?" are "judgmental" if not accusatory questions. We have already judged our clients and found them guilty as charged.

Coaches are not experts on other people. *Clients* are the experts on their own lives. Clients generally know what works best for them and what does not. They need to decide for themselves how they feel about their actions and their life paths. It is not your place to judge your clients or their actions. As soon as we start judging anyone, we appear that we are saying that we are better than them. We are analyzing people based on our preconceived values and beliefs. This behavior will strain our relationships with them. For our clients, feeling judged will prevent them from expressing themselves freely and moving forward. They will most likely respond to judgment with defensiveness, withdrawal, or even anger, thereby eroding the level of trust and respect in the coaching relationship.

When you listen to your clients, do you see them as an "A" (Outstanding) or as an "F" (Failing) or incomplete? Do you see them as works in progress and believe that your job is to help them succeed on their own? Or do you think that there's something wrong with them and it's your role to fix them?

Let's not judge our clients or impose our values, opinions, and prejudices on them. It is difficult to succeed if we're talking to a boss who's already formed judgments and conclusions about us rather than keeping an open mind. It is equally difficult to succeed if the coach listening to us—who's supposed to help us—cannot set aside his own needs, preconceived notions, and partiality in order to focus on the essence of what *we* are thinking, feeling, and needing.

In her online article, "The Power of Effective Listening," Jana Hollingsworth cited this example: If the speaker is telling you about how they just paid off their credit card debt, your empathic response would be something to the effect of, "That must be a huge relief!" or "You must feel so good!" If you acknowledge the person in this way, he feels heard. On the other hand, here is an example of *not* being an empathic listener:

Client: "I just lost 25 pounds. This is the first time in my life I've been able to lose the weight and keep it off."

Coach: "I remember the first time I lost a lot of weight. I was so happy until the pounds starting creeping back on." Notice that this listener has completely ignored the speaker's "win" and turned the focus back on himself. He's emphasized that he's more interested in himself than in the client. When the focus stays on the client, though, both people share a more meaningful exchange.

So what are we waiting for? Let's get our judgments out of the way and be mentally and fully present with our clients. Let's realize that everyone sees things differently and the gift that we can give to our clients is empathic listening. This will provide an opportunity for people to talk through their problems so they can clarify their thinking as well as provide a necessary emotional release. Lyman S. Steil, former president of the American Listening Association, refers to this as "cathartic communication." He says this kind of communication "requires caring, concerned risk taking and nonjudgmental listening. Truly empathic people suspend evaluation and criticism when they listen to others. Here, the challenge is to enter into the private world of the speaker, to understand without judging actions or feelings."

*A skilled listener takes information from others
while remaining nonjudgmental and empathic, and
acknowledges the speaker in a way that invites the
communication to continue.*
—Madelyn Burley-Allen

PRINCIPLE 20

Listen Deeply, Use Observation and Intuition

*The essence of mastering systems thinking as a
management discipline lies in seeing patterns where
others see only events and forces to react to.*
—Peter Senge

When you choose to listen rather than tell, you stay fully present for your client; you avoid jumping to premature conclusion; you remain impartial and nonjudgmental; and when you ask great questions, you are able to draw out a lot of valuable data from your client. When that happens, you need to use deep listening, observation, and intuition to make sense of crucial information, carry on asking great questions, and use your curiosity until your client discovers new insight. (Asking questions and curiosity were dealt with in the previous chapter.)

Here is an equation that serves as a model to help you conceptualize a very important process that takes place during an effective coaching conversation. We call this the "Crucial Conversational Process."

(Deep Listening + Observation + Intuition +
Curiosity + Great Questions)
+ Repetition = Insightful Discovery

This process, when used effectively over and over during a coaching conversation, unleashes insightful discovery for your clients. After that clarity has been achieved, you will be able to work through implementation plans with them. You can then support them in taking action to produce the desired results.

93

Deep Listening and Observation

Deep listening means listening in order to understand what the client is really saying, then being able to identify what is really important to them. Good coaches listen for what is significant. For example you listen for:

- Underlying thought patterns

- Habits

- Critical incidents

- Competencies

- Strengths

- Weaknesses

- Beliefs

- Values

When we listen deeply, we also listen for patterns of success and patterns of failure. When people can identify such patterns, it usually indicates that they are ready for the next step: working on solving their problems and producing better results.

Deep listening does not mean jumping to conclusions or being judgmental. When you hear something that you think could have significant implications, you respond by asking neutral and nonjudgmental questions to clarify and let your client come to his own realization about what he or she said.

Use deep listening alongside observation to identify strong emotions and reactions, as they could signal you that you need to go deeper with your client to bring new understanding to the surface. If what you are hearing and what you are observing are not consistent with one another, continue asking questions—there could be more things waiting to be discovered.

A client once told us that she was very motivated to complete her research project, but we observed that her tone of voice, gestures, and facial expression seemed to indicate a strong negative emotion rather than one of enthusiasm. As a result we asked her if there were other more important goals that might need her attention. It turned out that when she said she was motivated to complete her research project she was trying to please her husband (and us!) because she had verbally committed to do that research project earlier. By applying deep listening, observation and asking further questions, we eventually found out that her heart's longing was to pursue acting rather than academic research. Our coaching sessions became instrumental in her eventually pursuing a career as a successful actress.

Observation consists of receiving knowledge of the outside world through the senses. It is the process of filtering sensory information through the thought process. Input is received via sound, sight, smell, taste, or touch and then analyzed through either rational or irrational thought. Ira Chaleff, in her online article, "How to Choose A Coach," asserts that an effective coach is a keen, "hawk-eyed" observer. The coach observes the gesture, tone, hesitation, choice of words, body language, motion, innuendo, and tactics in listening to what people are saying.

Keen observation requires a clear mind. The coach listens not only with his ears but with his eyes and other senses to collect information. He gets a sense of what is going on, what is said and what is not said, and uses that to ask further without judging or jumping to any conclusion. As coaches we need to practice and hone our ability to observe, to notice even subtle clues to what might be happening inside our clients' heads.

Observation is not as simple as it seems. There are many brain processes, preconceptions, judgments, and even beliefs that can interfere with observing. Each one of us views the same thing differently depending on our backgrounds, our beliefs, and our values. Thus, it is always necessary to check our perceptions that influence the way we interpret what we see or hear. We have our own filters when we make observations and choose what we want to receive. This will affect the gathering of data and information during coaching. Be aware of these challenges when observing those whom you coach, and seek to be as objective as you can.

Intuition

In addition to deep listening and observation, experienced coaches learn how to use intuition to their advantage. Deep listening, observation, and intuition are all important components of the "Crucial Conversational Process," and they should all work in unison. When we practice good listening, we listen deeply and use observation. Our mind receives various inputs. As a result, there are moments when our intuition is ignited with a sudden revelation and a heightened sense of curiosity. We want to find out if our intuition is pointing us in the right direction.

Intuition is what happens when the accumulated mass of information, knowledge, and experience that we have aquired over the course of our life, comes together in one single spur of thought that relates directly to the stimulus of the moment. According to author and poet Robert Graves, "Intuition is the supralogic that cuts out all the routine processes of thought and leaps straight from the problem to the answer." *New York Times* bestselling author of *Blink*, Malcom Gladwell, introduces the concept of the "thin slice"—intuitive abilities that refer to the way that our unconscious minds can make what are in many cases highly accurate assessments in a very short amount of time, often in a matter of seconds.

There are times during the coaching conversation when after listening deeply and observing, your intuition is activated. Instead of making statements and passing judgments to confirm that your intuition is accurate, keep that in suspense and notice that it makes you feel really curious. That is when you should contuinue asking great questions; at the same time let your client take your intuition and apply it to her situation to see if it is useful to her. Don't be too attached to your intuition, no matter how certain you feel; always be ready to let it go. It could very well be that your intuition is inaccurate or does not apply to your client.

Malcolm Gladwell asserts that when we allow our unconscious prejudices and biases to circumvent the "blink" process, our more considered judgments are often inaccurate. Getting too much information, removing a problem from its normal context, or asking people to decide something that is outside of their range of knowledge can cause inaccurate judgments.

Keep using your intuitive abilities as you apply the "Crucial Conversational Process" and you will find that it does at times benefit your client greatly. The following coaching scenarios show how intuition can add value to the people you coach.

Scenario 1

Françoise was expressing her great disappointment in the many business and strategic partners with whom she had collaborated over the years. She had great difficulty sustaining any collaborative efforts and had resorted to rejecting any further collaboration with external parties. This had weakened her business tremendously. The coach felt intuitively that Françoise showed poor judgment in selecting whom to collaborate with. On deeper analysis, though, it was found that this was not the case—in fact, those people who had terminated their relationships with Francoise had very successful collaborations with many other people.

The coach continued to ask great questions and listened deeply. Eventually he used his intuition to accurately identify a limiting belief that revealed that due to the failures in her many past relationships, Françoise did not trust others. That had seriously offended most of the people with whom she partnered. Realizing this limitation allowed Françoise to work with her coach to release this pattern of distrust and eventually helped her to establish one of the strongest networks of partners in Paris.

Scenario 2

Boris complained continuously to his coach about how much he hated his job. After observing and listening to him deeply, the coach felt intuitively that Boris's boss was the main problem. The coach was curious and continued to ask him questions. From Boris's answers, it emerged the issue was not about the boss but something else not yet identified.

The coach kept an open mind, listening, observing, and using his intuition. At one point, he had a strong intuitive feeling that Boris's talent and the competency requirements of his job were in conflict. Boris was gifted with the ability to relate to people and to influence others, so the job of a systems analyst was dreadful for him, as it focused on his area of weakness. When he took a new role as a sales consultant under the same boss, his job became satisfying; he began to flourish and eventually became one of the top performers on the Moscow team.

Listen deeply, use observation and intuition, and there will be more and more moments when you can rejoice in helping people gain insightful discovery. "Follow your instincts. That's where true wisdom manifests itself." These are the words of the legendary Oprah Winfrey.

Often you have to rely on your intuition.
—Bill Gates
Founder of Microsoft

CHAPTER 5

FEEDBACK AND AWARENESS

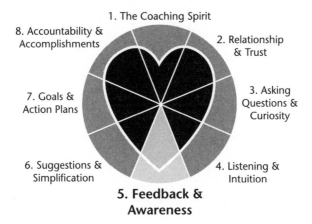

1. The Coaching Spirit

8. Accountability & Accomplishments

2. Relationship & Trust

7. Goals & Action Plans

3. Asking Questions & Curiosity

6. Suggestions & Simplification

4. Listening & Intuition

5. Feedback & Awareness

PRINCIPLE 21

Embrace Feedback to Triumph

Feedback is the Breakfast of Champions.
—Ken Blanchard

Feedback and Its Importance

The word "feedback" started in the early twentieth century and grew out of the broadcasting industry with the advent of microphones. Since inputs into the mics were called "feeds," if there were "feeds" that came back through the system (usually when the mics too close to speakers or the volume of the mic was set incorrectly), you'd get an unpleasant, high-pitched sound. That sound was named "feedback." After several decades the term was borrowed to refer to the reaction to information, a situation, or a relationship.

BusinessDictionary.com defines feedback as the information sent to an entity (an individual or a group) about its past behavior so that entity may adjust its present and future behavior to achieve the desired result. Feedback occurs when an environment reacts to an action or behavior. For example, "customer feedback" is the consumer's reaction to a company's products, services, and policies. "Operational feedback" is the internally generated information on a company's performance. In both cases the reaction and information is returned to the company and "fed back" to modify the organization's next action.

Even though it began life as an unpleasant and often ear-splitting sound, feedback is not inherently negative. What *is* negative is criticism. When we "criticize," there is implied some type of evaluative judgment, censure, or disapproval of the merits and faults of one's work or actions. People don't feel helped by criticism when it comes across as a personal attack that is destructive rather than constructive. This is also the reason why we avoid using "constructive criticism;" something that puts you down and judges you cannot raise you up and help you improve.

Feedback, on the other hand, is generally positive in that it can improve someone's performance. In a coaching conversation, feedback on whether the client is "on course" or "off course" based on his objectives is extremely valuable. People sometimes cannot see themselves, or when they are too deep in a problem or overly engrossed, stressed, or anxious, they cannot see the solutions, resources, and opportunities right in front of them. The coach can act as a "mirror" for the client, showing them where they are, how they are doing, and what they can do better. The coach guides the client to discover what is usually right in front of them. Because people are not able to easily observe themselves, the feedback from others, including their coaches, can be very valuable.

Giving Great Feedback to Clients

Kevin Eikenberry, in his online article on "Coaching and Feedback," asserts that the key to successful feedback is intent. When our intent is clear and pure, when we are really giving feedback and coaching with the very best for the other person in mind, it will be more success-ful. But if our purposes are vindictive, punitive, meant to "fix" some-one, or come from our frustration or anger, the feedback will be less successful. In other words, coaching and feedback shouldn't be about us, but about the other person and their success. When the client senses that the feedback they are receiving is valuable and comes from a per-spective of wanting them to improve and move forward, he or she is more open to hearing and applying it.

As a coach, we have a responsibility to articulate and give feed-back on what we see would be helpful to our client. At the same time, we shouldn't feel too attached to it. In fact, *we should give up the need to be right*, because when we give feedback, we could very well be wrong in what we observe and perceive. If this happens, you must take responsibility. If the feedback was not helpful or was wrong, or the client took it in an over-sensitive manner, apologize: "I am sorry. I meant well and was trying to help with that. If what I said upset you, I apologize. I did not mean to do that."

Feedback can also be given in a form of a question or a statement followed by a question. Take a look at these examples and see which ones were communicated well:

1. You seem to be procrastinating. Don't you think you just need to make the decision now and then stick to it?

2. Do you think that something is causing you to procrastinate? If you want to get this decision done with, what would you do?

3. I notice that you are hesitating on making a decision on some-thing that you want to resolve. Could you tell me more about that?

Example 1 is not great feedback. It's more telling and prescriptive. Examples 2 and 3 are phrased better.

Let's take a look at another example:

1. You seem to be worrying about this unnecessarily. Isn't this causing you to lose focus on other more important things?

2. Is something causing you to worry about this? What can you do to focus on what's more important to you?

3. I sense that you might be worrying about this, but you would rather focus on things that are more important. Can you tell me more about that?

Similar to the first set of examples, Example 1 is not great feedback. It's more telling, if not judging. Examples 2 and 3 are better forms of feedback.

Feedback, followed by a question, helps the client find his own solution or answer. After the feedback is given, allow the client to address it. If it is really necessary to give suggestions, get consent first but minimize its use. It is more empowering to guide the client to find their own solutions rather that giving a lot of suggestions. (More details on giving suggestions will be provided in Coaching Principle 23.)

When to Give Feedback

When a client asks for feedback and needs it, you can share your honest reaction with them. It is essential for you to practice honest, direct, and respectful communication in giving feedback. Sometimes clients need to get feedback from others, and the coach needs to encourage them to ask for feedback from the appropriate people and support them to get it done.

A factory manager we once coached wanted to know how he was doing as a leader. We held him accountable to solicit feedback from those working under and around him. The feedback was valuable in helping him to focus on his strengths and to overcome his weaknesses. It enabled him to become a much better leader.

When the client doesn't ask for feedback but he needs it, you should find the best way and time to give it. When the client is upset, feeling down and highly sensitive, that might not be a good time to offer feedback, as he might not be receptive to it. Great coaches know when to seize a teachable moment to give feedback in the form of a statement followed by a question. This approach gets people to realize how they can do better and gets them to feel motivated to improve rather than resulting in lowering their self-esteem.

For example, if you are coaching a person who has been facing a lot of conflicts at home because of his lack of emotional control, asking direct questions arising from feedback given by family members could result in more defensive behavior and resistance to change. You can listen to him first and then choose the right time (when he talks about a conflict he would like to solve). At that time, offer some feedback, and ask him what he would like to do to handle his challenge. "It appears like whenever your wife gets stressed out, it makes you angry, and this is followed by a series of heated arguments. What could you do to react differently in these situations so that you could triumph over this emotional challenge?"

Responding to Feedback from Clients

Feedback is a two-way process. Just as the client can ask for feedback from his coach, you can also ask for feedback from your client. From the beginning, you must have a sincere desire to seek feedback in order to improve your coaching. Remember to receive feedback as a gift and as an opportunity to learn, achieve more, and be better than you are. Look directly at the person, listen intently, and ask questions if you are not sure or not clear about what he or she is saying. Instead of defending, rationalizing, or making excuses, take time to reflect and understand.

Sincerely thank the person for the feedback and offer her appreciation for caring enough and having the courage to share her thoughts with you. When you do this, you are more likely to continue receiving valuable feedback in the future. Respond to the feedback given by making improvements where necessary, and use the feedback to your advantage to continuously become a better coach. (Further techniques on giving and receiving feedback will be dealt with in Chapter 16.)

CASE STUDY: HENRY'S STORY, PART I

To exemplify the process of offering and receiving feedback from a client let's take a look at the first part of a coaching conversation with Henry, a business development manager of an automobile company.

Coach: Hi, Henry. I am really glad that you are able to make it today. How are things going with you?

Henry: Life seems to get more and more stressful, and I wish my team could accomplish more in a shorter time.

Coach: Is that something you would like to work on? Do you also have any other objectives?

Henry: I really want to work on this. I suppose the other main thing that I have stated in my coaching objective is to be a more effective leader.

Coach: Yes, we can certainly do that. What connection do you see between your stress level, the performance of your team, and being a more effective leader?

Henry: If I can better manage my stress level, I can focus on finding more ways to help my team deliver better results. That would enable me to be a more effective leader.

Coach: Sounds good. Which of the three related areas would you like to start working on first?

Henry: I guess the biggest immediate payoff is to get better results from my team. The sales volume of my team has been on a decline, and we have been way below our target for three straight quarters. My job could be at stake.

Coach: Agreed. What do you think is the main thing preventing you and your team from achieving the targets?

Henry: I believe it has a lot to do with my team members. There are eleven of them, and I wish I could have them all replaced with better team members.

Coach: I am curious. Can you say more about that?

Henry: Whenever I tell them what to do, initially they follow but then later they keep making more and more mistakes. It never seems to end.

Coach: Please tell me more.

Henry: What good can I be as a manager when every time I correct people, they just keep making more mistakes. It makes me feel like a fool and gets me really frustrated.

Coach: Can you give some specific examples?

Henry: One of my sales executives has a habit of making promises to clients to secure sales, and when we are not able to deliver the vehicles on time, customers get furious, and many just cancel their orders. The last time this happened I could not hold my frustration. I shouted at my staff and called him a dishonest, irresponsible phony. I felt better after I released my emotions, and I think I did the right thing to correct him.

Coach: What other critical incidents of this nature can you recall?

Henry: There are so many incidents. These sales people seem to be problem creators. One of the girls resorted to going out on dates with clients to win sales. This created a disaster when a client stormed into our office to demand that he be allowed to see more of her. I was furious and scolded her at one of our team meetings just to warn her and others not to repeat such behavior. Another staff member promised to do thirty sales calls and eight customer visits each week but only did 60 percent of what she committed to. I had to tell her off and emphasized that I cannot accept lazy, good-for-nothing staff members who fail to keep their commitments.

Coach: How do you feel before and after things like that happen?

Henry: When things don't go the way I want, I get very unhappy and stressed. When I do the right thing to reprimand them, my feeling of frustration is released and I feel better. But the issue is that I don't see improvements, and people just keep making more mistakes.

Coach: Can I have your permission to offer you some feedback?

Henry: Please do; that's why I hired you.

Coach: I might be wrong, but I notice a consistent pattern in your reaction to your team members in the way you have just described.

Henry: I think you're right but I have been doing the best I can. That's why I need a coach like you to help me.

Coach: My honest feedback is that, you have good intentions of solving problems but the methods you use seem to focus on punishing people and faulting their characters rather that motivating them to change.

Henry: What do you mean? Are you saying I am a bad manager?

Coach: I didn't mean that, and I am sorry if I gave you that impression. I am totally on your side to support your objectives.

Henry: So what should I do?

Coach: Have you asked for feedback from your team on how they feel and how you can help them improve?

Henry: I can't see the value of asking for feedback from the people who keep creating problems. What are you thinking?

Coach: My sincere feedback is that the people who create the problems . . . they also have the answers to them. What are your thoughts about asking them?

Henry: I will try and talk to them when the time is right.

Coach: I have a request that I believe will help you find solutions.

Henry: Please. I need solutions fast. I don't want to be out of a job.

Coach: Would you consider getting anonymous written feedback from your team about their problems and how you can help them solve them?

Henry: I could get help from my HR to do that.

Coach: Is that something that you would be willing to commit to?

Henry: Yes, I will commit to getting this done before our next meeting. After all, I want to solve this problem.

Coach: Is there anything else you'd like to do before our next meeting?

Henry: I want to reflect more on the feedback you gave me, especially on my consistent pattern and how it is affecting my results.

Coach: That would be great. Before we go, can you offer me some feedback on how the coaching session went today?

Henry: Sure. To be honest I expected more concrete ideas and suggestions from this session. I need all the encouragement and motivation that I can get to be on top of this problem.

Coach: I appreciate your open feedback. One of the leadership gurus that I admire most is Ken Blanchard. He said, "Feedback is the breakfast of champions." I love this phrase, and I love feedback, since I know it can help me serve you better.

Henry: Thanks for sharing this. I have Ken Blanchard's books. They are fantastic.

Coach: Is there any other way I can add more value to you?

Henry: Please help me find solutions faster so I can produce better results.

Coach: Point taken. I will work on it tirelessly, and together we will handle this.

Henry: Thanks, Coach.

Remember no one can make you feel inferior without your consent.
—Eleanor Roosevelt

PRINCIPLE 22

Awareness and Acceptance Cultivates Transformation

Transformational coaching enables people to become aware of what stops them from getting going and what gets them going.
—Jack Canfield and Peter Chee

When people are not aware of what is limiting their progress and happiness, they are oblivious to what needs to change; when they are in a state of denial, they will *resist* change. An effective coach works with her clients to create awareness and acceptance so that they embrace and initiate change willingly without needing to be coerced by anyone.

Helping people to create awareness and voluntary acceptance has the potential to change people's lives for the better. When a coach engages in asking powerful questions, listens effectively, offers valuable feedback, and the client articulates his thoughts openly, this often results in surfacing a new insight that energizes change.

CASE STUDY: HENRY'S STORY, PART II

To bring life to the coaching process that helps create awareness and acceptance that propels change, let's take a look at another coaching conversation with Henry.

Coach: Hello, Henry. How have things been going since we met two weeks ago?

Henry: Not too bad. I think I am beginning to get a much better idea about my pattern of behavior that is limiting my progress.

Coach: That sounds great. I am so eager to hear that, but just before we go there, can we revisit your action step from our last conversation?

Henry: Yes, I did send out the anonymous feedback forms to all my staff, and the response rate was close to 90 percent.

Coach: Well, congratulations on your success with this significant step. How do you feel about it?

Henry: At the beginning, I was sensitive about what many of them said about me, but since I was the one who asked for feedback, and since I have now adopted the phrase "Feedback is the breakfast for champions," I swallowed the pill. Now I feel better and am more prepared to face change, since I am no longer in a state of denial.

Coach: Wonderful. I am intrigued by what you just said about your pattern of behavior that is limiting your progress. Would you tell me about that?

Henry: It seems like every time things don't go the way I want, it makes me feel depressed. That triggers a pattern of criticizing and scolding people and attacking their behavior. This was also the essence of the feedback I got from my staff. I seem trapped in this behavior, and I don't know why. It just seems to happen automatically.

Coach: Tell me more about what impact this "trap" has on you?

Henry: Well, the feedback tells me that people are very unhappy working with me. They say it stresses them to the point that it badly affects their performance and their confidence.

Coach: Think deeper. Is there any other way that this trap is affecting your life?

Henry: My seventeen-year-old daughter seems to be having frequent outbursts and she avoids talking to me. I think it's just part of the "growing pains," you know, that "teenager thing." Hang on there! As I am talking to you, it just struck me that I have been using this same pattern of behavior when communicating with her. Oh my God! . . . You know I would rather hurt myself than hurt my darling girl, Erika. This really breaks my heart. . . . Sorry I just can't hold back my tears. This is getting too emotional for me.

Coach: I understand how you feel. Can we stay on this for a while more so we can get through this together? I believe you can create something good from here.

Henry: You know, I come from a tough family. I shouldn't cry like this. All right, let me just clear my eyes and nose.

Coach: I can relate with how you feel. Just imagine if you continued with this pattern for years to come: What could be the worst-case scenario?

Henry: I imagine being lonely, not progressing in my career, getting a demotion, and being the first laid off when tough times come. I have seen that happen to others. Erika's future would be jeopardized. I would be hurting my family and the pain would be too much to bear.

Coach: What are your thoughts about change?

Henry: I am fully aware now that I must change! I need help.

Coach: I am with you all the way. What would you rather have?

Henry: I would rather feel good about myself and others while having others feel good about themselves and about me too. Life would be much happier.

Coach: I agree. Could there be some need that you are fulfilling that sustains this pattern?

Henry: I don't know, but I want to kill this pattern before it drives me crazy.

Coach: All right, let's kill it. Let's search deeper. Who is the wisest person you know of?

Henry: Ben Franklin. I've studied his life. Plus he comes from a town not that far from where I grew up.

Coach: Yes, I understand. Now fix an image of Ben Franklin in your mind. Remember some of your favorite quotes from his writings. And now visualize him bestowing his wisdom on you. If you were to think like Ben Franklin, what would you be saying?

Henry: Let me think about this. ...

Coach: Just keep articulating; the answer will come to you.

Henry: The Ben Franklin in me is saying that when I put others down and attack them, it seems to make me feel bigger, smarter and more powerful in comparison to others. I feel good initially; it fills my ego needs but leaves a terrible effect on people that creates even more problems for everyone.

Coach: Great. That's an insightful observation. Is there anyone you know who has this similar pattern?

Henry: Wow, I just remembered now. My mom had this behavior. She used to scold me nonstop and put me down in front of others to tame my "wild" behavior. That made me feel really small and embarrassed, and later I would hide in the attic.

Coach: Thanks for sharing that. What was the good side of your mom?

Henry: She fought hard to keep our family alive. She's a very tough woman who had to raise four kids single-handedly after my dad died in a plane crash. I was proud of my dad. He was one of the best pilots in the navy flying the F/A-18 Hornet fighter plane. I know my mom loved her family immensely and I don't blame her. She had a very tough life, and she did not realize her way would negatively impact me. Furthermore, she didn't have a coach.

Coach: What an interesting observation. Shall we work on creating a brighter future?

Henry: Definitely. I am fully aware of my problem and I accept that I have to do something about it. I am ready and determined to exterminate this nasty "bug" in my head.

As you have just seen from Henry's experience, the right feedback and questions from his coach enabled him to discover things that were limiting his progress in his work and his life which he was not fully aware of. Creating awareness was the necessary step to stimulating his desire to change. You can see how his coach used the right guestions to help spark this self-awareness and self-acceptance. His coach did not have to push him to change or tell him what to do. Instead, she took him on a journey of self-discovery which motivated him to invent his own solutions.

When you coach, use your curiosity and ask powerful questions and then listen deeply, observe and use your intuition to take notice of patterns of behavior, and observe its effects. Then ask more powerful questions such as, "Are these the effects and outcomes that you want?" In the case of ineffective patterns, the answer is usually no.

Once you have identified a pattern, you can begin to deconstruct it and identify what's going on. Ask people to give an example of the larger issue being affected by their behavior pattern. Find out if there is a repeated sequence and a trigger that sets off an ineffective pattern. Ask about what negative effects the habit has on their lives, and what experiences they would rather have.

In the case of Henry, we see how facing and changing his limiting habit of scolding and attacking people's characters eventually transformed him into a better leader and a better father, significantly impacted the sales results he achieved with his team, and made him a much happier person.

What Are You Good At?

Apart from working with people on areas for improvement, another very important role of a coach is to help people become aware of their core strengths and how to engage in what they are really good at. People's failures have a pattern; therefore it can be studied and understood and then consciously not repeated when people become aware of how to avoid it. Conversely, helping someone understand how they have constructed their past successes helps them to replicate more of the same by focusing on their strengths and what they do well.

Too many times people achieve their goals and keep striving for more without taking stock of what they have already achieved and how they did it. People are often too engrossed in what they are doing to become aware. With so much going on, they lack awareness of things that may seem obvious to others.

Coaching helps to facilitate this awareness, by giving people the space in which to stop and reflect on what's going on around them. This, in turn, allows them to consciously improve their thoughts and behaviors so as to produce better outcomes. A client we once coached said, "Because I have been heard, I can now hear myself. Now I know myself better, and I know how I can do better." As a coach, when you help your clients know themselves better, it also helps them better manage their thoughts, emotions, and behavior. This has a huge impact on their success in all areas of their lives.

Daniel Goleman, in his book *Emotional Intelligence*, referred to "knowing thyself" as the first domain of emotional intelligence that facilitates the development of the other four domains that include managing emotions, motivating oneself, recognizing emotions in others, and handling relationships. Coaching has the power to raise people's emotional intelligence, and this in turn impacts their success.

> *Wisdom begins from knowing and conquering*
> *thyself and coaching makes that possible.*
> —Jack Canfield and Peter Chee

CHAPTER 6

SUGGESTIONS AND SIMPLIFICATION

1. The Coaching Spirit
2. Relationship & Trust
3. Asking Questions & Curiosity
4. Listening & Intuition
5. Feedback & Awareness
6. **Suggestions & Simplification**
7. Goals & Action Plans
8. Accountability & Accomplishments

1. The Coaching Spirit
8. Accountability & Accomplishments
2. Relationship & Trust
7. Goals & Action Plans
3. Asking Questions & Curiosity
6. **Suggestions & Simplification**
4. Listening & Intuition
5. Feedback & Awareness

PRINCIPLE 23

Get Consent Before Giving Suggestions

Believe that better answers are going to come from the people you coach so give suggestions only when it is absolutely necessary and after getting their consent.

—Jack Canfield and Peter Chee

To illustrate how a coach brings out the solutions from within the client, gives suggestions only when it's necessary to help the client, and minimizes making suggestions, let's take a look at the third part of the coaching conversation with Henry.

CASE STUDY: HENRY'S STORY, PART III

Henry: As my coach, what's your advice on how I can solve this problem immediately?

Coach: It could take some time to install a new habit. What are your thoughts?

Henry: I think you already have the answer so we can get right to it and kill the bug in my head right away.

Coach: You know, I was not trained as a magician. In reality, the best way I can serve you is to help you find your own solutions. That would be better than magic. (Henry and his coach started laughing.)

Henry: Please help me. I need your magic.

Coach: I will do my very best, but please keep in mind that the best answers are going to come from you rather than me.

Henry: I thought as a coach you would have the best answers and that you would advise me.

Coach: Remember, before we started coaching, I ran down with you what good coaches do. We ask powerful questions, listen deeply, and use our curiosity and intuition to draw out the best solutions from you. I explained to you that you know your life and your circumstances much better than I do. The answers you need are within you.

Henry: I remember, so please start with your questions and help me get out of this rut.

Coach: If someone were to ask you to give this self-defeating pattern of yours a name, what would it be?

Henry: Well, my movie hero is John Wayne. Let's see; who's a famous movie villain? Could this be the Peter Lorre pattern? No, I'm just kidding. I might call it the cruel, heartless, sadistic, and vindictive pattern.

Coach: Can I suggest that you give it a short, clear, and simple name so you remember instantly and can spot it every time it's about to manifest itself?

Henry: Good point. I'll just call this the "sadistic pattern." It's killing me. It's worse than cancer!

Coach: I believe you. How will you know the next time this "sadistic pattern" is emerging?

Henry: I am very aware of this feeling now. Whenever I feel really down and things don't go the way I want, this sadistic pattern starts creeping out.

Coach: What could you do to interrupt this pattern and stop it from emerging?

Henry: I really have no idea so far. Well, I guess I could use my willpower to fight it off. Just stop myself, count from one to ten, leave the room, or go kick a punching bag instead. What do you think?

Coach: What is something positive and fun or humorous that you could do?

Henry: That's a great question, I never thought of it this way.

Coach: Go ahead and see what you can come up with.

Henry: All right. I could do something physical and funny like spin three rounds quickly and put my hands up like superman flying up to the sky and then laugh out loud and say, "I am free." That would be funny enough for me. It would make me feel like a kid again and ready to install a new pattern. I could call this the "humor pattern."

Coach: I like this "humor pattern." That's a great way you just invented to interrupt the sadistic pattern. Can I suggest that you see if you can find a replacement for the sadistic pattern that also fulfills your ego needs so you also feel bigger and better?

Henry: Good idea, but what would you suggest?

Coach: You are capable of thinking of a solution.

Henry: All right, I am beginning to get the hang of your coaching approach. Go ahead ask me some more questions.

Coach: What do you love most about yourself, and what gives you the strongest feeling of love?

Henry: All these years my ability to make powerful presentations has been what I love most about myself. It's what most people at work appreciate about me. When I think about that, it makes me feel really great. About the strongest feeling of love, it comes from my wife Edith. Her warm embrace, her patience, her understanding, and her loving personality make my life worth living.

Coach: Wonderful. What name could you give this pattern?

Henry: I could simply call it the "love pattern."

Coach: I suggest that after you do your "humor pattern," you visualize this "love pattern" and anchor its feeling in your heart. I might

Henry: be wrong, but I believe your can use this to replace the sadistic pattern and over time to become your default pattern.

Henry: I'd like that very much. I love your suggestion. I will definitely work on it.

Coach: Anything else that you would like to do?

Henry: Yes—a lot of good ideas seem to be flowing from inside me. I like visualizing and feeling the love pattern. I can also work on making powerful presentations as often as it is practical, and I can call my wife to listen to her voice whenever I need to feel better.

Coach: That's a good move. Keep tapping into the wisdom that is within you. What else would you do to interact with your team?

Henry: The Ben Franklin hero in me says that I could talk to my staff individually to thank them for their feedback and let them know that I've become aware of this pattern and seek their support to help me change.

Coach: Great!. Tell me more.

Henry: I can also talk to them about how I can help them improve their performance. I'd like to get everyone to work together in a team to focus on their strengths and also focus on mutually coming up with solutions rather than just focusing on problems and mistakes.

Coach: That sounds wonderful. Anything else?

Henry: Yes; earlier you mentioned that it takes time to establish a new habit. I could make it a routine every week, when I review my staff performance, to get feedback from them about how I can lead them better, what they would like to do to improve their performance, and how we can all support each other to take the necessary actions and keep improving. I know you are going to ask me, so I will name these behaviors the "nurturing pattern."

Coach: These are excellent plans, Henry, and I believe you're going to see significant improvements.

Henry: Thanks for believing in me and for helping me come up with these solutions.

Coach: You are most welcome. I am glad to see you solving your own problems.

Henry: You remind me of a well-known magician. (Henry and his coach laugh.)

Coach: Your solutions are better than Houdini's illusion of breaking free from the chains; these chains of yours are real, and breaking them will make a huge difference in your life.

Henry: Agreed. I was able to access the wisdom of Ben Franklin and not Houdini within me. And thank God I have a great coach who is not a magician. (Henry and his coach continue laughing.)

———————————

You might notice that in all the conversations with Henry, the coach seldom gives suggestions. Rather she'd prefer to draw out the answers from him. In this particular part of the conversation, Henry felt that he really needed advice from his coach, and yet she was still able to resist the temptation of giving advice. She only gave suggestions when it was absolutely necessary and after getting his consent.

One of the few suggestions that the coach made was for Henry to give clear simple names to his problematic patterns and his desired patterns of behavior. This naming technique helped Henry to clearly distinguish between what he wanted and what he did not want each time the behaviors emerged. As it turned out, the suggestion was helpful to Henry. As a coach, you should be aware that there are times your well-intended suggestions may not turn out to be suitable or helpful to the client. When that happens, remember that since you are only giving suggestions, you must allow your client to decide what's best for her or him. When we give suggestions, they are based on our own opinion, knowledge, perception, and experience. These may not be relevant to the client's situation, and we could very well be wrong.

Instead of giving advice, which might make people feel they were obligated to follow it because you are their coach, or might result in you being unduly attached to that advice, instead, after getting consent, offer suggestions. Leave it to the client to consider what he would like to do about it. The act of getting consent shows respect and a belief in the capability of the people you coach. It keeps you from giving unsolicited advice and reminds you as a coach to keep suggestion-giving to the minimum and let people come up with their own more empowering and motivating solutions.

If your client keeps asking you questions, bounce the questions back to them, and assure them that they are capable of finding their own answers. If they persist in asking you, confirm that what you're offering is only a suggestion. In any case, give suggestions sparingly; otherwise, you can unconsciously change your role to a consultant or advisor; that's not the role of a real coach. If you assume the role of consultant or advisor, clients become increasingly dependent on you, and the responsibility for their solutions (and their failures) shifts to you. Your clients will become less empowered and have lesser owner-ship of their goals and solutions.

Coaching prioritizes buy-in and motivation over giving people the right solution. That is why effective coaches give very little advice and make very few suggestions. This may differ from some people's expectation that professionals such as coaches, doctors, lawyers, and consultants are paid to give good advice. If you understand that this isn't the case, it will revolutionize the way you work with your clients. You can tell people what to do, but real motivation comes only from within them.

If you believe the critical factor in taking action is motivation, you'll ask questions and encourage people to come up with their own solutions because you know that buy-in and motivation are the high-est for plans that people develop and choose on their own. That's why the coaching approach to listening and asking questions and believ-ing in people is ultimately more empowering and effective in fostering change than the advice-giving approach.

> *A boss might give instructions and bark orders,*
> *a consultant would analyze data and give advice,*
> *but a coach would use curiosity to ask, listen and*
> *draw out the best from people.*
> —Jack Canfield and Peter Chee

PRINCIPLE 24

Use the Power of Simplicity

Genius is the ability to reduce the
complicated to the simple.
—C. W. Ceran

What is simplicity? The dictionary meaning of "simple" is *easy to understand* or *plain without anything extra or unnecessary.* The word simplicity itself makes it sound as if it's easy to attain. But the concept of simplicity should not be confused with little effort. Nor is it the same as "simple-minded," which to some people means ignorant, gullible, naïve, or even foolish. No wonder some people fear being simple and do not see simplicity as a positive. They would rather create complexity in their lives and focus on the details of the problem instead of the main thing. Such people often miss seeing the simple solution staring them in the face.

When do we simplify? We see the signals when we are in a state of anxiety, chaos, or confusion. We experience forgetfulness, overload, or fatigue. There is lack of time, concentration, and focus. We live an imbalanced life, not clear about what we want, where we are going, and how we are going to get there. A lot of us suffer from the paranoia of omission—not wanting to miss out on anything and striving for perfection. We're afraid something will go wrong if we miss out on something, but we end up feeling overwhelmed, lost, and forgetting our priorities.

Why do we need to simplify? A simplified life consists of having what matters most, instead of just having more and more. If we live a cluttered life, we find that there is a constant overload of information and "stuff" everywhere—a cluttered and chaotic workplace, a crowded home, and a disorganized mind. When we simplify, we get the most important things done on time. We have time to do what we want to do, not just what we have to do. We can relax for a while and enjoy life without feeling guilty that we should be doing something else. We experience clarity of thought and happy stress-free living.

As Edward de Bono, author, inventor, and consultant, said, "Dealing with complexity is an inefficient and unnecessary waste of time, attention, and mental energy. There is never any justification for things being complex when they could be simple." How true! A lot of people still do not understand and appreciate, let alone use, the power of simplicity. Perhaps they think that complex things are more impressive as they are more difficult. Perhaps they get lost in the details and do not know how to think simple. Perhaps they want to avoid seeing the reality and live complex lives in denial or out of fear. Whatever the reason, simplicity clears the unnecessary and helps people see things from a clearer perspective and to focus on the more important things in life.

Bottom-lining

How do we capitalize on the power of simplicity in coaching? One of the very important roles of a coach is to help people to see through the fog that makes it hard for them to see things objectively, missing out on solutions and resources that are at their disposal. Many clients tell the coach about lots of things and give long explanations, but in the end they forget to answer or avoid the coach's question. Instead, they tell stories filled with increasingly irrelevant details that multiply in complexity even as they keep repeating themselves.

In his online article, "How Can You Move the Client from Complexity to Simplicity in Coaching?" Hakan Arabacioglu, a life coach based in Istanbul, Turkey, gave this analogy: Imagine that the client is lost and trying to find his orientation in life. He is trying to find the answers to the questions: Where am I now? Where do I want to go from here? He is looking at Google Maps and his zoom level is 18 where he sees himself stuck between the buildings and the streets. He does not even know which city he is in.

The coach's first duty here is to help the client "zoom out" and discover where he is. When the client zooms out, assuming he is familiar with the environment, then he can locate himself. He can identify which city he is in. If he is not familiar, then he needs to keep zooming out till he sees the planet as a dot. He is now focused on the big picture (in fact, about the biggest picture possible). At this time, the client's hour-long story is cut to a single sentence. Also, since he knows where he is now, he can choose where to go from here.

In accounting, the bottom line is the final figure. You can have a spectacular income, but if your costs are not well managed, you'll have nothing to show for all the hard work. So the bottom line has a lot to do with what really matters. In coaching, it's about getting to the core of the issue or the problem, the gist of a discussion that is most important, the critical actions to be taken, and the end result that the client is looking for. These points have to be clear, simple, and powerful.

As coaches, let's ask clear and simple questions and offer clear and simple feedback and suggestions, when needed. Let's avoid complex language, as this will cloud our clients' mind. Let's ask them about the gist, the essence, the core. Let's listen for critical inputs and help the clients simplify and identify the critical issues, main problems, and key solutions. Let's discover what matters most to them and what would make the greatest difference for them. Let's provide an opportunity for them to leverage their strengths and prioritize their most important goals related to the different aspects of their lives.

CASE STUDY: MEI YING'S STORY

Take the case of Mei Ying, an HR manager of a leading shoe manufacturing firm in Shanghai. When asked about the toughest challenge she encounters at work, she started to give a laundry list of all the things that require her attention. She joined the organization six months ago, but there is still so much information she has to learn and many options she has to consider. She shared about the perceived lack of support she felt from management and the perceived lack of cooperation she experienced from the other line managers. One of her team members was going on maternity leave, and another had just submitted his resignation letter. She didn't know what to do or where to start. She was caught up in the complexity of things and couldn't see the possible solutions and resources that were within her reach.

Mei Ying's coach asked her to first relax and breathe deeply. The coach saw the signals that she was in a state of anxiety, chaos, and confusion. Mei Ying was overwhelmed, stressed, even hopeless. The coach needed to "zoom" her out of the story where she was stuck so she could be free from all the confusion and complexity in her story. He did this by asking Mei Ying to zero in and focus on the essential—what was the core of the issue or the problem? By working with her coach, she realized that she hadn't asked for or received any feedback from her boss, peers, and staff since she joined the organization. This was causing the stressful anxiety, undue pressure, and lack of confidence in getting the job done. A simple solution, getting feedback from important people in her workplace, allowed Mei Ying to learn about the most important things, and led her team to producing better results. Simple and effective solutions generated from coaching eventually enabled Mei Ying to excel in her new job.

A coaching session during which you encourage simplicity becomes time efficient. It consumes less mental energy and brings clarity for both you and the client. When we choose to talk simply, without anything extra or unnecessary, we cleanse our minds. Without the chaos and clutter of complexity, we can more easily find what we are looking for—the solution that is readily visible. Using the power of simplicity helps the coach to create more breakthroughs and "Aha!" moments for the client.

> *The business schools reward difficult complex*
> *behavior more than simple behavior, but simple*
> *behavior is more effective.*
> —Warren Buffett

CHAPTER 7

GOALS AND ACTION PLANS

1. The Coaching Spirit
2. Relationship & Trust
3. Asking Questions & Curiosity
4. Listening & Intuition
5. Feedback & Awareness
6. Suggestions & Simplification
7. Goals & Action Plans
8. Accountability & Accomplishments

PRINCIPLE 25

Establish Goal Ownership and Commitment

*Living your best life begins with knowing
what you really want out of life.*
—Jack Canfield and Angelina Cheong

Coaching is a goal driven process, and the main purpose is to enable your clients to achieve better results in their work and lives. The stronger the level of ownership and commitment toward the goals, the better the results will be. One of your key roles as a coach is to take people through an effective goal-setting process while letting them decide on the goals that they are motivated to pursue.

As an effective coach, you must refrain from setting goals for the person you *are coaching. You are not responsible for setting their goals.* Your role is to support them in clarifying their real needs and desires. Ask the right questions and enable your clients to create their own goals and action plans. When you do that, the client will establish a much stronger sense of ownership and commitment toward the goal.

Remarkable things happen when people are strongly driven to take action as a result of setting an effective goal that they own and are committed to. Letting others take responsibility to manage themselves to make worthwhile achievements is a big part of the power of a coaching relationship.

There are three important aspects to the goals you must help your clients create:

1. The goals must be specific and measurable with a clear timeline for completion.

2. The goals should be achievable and yet challenging enough so that the outcome obtained from completing the goal is worth pursuing.

3. The goals should enable the client to grow and develop in the process of working toward them.

To ascertain and to heighten the level of commitment toward people's goals, you can suggest that they do a visualization exercise. Ask them to describe as vividly as possible, what it will be like when they have realized their goals: what outcomes and benefits they will enjoy. Ask them to imagine how they will celebrate their achievement and what sort of enduring satisfaction they will experience after the goal is realized. Finally, ask them to assume the goal is already accomplished and to look back to see what they did to achieve the goal, and to see how they grew in that process.

This will help your client own his goals and be fully committed to achieving them. (Further techniques on effective goal setting will be dealt with in Chapter 13.) To see an example of this, let's return to the coaching session with Henry.

CASE STUDY: HENRY'S STORY, PART IV

In Part IV of the coaching conversation with Henry, the coach works with him to clarify his goals and ensure that they are well formulated.

The coach also helps to confirm that Henry has strong ownership for the goals and is committed to accomplish them.

Coach: Now that you have identified what I believe to be some good solutions, how do you feel about it?

Henry: I feel excited and really empowered since you enabled me to find my own direction—in spite of the fact that I kept pushing you every now and then to give me the answers.

Coach: I am happy for you. Think about the goals that you decided on since we first started our coaching sessions; do you feel that you have ownership over the goals and the solutions that come with them?

Henry: Absolutely. I was the one who decided to work on getting a better performance with my team first, and I created the solutions myself with some help from you. The goals and solutions feel like my babies since I gave birth to them.

Coach: Do you think that getting better performance from your staff will help you achieve your other goals?

Henry: Yes. Come to think of it, the main source of my stress has been from the nonperformance of my team, so when I achieve this goal, my stress level should be greatly reduced. I'm confident that when this issue is resolved, I will have become a better leader of my team.

Coach: It's good to know that. Do you think you could benefit from making your goal more specific and measurable?

Henry: Sure. Goals that are specific and measurable would make me more clearly accountable. Better performance from my sales team would be to meet the target of at least 30 million in sales for this year. Last year we only did 20 million.

Coach: Do you think that 30 million is achievable and within the capability of your team under your leadership?

Henry: With a strong team we can easily reach the target. Our company has 20 sales teams of similar size under different leaders and 15 teams exceeded the 30 million mark, with the top team achieving 50 million.

Coach: What would you consider a breakthrough goal that would be achievable and yet would stretch you and your team in the process of achieving it and result in a quantum leap in your success?

Henry: A breakthrough goal would be 40 million. It's possible but it would require tremendous effort and improvement from everyone in our team.

Coach: True. But how do you feel about setting this as your breakthrough goal?

Henry: I'd like to take on the challenge to make it happen. I believe this coaching process has made a big difference for me and that we can do it.

Coach: Wonderful. How will you engage your team to work together to achieve this breakthrough goal?

Henry: I plan to use the same coaching process that you are providing to me. I'll ask good questions, listen to the answers, and draw out the best from the team members. I'll ask them to visualize the benefits of improved performance and a high-performance work culture. I'll also get everyone involved in creating the goal and then let them commit themselves willingly to our breakthrough goal. Once they fully buy into the target, then I'll work with them on more detailed goals and the roles for each team member.

Coach: That's very good. I guess you already can foresee my next question: Imagine that your breakthrough goal is already realized. How will you feel, what will you be doing, and what benefits will you be enjoying? Go ahead and just relax and visualize that.

Henry: Okay. Let me relax and close my eyes and begin to visualize. Yes, I can see my daughter Erica laughing with me and living a happy life. My wife Edith embracing me and congratulating me as we celebrate together in Paris. My team members grow and develop into effective sales professionals; they reap handsome rewards and look up to me as a good leader who made a difference for them. I receive a promotion and a hefty profit sharing from the great performance. I celebrate together with my CEO at the coming New Year's party. I look in the mirror and smile to myself, saying that I have been transformed and become a much better and happier person.

Coach: Wow! That sounds exciting. What's your level of motivation and commitment toward achieving this breakthrough goal?

Henry: I believe you already know the answer, even though you are still not a magician. (Laughter from Henry and his coach.)

Coach: I'd love to hear your answer.

Henry: My breakthrough goal is to improve the performance of my team and meet the 40 million mark in sales by 5 p.m. on December 31 of this year. I am fully motivated to achieve this goal, and I am totally committed to do everything in my power to achieve it as I take this journey with a great coach who believes in me.

Coach: That's fantastic. I can already feel your victory.

The stronger the level of ownership and commitment to the goal, the greater the achievement will be.
—Jack Canfield and Peter Chee

PRINCIPLE 26

Create Strategies and Action Plans for Goals

Chunk down your goals with the right strategies and action steps and ensure that they are aligned to enable maximum achievement.
—Jack Canfield and Angelina Cheong

Once the overall goals of the person you are coaching have been clearly identified, work to help them identify the main strategies that they will employ to meet the goals. Follow this by identifying more specific action steps or tactics for each strategy.

Action steps are an important output of a coaching conversation. Using them, you as a coach can follow up with people to support their task and goal completion. Breaking a goal down into all the action steps that need to be taken helps people to clarify the things that need to be done in order to achieve their goals. Without a plan of action, the coaching relationship would lack direction and accountability.

The act of setting down the goals and breaking them into clear, measurable chunks, allows people to see more clearly a step-by-step process of getting from where they are to where they want to be. It helps to get people started on the journey of realizing their goals and guides them to focus on what they need to do to achieve their goals.

A coach also works with people to ensure that their detailed action steps and strategies are clearly aligned with their goals so they can be more effective in achieving their intended result.

Develop action steps gradually as you progress with the coaching conversation instead of waiting until the end of the session when time might run out. Ask questions to help people identify what they need to do to achieve their goals, when they should start taking action, how often they should do it, and the target completion date. It's also beneficial to ask about the resources and people needed to produce the results.

Rather than telling your clients what to do, you can help them find a better way to achieve their goals. Focus on asking great questions to draw out the answers from your client. Give suggestions sparingly after getting consent. If your client is still unsure of what strategies and action steps to take to realize his goals, you can suggest that he talk to those who have accomplished similar goals to get some ideas that might be helpful to him.

While working on the strategies and action plans, encourage your client to be creative and explore various options first and then work with them to analyze and identify the better solutions, eliminate what is not necessary, and prioritize the goals, strategies, and action steps.

Also ask your clients about sacrifices: What do they need to forgo in order to implement the action plans to achieve their goals? You can also identify barriers that could prevent your clients from achieving their goals so that you can include strategy and plans to overcome them.

Don't be overly concerned about finding the "perfect" solution. In the process of coming up with strategies and action plans and putting them into action, new ideas will continue to emerge. Goals may be revised to reflect something that your client is more committed to pursuing. When this happens, you and the client can revise the strategies and actions steps to ensure that they are aligned with the overall goal. In fact, it's useful for you and your client to constantly review and update plans as needed.

It's good practice for you to work from your client's list of goals and action plans instead of maintaining the list yourself. This ensures that they take active responsibility and ownership instead of shifting the responsibility to you. Use the term "action steps to achieve your goals." Avoid the words "assignment" or "homework," as it suggests that you have given them a task and are telling them what they should do. People feel more empowered to take action when they have been responsible for creating their own "action steps."

Effective strategies and action steps are essential in enabling clients to achieve their goals. When they get things done, it creates momentum and increases motivation to achieve even more so that success breeds more success. When people meet their goals and make great progress, they get excited and begin to believe in themselves even more. Over time they become capable of achieving much more than they imagined possible.

CASE STUDY: HENRY'S STORY, PART V

In this part of the coaching conversation, Henry and his coach work together to specify in greater detail the strategies and action steps for the accomplishment of his breakthrough goal.

Coach: Shall we break down your goal into more detailed action steps and strategies to ensure your success?

Henry: You bet! I'm ready to get into action.

Coach: Would you like to list the things you would need to do to achieve your goal based on what you have identified so far?

Henry: All right, let me do that part by part. Part one of my strategy to reach my breakthrough goal is to transform myself. So from now on, I will use the "humor pattern" to interrupt my terrible "sadistic pattern." Part two of my strategy will be to replace the terrible pattern with the "love pattern" and then I will use the "nurturing pattern" with my team and my daughter.

Coach: For how long and how often will you do this?

Henry: I will do it as often as the undesired pattern emerges, and I will do this from now on until my undesired habit is gone and the new habit is fully installed in me.

Coach: Are there any further steps under part one or two of your strategy?

Henry: Part one is clear and specific enough for me. For the "love pattern" in part two, I will schedule powerful presentations to support my team and my customers at least two times each week for one hour, and I will call my wife to hear her kind words and warm voice every time I feel down.

Coach: And, what about the "nurturing pattern" in part two?

Henry: Yes, for this I'll do the following:

1. Thank each of my team members for their feedback and let them know I am aware of my limitations and that I am committed to improve.
2. Share my plan to improve and ask for their support to help me change.
3. Ask them to discuss further how I can help them to improve their performance.
4. Identify and focus on the strengths of each team member.
5. Conduct weekly performance reviews and team meetings that are focused on solutions.
6. Exchange weekly dialogue with individual team members on action steps for each person to deliver better results.
7. Facilitate a planning session to get buy-in and ownership from all team members on the breakthrough goal.
8. Equip team members with the tools and methods for better results through training and mentoring.

Coach: Wonderful! Is there anything that could prevent you and your team from achieving the breakthrough goal?

Henry: Let me think. Can I ask the Ben Franklin in me? (Laughter from Henry and his coach.) I feel strongly that my team lacks effective selling skills and has some bad habits. That could be a roadblock. I am glad you asked me this question because that got me to realize that I need to do something about this.

Coach: If you had all the power in the world that you need to change this, what would you do?

Henry: Ben, please help me! This is a tough question. Well, I do know that Zig Ziglar is one of the world's best sales trainers. If only I can tap into his "magic" (Laughter from Henry and his coach.)

Coach: Well, I know that Ziglar's company has a train the trainer certification program. Since you are very experienced in sales and you have powerful presentation skills, would you consider being certified to train for the Ziglar's Sales System and Ziglar's Presentation Skills programs?

Henry: That's a brilliant suggestion. This is something that would strongly motivate me. If I can be a great trainer for my team, this will also help me become a better leader for them. I'll add this to my action list.

Coach: Anything else you would like to do?

Henry: Yes. I'm beginning to love this coaching process. I would also like to learn how to coach my team members to help them establish new habits.

Coach: I am so pleased to hear that. Yes, I can certainly help you find a way to get certified as a professional coach. How would you rank this action step in terms of priority compared to the other items you have stated in your list?

Henry: I would say that this is a high-priority item in the mid-term and the other items on my list are of a higher priority in the immediate term, so I would focus on them first.

Coach: Well, it looks like we have a plan. How do you feel?

Henry: I feel clear about what my goal is and how I am going to achieve it, and I believe that I have been able to come up with a very good plan with your help. Thank you very much.

Coach: You are most welcome.

Knowing where you really want to go, how you are going to get there and taking action to get there is the essence of the psychology of achievement.
—Jack Canfield and Peter Chee

PRINCIPLE 27

Keep Score of Goals and Action Steps

*People can make adjustments to stay on course
when they know how they are progressing
toward their goal at any given time.*

—Jack Canfield and Peter Chee

CASE STUDY: HENRY'S STORY, PART VI

In this part of the coaching conversation, Henry and his coach plan out a system that will help him to keep track of his progress and the completion of action steps that enable him to achieve his goals.

Coach: How would you know how things are progressing with you and your team on the breakthrough goal and the subgoals?

Henry: Well, I could devise a scorecard that will help me keep track of things.

Coach: Tell me more about the scorecard.

Henry: I would like to have three scorecards: One for the breakthrough goal that all team members can see clearly on our notice board in the office as well as on our intranet. I will have another scorecard for my own personal action items; I'll keep it on my organizer and carry it with me all the time at work. The third one for each team member for them to keep score of their own action items related to our breakthrough goal.

Coach: What will the first scorecard look like?

Henry: It will show our breakthrough goal, the latest score updated each week, the difference between the latest score and the breakthrough goal, and the time period indicated.

Coach: That's a good one. What would the other two scorecards look like?

Henry: For my team members, they will each have their targets that align with the overall breakthrough goal and a list of action items updated weekly. One scorecard will show action steps pending and in progress, with a target date for all of them.

Another scorecard will show items accomplished, with date of completion. I will review each team member's scorecard and plan with them at the beginning of each week. I plan to practice the coaching method each week when I have meetings with individual team members.

Coach: That would be great. What about your personal scorecard?

Henry: For me, I will use the same format that I just described for my team members; I'll update you during each coaching session on how I am progressing.

Coach: You'll have a lot of items on your scorecard and action list. How will you know which tasks are of higher priority?

Henry: Well, the target dates on each item will in a way indicate the priority since only important tasks will be included. In addition I can still add a column to indicate a 1 to 10 rating on each task, 10 indicating the highest level of importance.

Coach: That would be good. In fact, devising and implementing the scorecard that you have just described is in itself an action step for you.

Henry: Yes, indeed, an important action step. I will add this to my list.

Coach: What value do you see from having the scorecard?

Henry: I see tremendous value. All team members will be able to know clearly at any point in time where we are going, how we are going to get there, and where we are at any point in time. We would be able to continuously make adjustments and improvements to achieve more. I believe this can help us realize our dreams.

Coach: Could you please e-mail me a copy of your scorecards before our next coaching session so that I can review them before we meet?

Henry: Certainly. I'll send you the format first for your feedback. Then you'll get my fully updated scorecard a day before each coaching session. I will add this as another one of my important action items.

In the process of coaching, we need to help our clients create and use a scorecard. This will serve as a guide to show how close or far they are from accomplishing their goal, what steps are to be taken, and what has already been accomplished. By setting a scorecard, they will be able to keep track of their goals and achievements in an organized way. According to Dr. John Maxwell, "Competing without a scoreboard is like bowling without pins. You may be working hard but you don't really know how you are doing."

Keep Your Eyes on the Prize

Staying focused on the goal will give people a reason to wake up every morning filled with energy and the anticipation of what is to come when they achieve their goals. It is essential that people are able to measure their goals. This way, they keep score of exciting progress, positive outcomes, and beneficial gains. Score-keeping, as any sports fan can tell you, stimulates us to create more and more positive outcomes and gets us motivated to want to achieve more. It creates a "structural tension" in our brain as a result of the apparent gap between where we are and where we want to be. This increases our receptiveness to available resources, the generation of creative solutions, and drives us to act in order to resolve the structural tension that has been created.

Without a scorecard, people often forget what they've achieved in the past. Reviewing and visualizing past accomplishments as victories gives a boost to a client's self-esteem and motivation. When you evoke emotions of joy and pride from their past achievements, it reminds them how capable they are and gives them the energy to do and achieve more. In reviewing scorecards, you should constantly acknowledge and reinforce what your client has already accomplished.

When people do better than expected or when they are on target, celebrate with them and challenge them to see if they want to aim even higher in the future. When their scorecard shows that they have fallen short of their target, review their goals and action steps with them and focus on helping them find their own solutions to achieving their intended result. At times, this could entail a reformulation of goals and action steps; at other times what they need is continuous support, encouragement, and motivation.

After reviewing the scorecard, help people learn how they can do better once they have a clear understanding of the outcomes they are getting as a result of what they have done. Scorecards offer valuable feedback and significant lessons when we take time to reflect and uncover the reasons behind the scores that we are getting. (We have further thoughts on keeping score of goals and action plans in Chapter 15.)

In the case of Henry, the use of scorecards proved very beneficial to him and his team. The scorecard allowed Henry, his coach, and his staff to know how they were progressing at any point with their breakthrough goal as well as individual goals that were clearly aligned with each other. The scorecards made a big difference that helped Henry and his team to stay accountable and to take action to continuously be on top of their game for producing even greater achievements. That's the value of keeping score of our goals and action steps.

The game plan tells you what you want to happen.
But the scorecard tells what is happening.
—John Maxwell

CHAPTER 8

ACCOUNTABILITY AND ACCOMPLISHMENTS

1. The Coaching Spirit

8. Accountability & Accomplishments

2. Relationship & Trust

3. Asking Questions & Curiosity

4. Listening & Intuition

5. Feedback & Awareness

6. Suggestions & Simplification

7. Goals & Action Plans

PRINCIPLE 28

Support Goals Completion Continuously

To maintain old habits requires little effort but to inculcate new habits requires support structures and persistency.

—Jack Canfield and Peter Chee

Sometimes when people begin to take action toward realizing their goals and objectives, they realize that the amount of effort and sacrifice required for them to get what they want is much more than they had anticipated. On some occasions their energy begins to diminish, especially when they are faced with obstacles and difficulties. When this happens, people often slack off and have problems completing their planned tasks. And when it comes to replacing an old habit with a new one, the challenges are usually even greater.

Getting started on something new is much harder than persisting in an established pattern of behavior. It's easy for someone to revert to his old habits: for example, getting angry and shouting at his spouse when something activates his trigger button. Permanently inculcating the new habit of staying calm, understanding, and loving when the old trigger is pulled requires a lot of effort and determination.

One of your important roles as a coach, in addition to championing your client's goals and providing continuous encouragement and affirmation, is helping them establish support structures that will maximize their chances of succeeding. Coaching enables people to sustain change and achieve more because it offers a support system that keeps the client motivated and on track.

Self-Esteem Takes a Hit

When people do not achieve the changes they want, their self-esteem is affected because of their failed effort. When this happens, a bad habit can become even worse. People try to change and take action, but when life's challenges knock them down, they may lack the energy and determination to get back up to continue the effort. That's when excuses usually crop up:

- "I can't spend more time with my kids when my work keeps expanding."

- "I can't get regular exercise because I don't have the equipment and the gym is too far away."

- "When I am nice to people, they take me for granted and do not follow my instructions."

When effective support structures are built into your coaching, such problems can be prevented or resolved as soon as they arise.

As with advice, a point we touched on earlier, it's better to help your clients come up with their own support structures rather than telling them what to do. As a coach, you might offer some ideas, but only if it's really necessary and after getting their consent. Leave it to people to choose what works best for them. There are many different forms of support that clients can utilize. The ongoing coaching session is itself a crucial form of continuous support. At the beginning of every session you should ask them for a progress report on what they've accomplished since you last met.

Other forms of support structures can be used by your client, depending on the situation and their needs, include:

- Follow-up e-mails

- Short phone calls to or from you

- Submission of written progress reports in between coaching sessions

- Meeting or talking with accountability partners who are regularly in contact with the client at home and at work

- Using planners, electronics devices, and software to schedule tasks and reminders

- Celebrating the completion of tasks that mark milestones with family, friends and coworkers.

The frequency and time frame required for utilizing support structures would depend on the nature of the goals and solutions needed—some monthly, fortnightly, weekly, daily, and so on.

Encourage people to come up with simple and creative solutions that work. Stay open to devising different support structures relevant to different goals. For example, we had a client who used a Post-it® note on his steering wheel to remind himself for 60 days to be a safe and caring driver. This helped him to change his dangerous driving habits, which had caused him to have several nearly fatal accidents. After successfully changing his driving habits he continued to use several different support structures to develop a series of new habits that also transformed him into a much more considerate and caring father and husband—in addition to being a safer driver.

A client needs to work on a new habit for a minimum of 30 to 90 days before it sticks. That's why suggesting, providing, and gaining commitment to use support structures is a very important aspect of successful coaching. For example, here are some significant habit changes that could require support structures:

- Changing from watching TV every day to reading beneficial books

- Changing from always doing things at the last minute and being late to being well planned and starting and completing things before the deadline

- Changing from getting angry easily to being calm and centered even under pressing situations.

Change is something that is difficult to do on our own, but with support from others, we are able to do much more. The people whom we see become the most successful in life are the ones who learn to ask for and accept support from others rather than trying to go it alone.

In a coaching relationship, the coach needs to provide continuous support, encouragement, and accountability to the client. Helping a client to put support structures into their lives is one of the most beneficial things you can do as a coach.

CASE STUDY: HENRY'S STORY, PART VII

The ongoing coaching conversation between Henry and his coach every two weeks is in itself a very important form of continuous support. This part of their coaching conversation demonstrates other forms of continuous support that were put into place to enable Henry to achieve his desired results.

Coach: Now that you have a clear and compelling breakthrough goal and a substantial list of action steps, what support structures do you think could help ensure that you get these things accomplished?

Henry: That's a fantastic question, but I am not sure if I have an answer.

Coach: So far you have already proven that you are far more capable than you imagine at coming up with good ideas.

Henry: Well, for one thing, I feel that your constant support, encouragement and belief in me are definitely helping me.

Coach: Good. I am happy to do this, and I'm glad its helping you.

Henry: In regard to your question, can I try and think like another wise person? How about Tony Robbins?

Coach: Please, whatever works for you.

Henry: Support structures? Let me go through my list of action steps again. All right, I know establishing new habits take time and can be quite challenging, so I will schedule the future action items into my weekly planner on my iPhone and schedule reminders to ensure that I get everything done on time.

Coach: I get excited when you start thinking like Tony Robbins. Tell me more.

Henry: I will send a progress report to you by e-mail at the start of each week.

Coach: Great. Would you like me to enter this into my calendar program? That way reminders will be automatically sent to you and me when a progress report is due.

Henry: That would be fantastic.

Coach: Any more ideas?

Henry: I think I'll need someone in my workplace who can be my accountability partner. My CEO mentioned something about this a while back.

Coach: Great idea. I've found that having an accountability partner really assists people in staying focused and getting results.

Henry: I am thinking of asking my assistant manager; she's really good with details and always follows up on things.

Coach: What would you like her to help you with as an accountability partner?

Henry: The "nurturing pattern." There are eight very important action steps I need to take to accomplish that. She can help me to be accountable by having a follow-up meeting with me to ensure that I get things done according to my plan. Let me add this to my action list right now.

Coach: Very good, anything else?

Henry: I need someone to remind me to call my wife, whenever I am feeling depressed. My secretary is very good at sensing when I am down. She always asks me how I am. I am confident she can support me by reminding me to call my wife.

Coach: And, what do you think if in addition to our 90-minute conversations every two weeks, I call you, for a 15-minute chat at the end of each week, just to see if I can support you in any way? Would you like that?

Henry: I would be very grateful if you would do that. Thanks for going out of your way to continuously support me.

Coach: I'm happy to do it. Now let's look at what you think should be your first major milestone to reach in working toward your breakthrough goal of 40 million in sales?

Henry: That would be when I have successfully replaced my sadistic pattern with the love and nurturing patterns.

Coach: How would you know when you have accomplished that?

Henry: The best way would probably be to gather another written feedback from my team members three months from now.

Coach: If the feedback shows the results that you are aiming for, how do you want to celebrate that accomplishment?

Henry: Well, my family and I love to eat and drink, so I think it would be great to go out for a fabulous celebration feast at our favorite gourmet restaurant.

Coach: Good. Schedule that on your calendar, and I look forward to congratulating you on that occasion. Well done !

Providing continuous support, encouragement
and accountability in coaching has the power to
literally change lives.
—Jack Canfield and Peter Chee

PRINCIPLE 29

Accountability Drives Accomplishments

Sustainable accountability is not inflicted, it is voluntary.
—Jack Canfield and Peter Chee

Accountability is one of the most valuable outcomes of effective coaching. People who have been well coached become responsible and committed to execute what they have agreed to, and capable of accomplishing much more than previously. Coaching is about focusing forward and getting things done. Constant follow-up by the coach and an accountability partner helps to ensure that people are kept on track. Getting regular progress reports from your client keeps them responsible and serious about getting things done. Always keep an updated list of goals and action steps from your client, and ask them to review it and update it with you on a consistent basis.

When the Client Doesn't Deliver

At the beginning of each coaching conversation, ask your client if he has delivered on what he committed to do during the last session. If the answer is yes, congratulate him and celebrate with him. If the answer is no, you should not scold, threaten, or shame him. Instead ask questions like:

- What happened?

- Is this still important to you?

- If it's still important, do you still want to do it?

- What would it take for you to get it done?

- What help do you need? Who can you ask for that help?

- What benefits would you be enjoying when you get this completed?

- How do you think you will feel when you accomplish this?

- How do you feel about your sense of ownership related to this task and goal?

- Are you willing to recommit to getting this done?

- By when would you like to have this completed?

If people don't keep their commitments, don't belittle them. Just ask powerful questions that will help to move them forward. Find out if it's necessary to revise their goals and action steps. Give some flexibility if needed, but avoid lowering standards. If high expectations in your coaching relationship begin to erode, coaching starts to lose effectiveness. If you don't hold high standards, your client could lose respect for both the coaching process and you as a coach. This is not the same as forcing people or telling them what to do; it's about helping them to get what they really want. It's about holding people accountable for their own decisions. There is no need to coerce them, but when they slack off, help them get back on track as soon as possible.

Tell the people you coach that you want them to come up to a level where they succeed in each and every step they set out to do. Ask them, "What can we do to make sure you reach that standard?" The *we* in the statement is key. As a coach, you must continue to believe in your client's potential for greatness and continually focus on a brighter future. Your morale should not be dampened when your client faces problems and setbacks. Many times we have seen *breakdowns* turn into an opportunities for *breakthroughs*. When we see ongoing breakdowns, we also see habits and issues that need to be resolved, and when they work through and replace those undesired patterns, the client experiences significant transformations that will enrich many aspects of his or her life.

The Importance of Accountability Partners

Accountability is especially helpful in changing habits and accelerating the completion of goals. A good way to deliver added advantage to your client is to help her get the best from her accountability partners. In this way she can take advantage of being held accountable by others rather than relying only on themselves and you. It's a good idea for accountability partners to be someone already in the client's work or personal life since they are already in constant contact with each other and the partner (or partners) are closest to where the client's behaviors occur. However, we don't advise people to use their wife or husband as their accountability partner because there can often be too much invested in having their partner change quickly, which can lead to pressure, resistance, and fights.

Accountability partners who are most effective are those who can be relied upon and who have the courage not to let your client neglect what is important. It's also good to formalize the relationship: Ensure that those who act as accountability partners know what to do, when to do it, and are equipped with specific accountability questions to ask. Encourage your client to develop his or her own accountability questions and make sure his or her accountability partners have those questions.

Here are some examples of questions relating to accountability partners that you can ask your client:

- Would you like someone to help you be accountable for your own success?

- Would being held accountable increase your chances of success?

- What qualities would you need in an accountability partner?

- Who would be an effective accountability partner for this task?

- What would you want from this person?

- What accountability questions would you like this person to ask you?

- When and how often would you need to check in with this person?

The best form of accountability is voluntary and not inflicted. *It works better* when people choose to be accountable, and they want their coach, their accountability partner, and their team members to hold them accountable.

Hold your clients accountable in a firm, encouraging manner. Never use fear or threats. When people are accountable, it means they are part of a team, and they can't easily let themselves off the hook for not meeting their obligations. When people are tired, stressed, and feel like giving up, they know that in the next meeting, the coach is going to ask how they are doing. Knowing that they are going to be held accountable by someone helps them keep going when they feel like giving in or giving up. Make sure that when people haven't kept their commitments, you don't waste time listening to them indulging in blaming, complaining, or making excuses. Simply ask them if they are willing to recommit to taking the action before the next coaching session.

We once had a client who procrastinated on submitting his research work that he wanted very much to complete. He agreed that if he did not submit by a set date, he would have to pay his best friend $100. His best friend held him accountable, and the researcher scored a significant achievement in his life. Allow your client the freedom to decide on what negative consequence to attach to the noncompletion of a task so that he or she can devise an approach that will work for them.

There were times when our client would have given up on his own, but he knew that his friend was going to call every week with the accountability question, so he persisted with his efforts. Rather than see it as a burdensome imposition, the client accepted his friend's call as a gift that helped him succeed.

Unhealthy accountability is when you are forced to be accountable to someone else and you do it unwillingly. Healthy accountability is a proactive commitment to encourage and empower the client (or anyone else) to accomplish what they have set out to do.

CASE STUDY: HENRY, PART VIII

To demonstrate the importance of accountability let's go back to our friend Henry and his coach.

Coach: Can we talk a little more about your accountability partners?

Henry: Yes, that will be my assistant manager and my secretary. The assistant manager will follow up to ensure that I implement all the steps for the "nurturing pattern" and my secretary will remind me to call my wife when I am depressed so as to replace the sadistic pattern with the love pattern.

Coach: That's very clear on your side. Can you elaborate on how you will talk to them about being your accountability partner and what accountability question you want them to ask you?

Henry: Good question. I'll explain the problem of my undesired habits to my secretary and how I intend to solve them. I sense that she knows me well enough not to be surprised. The accountability question I'll ask her to put to me is: "Henry, are you starting to feel down?" If my answer is yes then she will follow up with the second question: "Would you like to call your wife right now?"

Coach: Well done. How will you set up your next accountability partner?

Henry: With my assistant manager, I'll shart by sharing my eight-point action plan to implement the "nurturing pattern." I am confident that she'll like it a lot. The accountability question for her to ask me will be, "Henry, for the whole of last week, how many of the action items have you fully accomplished?" If all of the eight items have not been fully accomplished then her next accountability question will be, "What would it take for you to accomplish all of the action items this week or should you revise the items?"

Coach: Well done again. Is there anything else that you would like to be held accountable for?

Henry: Yes, there are two more very important things. First, is to ensure that in the next two months I am certified and start training my team on the Ziglar's Sales System and Presentation Skills program. Second, I need help to ensure that the scorecards are well implemented for me and all my team members.

Coach: Excellent point. You want to be accountable for these two important goals, so who else can help you with this?

Henry: On the first item, I will have my training director ask me weekly, "Are you on target with your certification and training delivery?" If I am not then he will follow up with the next accountability question: "What will you do to stay on target?"

On the second item, I will have our finance manager ask me each month, "Is the implementation of the scorecard up to expectation?" If my answer is no, then he should ask me, "How can I help you make it work better?" I will then ask for his support if needed to improve on the scorecard and its implementation.

Coach: Well, we are almost coming to the end of our coaching session for today. There are plenty of action items for the next two weeks. I have noted them down. Would you please put them all together in one list indicating the timeline and status of each task and e-mail them to me by tomorrow morning?

Henry: Definitely. I'll send this to you first thing tomorrow morning. I am highly motivated about what this is going to produce for me, my family, and my team. My life feels more exciting than ever before. Thank you very much.

Coach: You are always welcome. All the best wishes in getting things done. I will see you in two weeks to evaluate your progress.

Two weeks later:

Coach: Hello, Henry. How're you doing?

Henry: Better than ever. I'm excited to talk to you again.

Coach: Very glad to hear that. I have looked through the progress report that you sent yesterday and from our fifteen-minute conversation last week, I gather that you are making considerable progress. I am keen to know more.

Henry: Looking at the positive side, I have implemented the strategies and most of the action steps that I wanted to be held accountable for.

Coach: I have to say, I am impressed with your progress. I admire your commitment. What would you say were your most satisfying accomplishments in the past two weeks?

Henry: Three things stand out. First, after I thanked my staff for their feedback, and let them know that I am committed to improve, I shared with them my plan and asked for their support. They were surprised, but it touched them, and they all pledged their support; they committed to work together as a team to help each other improve. Deep inside, everyone had the desire to be better than they were. Later, three of them came to ask for my forgiveness for some of their problematic behavior. We were in tears when I also apologized to them for the way in which I had treated them. The process of reconciliation was very successful.

Coach: That was a good one; what was the second thing?

Henry: When I asked all of them to list their strengths and how they can contribute more to our team results, we got some very powerful input. For instance, two of our team members are gifted when it comes to gathering and analyzing data on target customers. When they started churning out the top target customer's information last week and our team zoomed in on that, the sales surged 40 percent higher than the previous week.

The third great thing was that when I used your coaching approach of asking great questions and creating buy-in. Each team member anonymously submitted their reply slip to me. They said they felt a strong sense of ownership toward our breakthrough goal, and we were able to all happily agree on the 40 million sales target for this year.

Coach: Well, congratulations on your many achievements. How do you feel?

Henry: I feel on top of the world but not complacent. There is still a lot more to do. I missed out on two things, and I need help to solve this.

Coach: Sure, let's work on it.

Henry: In the past two weeks, I was overloaded with things to do and did not get in touch with Ziglar's company for the certification program.

Coach: Is this something that you want to do?

Henry: Yes, of course. It's very important to me. I will keep this on the list for the next two weeks.

Coach: Do you feel as if you are accountable to complete most of the tasks on your own, or can you get some help to handle things like this?

Henry: You're right. I need to delegate some tasks so I can accomplish more. I'll pass the task of calling the people at Ziglar to my training manager.

Coach: Very good. What's the second area?

Henry: In the last two weeks, I noted at least five times when I felt depressed after problems emerged. I managed to interrupt the sadistic pattern with the humor pattern and replaced it with the love pattern four times but on the fifth time my sadistic pattern got hold of me and I had an outburst with a nasty supplier.

Coach: I am curious. Please tell me how the creature managed to survive?

Henry: My accountability partner, was on leave, and I lost the support that I needed to help me keep my new habit. My secretary wasn't around to remind me to call my wife on the day the supplier fouled up.

Coach: So put yourself in the shoes of Tony Robbins. What would you do if you were Tony Robbins?

Henry: Well, Tony's personality always knew what was important and what to do first. Let me think. (pause for 10 seconds) Yes, I got it. I will ask my assistant manager or admin assistant whenever she is not around, since I know that in the next two to three months I'll still need support to totally absorb my new habit.

Coach: Fantastic, I am confident that you will beat this.

Henry: Thanks. This accountability stuff's really helping me.

Coaching breeds accountability and accountability breeds accomplishments.
—Jack Canfield and Peter Chee

PRINCIPLE 30

Acknowledge Efforts and Progress

When we sow the seeds of recognition and appreciation, we reap greater accomplishments from people.
—Jack Canfield and Peter Chee

A great coach never misses the opportunity to appreciate people for giving good answers to the coaching questions, for making progress with their goals, and for their efforts to improve and learn. You don't have to wait until people accomplish their entire goal to acknowledge them. Do it sincerely and often along the way as people make notable advancement in improving themselves and completing their tasks. Be a cheerleader and a huge fan of your clients' successes. Reinforce their achievements in a way that they might not do for themselves. Coaches can greatly enhance people's self-esteem and confidence if they seize the opportunity to acknowledge and celebrate people's progress. Ask your clients to share their feelings after a success and identify the rewards and benefits that they are already enjoying. Encourage them and reward their "inner child" with words, high fives, and hugs where appropriate.

Now that we've reviewed the 30 principles of effective coaching, we are pleased to share with you our "Five As of Coaching Effectiveness." These are:

- Accountability

- Action

- Affirmation

- Acknowledgement

- Achievement

Ensure that *accountability* is voluntary and strong. Support your clients continuously to take massive *action* on effective plans that they have developed. In the face of inevitable challenges, use *affirmation* and words of encouragement continuously. When they make progress and complete important tasks, *acknowledge* them, congratulate them and rejoice with them. The first four As will then empower and motivate people to gain even greater *achievements* thereby completing the "Five As" of coaching effectiveness.

CASE STUDY: HENRY'S STORY, PART IX

Starting from the early stages of the coaching relationship and throughout the engagement, Henry's coach continuously acknowledged the efforts and progress he made. This, together with the coach's unwavering belief in him, continuous support, encouragement, and accountability for action and goal attainment, became profound motivational factors for Henry to transform, realize his dreams, and grow.

Henry worked with his coach over a period of eight months. Upon completion of the coaching engagement, he exchanged a number of letters with his coach that concluded one of the most eventful times in his life. As you read this last series of conversations, via letter, between Henry and his coach, we ask that you put yourself in the position of the coach. Feel the difference you can make in your life and the lives of the people you coach when you personify the coaching principles that live within you. Two of the following letters between Henry and his coach depict a most touching conclusion of this powerful coaching relationship.

COACH

Dear Henry,

Thank you for your heartwarming letters that capture the defining moments we had together. I feel deeply fulfilled when I know that my opportunity to take this journey with you made a meaningful impact in your life. The path we traveled together enriched me tremendously and the challenges faced brought out the best in me as a coach. I will always treasure our relationship.

I congratulate you for choosing to take the path of becoming a coach for others. I really appreciate you for your dedication in passing on the gift of coaching to your daughter and your team to make a difference in their lives and to help them make their impossible dream possible.

Wishing you love and joy in abundance,
Your Coach

MY DEAREST COACH,

Greetings! The New Year celebrations have come and gone but one thing remains: the memory of my transformational journey with you by my side. I was in Paris recently with Edith and we had one of the most wonderful celebrations of our life. We entered the majestic Notre Dame Cathedral, and as we knelt down to pray, I felt very thankful for how my life has changed. Later, we stopped to marvel at the Arc de Triomphe, which recognizes heroes who fought for the country. In my mind, that monument was symbolic of our triumphant coaching journey.

I am so gratified that as a result of my coaching encounter with you, I was able to accomplish much more than I ever imagined. My team managed to achieve total sales of 53 million last year, which exceeded our breakthrough goal of 40 million. We became the top performing team in the company. At a celebration party, my CEO called me a "renaissance leader" as he handed me a surprise letter to announce my promotion.

We have come a long way from where we started when I said that I wanted better performance from my team. The most recent written feedback from them was full of glowing praises of how I had transformed from a terrible boss into a nurturing leader who really adds value to people. I have also been amazed how my stress level and hypertension have been reduced, and I am now enjoying the benefits of emotional, mental, and physical well-being. Looking back, I realized that in the past nine months, I have grown more as a person than I did in the previous forty years.

Nine months ago, when I met you, my greatest enemy was me! I felt small about myself and my self-esteem was low, but I faked it by showing a tough and aggressive front as I victimized others. I had a "nasty sadistic creature" living inside me, which, when released, inflicted emotional pain on others and put them down so that I felt bigger and more powerful in comparison. I was also unaware that my daughter was slipping into a depressed state due to my problematic behavior. My team members detested my bad habits, my job and my future were at stake, and I was faced with a formidable challenge to turn this around.

Then you came into my life and accepted me with all my limitations and problems. You never gave up on me even when I was unreasonable, crude, impatient, and rebellious. You rose to every challenge and you were strong for me when I was weak inside. You resisted the temptation of telling me what to do and refrained from giving me advice even when I tried to coerce you. You motivated and empowered me to take charge of my own growth and you influenced me to act willingly rather than using your position to force me to improve.

You helped me find ownership in my goals and dreams, and allowed me to find my own solutions as you guided me to put them into action. You enabled me to be fully accountable to achieve the results that I wanted, and you helped me put in place scorecards and support structures that ensured my success. You continuously supported me, and in 90 days I was able to successfully replace my undesired pattern by developing new habits that brought love and joy to me, my team and my family. I am now able to nurture and add value to others rather than push them down.

Thanks for always doing what you said you would do, and for maintaining rapport and humor even when I felt bad and did not know what to do. You cared for me and appreciated the good that was in me—even though at times I was stressed, pushy, and rude. You championed my cause, encouraged me when I felt down, and you recognized my efforts each step of the way, rejoicing with me in each victory. Because of you, my life is more beautiful and meaningful.

In the midst of a cold winter, I am sitting by the warm fireplace, and as I review our moments of truth, it brings me great joy and happiness. Erika just gave me a lovely smile.

We are about to leave home for a skiing expedition over the weekend. Edith and Erika have both asked me to tell you that you have made a difference in their lives too. I told them the whole story of our coaching journey and we know that in all the remaining winters of our lives, our hearts will be warm when we recall what you have done for us.

You have truly been a great coach. Did I ever tell you that you are my hero? I am strong when I think of you. You raise me up to be more than I can be. You let me fly high against the sky, so high I almost touched the sky. Thank you, thank you.

With deepest gratitude,
Henry

There is more hunger for love and appreciation in this world than for bread.
—Mother Teresa

PART II

SITUATIONAL COACHING MODEL (SCM)

The Mind of a Coach

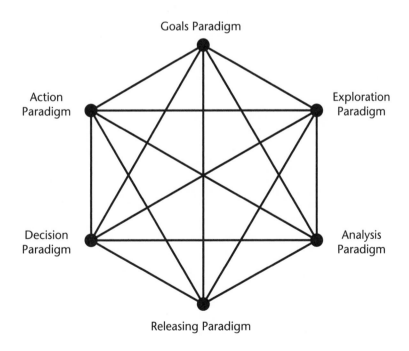

CHAPTER 9

THE SIX PARADIGMS OF SITUATIONAL COACHING

A genius coach knows how to shift seamlessly from one conversational paradigm to another, to best meet the needs of the situation for optimum results.
—Jack Canfield and Peter Chee

The Coaching Principles (TCP) are symbolized by the heart of a coach: it's steadfast and forms a solid foundation of life-impacting values, beliefs, and philosophies. Together these permeate successful coaching relationships.

The Situational Coaching Model (SCM) is a conversational model that uses effective paradigms in any given coaching conversation. It consists of six crucial paradigms that a coach can use in a flexible manner to navigate through a coaching conversation, shifting smoothly from one paradigm to another so as to best meet the needs of the client and the situation.

Great coaches know how to seamlessly combine different situational coaching paradigms while adhering to TCP. The mind of a coach (SCM) builds on the heart of a coach (TCP); together they make coaching even more powerful.

The following section provides you with a clear explanation of each of the six crucial paradigms of situational coaching as well as some exemplary coaching questions and guidelines about when to shift in and out of a particular paradigm.

The coaching questions are meant to provide you with a base of good questions to ask. Review them as you prepare for your coaching conversation rather than during the conversation itself. Use them to create the most appropriate questions for your client and the situation.

As an overview, here are the key questions and brief descriptions relating to each of the six paradigms of situational coaching:

Table 9-1 **The Key Questions of Situational Coaching**

Paradigm	Key Question	Brief Description
Goals	Where are you going? What have you accomplished?	Goals and accomplishments in coaching.
Exploration	How are you going to get there? What else do you need to consider?	Generating more ideas and possibilities, and seeing wider perspectives.
Analysis	Where are you now? What is the best way of getting there?	Knowing the reality of where you currently stand and finding out the best options for goal attainment.
Releasing	How do you feel? How can you feel better?	Releasing and letting go of negative emotions that are blocking you, and evoking positive feelings.
Decision	Which path are you taking?	Making the best choices among alternatives.
Action	What action steps do you need to take? By when?	Developing and committing to an action plan with a timeline.

Goals Paradigm

Key Questions: Where are you going? What have you accomplished?

Goals and accomplishments in coaching

The Goals Paradigm is crucial in coaching as it ensures motivation, clarity, and focus on goals so as to enable your client to achieve their desired results. When you shift into this paradigm, you focus your conversation on your client's goals: what they want out of a particular coaching conversation and what they want from the coaching relationship as a whole. You ask questions designed to get the client to clearly articulate their dreams and goals.

In a coaching engagement that involves only one conversation, the client's goal needs to be narrowly focused on what can be realistically achieved within the one conversation. On the other hand, if you are working with a client over a six-month period, the two of you would work on a bigger goal or on several goals.

For example, a client working with you over nine months with a 90-minute conversation every two weeks might choose to focus on discovering her life purpose, setting goals that are aligned with that, and then working to realize some of them. Another client might want to have four conversations with you over the course of two months to help him complete an important project at work. In that case, his goal will be specific and narrowly defined.

In most cases, a coaching relationship involves more than just one conversation and has a specified duration, frequency, and contact time. The first conversation in the series typically covers the overall goals of the entire coaching assignment; that particular conversation may also result in declaring some specific goals, time permitting.

In every subsequent conversation, you must shift into this paradigm to review your client's goals and the progress he has made from the last conversation. Ask questions to identify the client's recent accomplishments and then recognize and appreciate him for those. Ask him how he celebrated his achievements, what benefits he obtained from accomplishing them, and how he feels about his success. (To see what this looks like in practice, refer back to the end of Henry's coaching session, detailed in the previous chapter.) This review of achievement will motivate the client to achieve even more in the future by building his self-confidence.

If your client is behind target on achieving his goals, ask questions to ascertain his current level of commitment to the goal. If the goal is still important and he wishes to continue pursuing it, provide encouragement for him to carry on. After that, talk about the goals to work on during the current conversation. When relevant, you and your client can also review the overall goals of the entire coaching assignment that were identified in earlier conversations. Based on the client's progress, you can set short-term goals to be explored in future conversations, making sure they are aligned with the overall long-term goals.

Achievers Coaching Techniques (ACT) related to life purpose, vision, setting effective goals, visualization, and affirmation will be dealt with in Chapters 12 through 14. These techniques are an extension of the Goals Paradigm and will take it to a more advanced level.

Exemplary Coaching Questions for Goals

Goals to be pursued in coaching

1. In what ways can you best use your strengths and talents to serve your organization and the world?

2. What is your greatest passion and talent that you would like to use to serve others?

3. When you look at your life as a whole, what do you think is your main purpose for being in this world?

4. What do you know about your life purpose? Your destiny? What were you created to do?

5. What are your most important goals in the following seven areas of your life? (Professional, financial, relationships, health and fitness, recreation, possessions, and contribution.)

6. In what ways are your goals aligned with your life purpose?

7. What are your goals in your current job?

8. What are your career goals?

9. What are your other main goals beyond your job and career?

10. What do you want to be in the future?

11. What things would you like to do and experience in the future?

12. What do you want to have in the future?

13. If you were granted three wishes, which goals would you choose to fulfill?

14. What overall goals would you like to work on during the entire tenure of our coaching assignment?

15. From all the goals you've identified so far, how would you rank them in priority order?

16. Which are the top three goals that you would like to focus on?

17. Which goal would you like to start working on first?

18. Which of the goals would you consider to be the most challenging?

19. Among all the goals you've listed, which one would make the biggest difference for you?

20. What connection would there be between achieving this goal and your other goals?

21. How do you feel in terms of ownership and commitment to your goal?

22. On a scale of 1 to 10, how motivated are you to pursue this goal?

23. How can we make this goal more specific and measurable so we know when you have achieved it?

24. In what way is achieving this goal within your control? Is it achievable?

25. By what date and time would you want to achieve this goal?

26. What's on your agenda for today? What do we need talk about?

27. What do you want to achieve from today's conversation?

28. Is this something that you would really like to work on now, or do you have other more important objectives?

29. What is your most important and immediate goal for us to work on today?

30. What specific outcome do you want to obtain from this conversation?

Goals accomplished and goals pending completion

1. What have you accomplished since our last session?

2. Shall we take a look at the action steps completed since we last met?

3. What goals have you achieved so far?

4. Congratulations. How do you feel about what you have achieved?

5. I imagine that you feel like a champion. What did you experience after fulfilling this objective?

6. In what way have others noticed and recognized your accomplishments?

7. You completed this goal. In what way can you reward yourself? When will you do that?

8. How will you celebrate and rejoice in your achievements?

9. What benefits have you enjoyed since achieving the goals?

10. What other pending goals do you have to achieve?

11. Which of the pending goals are still important to you?

12. Which of the pending goals are you committed to continue pursuing?

13. How can we work together to reach a point where you will succeed with every action step that you set out to accomplish?

14. In what way would you like to be more effective in setting goals?

15. Shall we revisit our overall goals for our entire coaching assignment? How are we doing so far?

16. In what way does the completion of your goals so far contribute to your overall objective of our coaching assignment?

17. Considering the big goals that we have set for our whole coaching engagement, what subgoals would you like to work on in the coming sessions to ensure that we are on target?

18. In what way might you want to revise some of the goals in light of the latest developments?

Shift into the Goals Paradigm When

1. You begin the coaching relationship and you need to establish the overall goals of the coaching assignment.

2. Your client needs to establish the goals for a particular conversation.

3. Your client needs to identify the goals of future conversations.

4. You need to review your client's progress on her goals from the last conversation or from past conversations.

5. Your client loses focus and direction and needs to review his or her goals.

6. Your client wants to make changes to the goals he or she's set.

Shift out of the Goals Paradigm When

1. People confirm that they are clear enough about the goals that they wish to work on.

2. Your client indicates that she wishes to explore and analyze ways of how she can achieve the goal (shift to the Exploration Paradigm and then to the Analysis Paradigm).

3. She feels the need to express her problems and worries before talking further about goals and solutions (shift to the Releasing Paradigm and then back to the Goals Paradigm).

4. Your client wishes to decide on plans and work out action steps to achieve her goals (shift to the Decision Paradigm and then to the Action Paradigm).

5. She has finished talking about her goals and accomplishments.

Exploration Paradigm

Key Questions: How are you going to get there? What else do you need to consider?

Generating more ideas and possibilities, and seeing wider perspectives
This is also a crucial paradigm as people do need help from their coaches to engage in creative and "big picture" thinking so as to capture a wider range of good and innovative ideas that can enable them to achieve better results in a shorter time.

It is important to stay open to different ideas, ways of thinking and looking at things. Allow the people you coach to explore different perspectives and viewpoints and work out the implications of their goals and actions. In this way they won't miss any useful ideas for consideration before they have to narrow down their options and arrive at a decision.

As a coach, you add great value to people when you become his sounding board as well as brainstorming and thinking partner. This is one paradigm where you need to be very open to stimulate out-of-the-box thinking and maximum creativity from your client. Be ready to ask him for outrageous and disruptive ideas; it is often from here that the most innovative ideas emerge.

You want to engage him in lateral thinking, which involves looking at the same issue from different angles: scenario planning, options generation, and so on. Ask questions to help him see the connections and relationships between different success factors. Help him to identify potential problems and roadblocks and possible solutions for dealing with them when they arise.

Be aware of what ignites your curiosity. Use observation and your intuition to keep asking great questions. Listen for what appears to be more significant for your client's success and listen for potentially innovative ideas that could quantum leap his progress.

Exemplary Coaching Questions for Exploration

1. What are the wider benefits of pursuing and achieving this goal?

2. How will achieving this goal help you to achieve other goals?

3. In what way would the realization of this goal impact the other aspects of your life?

4. What value could you add to others by accomplishing this mission?

5. How would achieving this goal directly or indirectly serve the wider community?

6. What part of your dream have you not explored yet?

7. What are all the possible solutions that you can think of?

8. What other solutions can you think of?

9. If you looked at this issue from all the different angles, what would you see?

10. What other opportunities could there be? How can you tap into them?

11. What are all the possible threats?

12. What are all the things that could possibly go wrong?

13. How can you leverage all your strengths?

14. What are all the possible options that you can imagine?

15. Sketch a map showing your goal in the center and the strategies and tactics for achieving them radiating outward from the center. Please describe, how does this look like?

16. If you were to practice holistic thinking, how would you piece together all the information into a complete solution?

17. When you take a step back and look at the big picture, what are all the elements that you can see? How about drawing a map of this?

18. What connection can you see between all the different elements?

19. In what way would one element influence the other?

20. Let's aim for at least five potential solutions. What else could you do?

21. Assuming you had unlimited resources and you couldn't fail, what would you try?

22. Who are all the people who might be able to help you?

23. How will this affect others? What impact would it have on them?

24. Think like Einstein; what other ideas would you come up with?

25. Put on the hat of a highly creative thinker. What new ideas would you create?

26. Put yourself in the shoes of an innovator like Thomas Edison. What would you do?

27. Paint all the possible scenarios of how things could turn out. What would they be?

28. What would the best-case scenario look like?

29. What would the worst-case scenario look like?

30. What would you do under each of these scenarios?

31. What are all the different resources that you would need?

32. What would be a truly outrageous solution that could literally astound others?

33. If you looked 10 years into the future, what new solutions could there be? How could you speed it up to make it happen in the next year?

34. When you remove all assumptions and limitations, what else would you consider as possible solutions?

35. Think about when you are most creative. Imagine you are in that state now. What would you do?

36. Shall we explore further? I am very curious; please tell me more.

Shift into the Exploration Paradigm When

1. Goals are set and people need more creative and innovative ideas on how to achieve their goals.

2. Your clients need to generate a wider range of solutions and expand their possibilities.

3. A person's thinking is restricted and they need to think out of the box.

4. Your clients need to consider different viewpoints and perspectives to help them make better analyses and decisions.

5. People need to see the big picture to appreciate how things come together and how they connect to each other.

Shift out of the Exploration Paradigm When

1. You and your client feel that sufficient ideas have been generated (shift to the Analysis Paradigm).

2. People have shared as much as they can and have no further new inputs to offer.

3. Problems and worries block their ideas from flowing (shift to the Releasing Paradigm and then shift back to the Exploration Paradigm).

4. Your clients are ready to begin analyzing options and making key decisions for action (shift to the Analysis Paradigm and then to the Decision and Action Paradigms).

5. You and your client discover that they are still unclear about their goals and are not yet in a position to generate good enough ideas to achieve the goal (shift to the Goals Paradigm and then back to the Exploration Paradigm).

Analysis Paradigm

Key Questions: Where are you now? What is the best way of getting there?

Knowing the reality of where you currently stand and finding out the best options for goal attainment

The Exploration Paradigm is usually followed by the Analysis Paradigm. After exploring a lot of ideas and options and listening for what is significant, it is necessary to identify the ones that are most important to your clients and would produce the best outcomes for them.

The time available in a typical coaching conversation will usually not allow you to evaluate all ideas and options in great depth; furthermore, it would be a waste of time to do that. Therefore, you need to work with your client on selecting the best ideas and then more thoroughly evaluating those. You can identify their current status so as to be firmly grounded in the reality of where the client is versus where he or she wants to be.

The objective of the Analysis Paradigm is to put your clients in a better position to make good decisions for taking action. Ask questions that go deeper into the various areas that are important to your client so that they derive maximum mileage from being an effective analyst.

Exemplary Coaching Questions for Analysis

1. Of all the options that you have identified so far, which are the ones that you would consider to be really important?

2. Why would you consider them to be most important?

3. Deep inside, what really motivates you to pursue this goal?

4. What would be the best thing you could do to conquer this challenge?

5. Among all the different strategies for obtaining your goal, which ones stand out as the most powerful?

6. Narrow down your strategies to what you think are the three most effective ones. Which ones would they be?

7. Which one do you think is best?

8. What is your assessment of this?

9. What would you consider to be the best option to pursue?

10. What do you think would be the top 20 percent of things to focus on first that would produce 80 percent of the results?

11. If you were to rank the solutions in terms of priority, what would it look like?

12. What do you think would be the one product, service, process or strategy that could become a breakthrough innovation?

13. What factors are most important in terms of impacting the results?

14. Search deeper using all the wisdom that is within you. What could be the root cause?

15. Please share with me, what would be some of the critical incidents along the way?

16. From your observation, what patterns of behavior consistently emerge?

17. Looking at all the facts of the situation, what aspects really stand out as "red flags?"

18. What would be your greatest strength to focus on?

19. What would be your number one area for improvement?

20. What's the greatest opportunity here?

21. What would be the three most critical threats?

22. Have you checked the facts of the case? What are they?

23. What concrete evidence have you been able to gather?

24. Where do you stand now? What's the distance between here to your destination? What steps do you need to take?

25. To what extent are the goals achievable and within your control?

26. On a scale of 1 to 10, how realistic do you think we have been here?

27. How many times have you done this in the past?

28. When was the last time you did that?

29. What kind of similar things have you done in the past?

30. What's the gap between where you are now to where you want to be?

31. What are the chances that you will be able to close the gap?

32. How have you been doing up to now?

33. What have you already tried, and what difference did those things make?

Shift into the Analysis Paradigm When

1. Your client already has a lot of good ideas and needs to narrow them down to the most important and effective things to do to attain their goal.

2. People need to know where they currently stand and the gap between where they are and where they want to be.

3. They need to understand in greater depth what it really takes to achieve the goal and what is realistically possible and within their control.

4. They need to know in deeper detail the pros and cons and implications of the actions to be taken.

5. They need to evaluate the best ways of achieving their goal.

Shift out of the Analysis Paradigm When

1. They are clear enough about where they stand and the most important things they have to do to accomplish their goal.

2. People start to talk about when they are going to start executing and they are ready to get into a final decision and action (shift to the Decision Paradigm and then to the Action Paradigm).

3. They are still lacking good enough ideas about how to achieve their goal (shift back to the Exploration Paradigm and then back to the Analysis Paradigm).

4. They are still not clear enough about their goals (shift to the Goals Paradigm).

5. Negative emotions and problems block their ability to analyze effectively (shift to the Releasing Paradigm and then shift back to the Analysis Paradigm).

Releasing Paradigm

Key Questions: How do you feel? How can you feel better?

Releasing and letting go of negative emotions that are blocking you, and evoking positive feelings

The Releasing Paradigm makes possible one of the great benefits of coaching. Many people live in a negative world; they're surrounded with negative forces and negative news that wears them out. In addition, many people also have their own internal problems. No wonder there is such a great need for coaching.

With all these negative forces combined, more and more people are highly stressed, lacking in motivation, under great tension and anxiety, worried, sad, angry, envious, rebellious, revengeful, remorseful, manipulative, unfair, fearful, saying things they shouldn't, inflicting pain on others, or suffering from hypertension, muscular pain, attention deficit disorder, chronic fatigue syndrome, and the like. Imagine the plethora of real challenges that the people you coach face.

Remember: *Coaching is not about fixing people.* It's about helping them help themselves. In this paradigm, you focus on being present, listening, caring, and understanding. You ask questions to get the client to articulate her feelings and emotions related to issues she is facing. This increases the client's emotional awareness and allows her to talk about and release any psychological pain that has been building up within her. In this way, you are lightening her burden and uplifting her spirits. While you are doing this, it is important that you yourself stay resilient and not to let the client's problems pull you down.

Practice using the exemplary coaching questions of the Releasing Paradigm to help people let go of the negative thoughts and feelings that are blocking their progress. Don't be surprised if some clients cry in front of you. It is usually a good thing, a cathartic release of emotion, and they will be much better afterward. Just make sure you have tissues ready. After the emotional release has occurred, ask questions that evoke positive feelings to replace the negative feelings.

In the case of some clients who are less expressive and more cautious about opening up to share their true feelings, it may take more time to build rapport and trust. Don't push people to express their emotions. Let it happen naturally, and at the right time. You will then be able to touch their hearts by sincerely supporting them and caring for them.

The Achievers Coaching Techniques (ACT), related to taking full responsibility, building self-esteem and removing roadblocks, will be explained in detail in Chapters 12 through 14. These techniques will enable you to take the Releasing Paradigm to a more advanced level.

Exemplary Coaching Questions for Releasing

Surfacing issues and releasing the pain

1. What's getting in the way of living the life that you want?

2. What might be stopping you from pursuing your dreams?

3. Is there any fear that might be holding you back?

4. Tell me, is there anything that really worries you?

5. What's frustrating your progress and holding you back?

6. What's stopping you? How do you feel about it?

7. Could you tell me more about how you really feel about this situation?

8. Imagine being in that situation. What thoughts and emotions does that evoke?

9. How do you feel about it?

10. How do you feel right now?

11. How would you describe your emotions and reaction to this situation?

12. Is there anything that you keep thinking about that negatively affects you?

13. What are you feeling in your body right now?

14. What are you feeling in your heart right now?

15. Relax for a minute and visualize that you are floating on top of the water in a quiet pond. You are totally relaxed and feel weightless. What feelings are you aware of right now?

16. I am here for you, and I really love to listen to your sharing. Can you tell me what you are feeling now?

17. I understand how you feel. Please tell me more about your deepest feelings.

18. What are your feelings toward this person?

19. What feelings did you have at that time?

20. How do you think you will feel the next time something like that happens?

21. Can you "turn up the volume" and let more of your emotions out? I am here for you all the way. How do you feel?

22. If one burden could be removed from your heart, what would it be?

Letting go of negative emotions and evoking positive feelings

1. Take a few minutes to breathe deeply and imagine the worry inside you is melting away and leaving your body. . . . (pause). . . What did you just experience? What were you feeling?

2. What would it take for you to let it go?

3. Could you simply welcome and allow yourself to experience that feeling as best you can?

4. Could you imagine your problem as something spinning inside you, but it's not you?

5. Could you just let it go?

6. Would you let it go?

7. When will you let it go?

8. Imagine you are sitting in the middle of a waterfall, and water is flowing all over you and washing away all your worries and anxieties. Take the next two minutes to visualize and feel the feelings of that . . . (pause) . . . What did you experience?

9. What is a better feeling you could create for yourself the next time that happens?

10. If you could wave a "magic wand" and entirely change your feelings toward that situation, what would that look like?

11. If this were a defining moment and you needed to change your feelings toward your problem to succeed, what feelings would you choose to evoke?

12. Imagine that it's just a matter of choice. How could you choose to evoke the strong positive feelings that you would rather have?

13. You have the power to decide how you feel. What feelings would you rather have?

14. What could you do to choose the feelings that you want to experience?

15. Eleanor Roosevelt once said, "No one can make you feel inferior without your consent." What do you think about that?

16. In the face of these challenges, what opportunities can you seize?

17. What's the possible silver lining behind that dark cloud?

18. Every negative event contains the seed of an equal or greater benefit. What's good in this situation?

19. What positive qualities do you see in this person?

20. Considering that you have also made mistakes in the past and knowing that human beings are never perfect, how might you find the strength to let this go?

21. Imagine the strongest feeling of love flooding your heart right now. How would that change your reaction to this issue?

22. Close your eyes and imagine that wherever those feelings you just released were stored in your body is now filling up with a beautiful soft white light. How do you feel?

23. I believe that you have the power within you to conquer this challenge. I want you to access your deepest wisdom. How would you react?

24. Visualize being in a state of love, forgiveness, and gratitude. What could you do to experience this more of the time?

Shift into the Releasing Paradigm When

1. People want to or need to express and release their feelings and emotions.

2. You need to draw out people's emotions and feelings and enable them to express themselves openly for a greater awareness of what is blocking them and keeping them stuck.

3. They feel unhappy, misunderstood, angry, disappointed, and stressed.

4. They need someone to listen to and care for them and understand the difficulties they are going through so that they can start to feel better.

5. Your clients need to let go of negative emotions that are preventing them from functioning more effectively.

Shift out of the Releasing Paradigm When

1. Your clients have sufficiently released their emotions and feelings and they feel better.

2. They are in a positive emotional state and they wish to focus back on their goals (shift to the Goals Paradigm).

3. People have had enough time to express their feelings and now need to identify more ideas and effective solutions to the challenges they face (shift to the Exploration Paradigm and the Analysis Paradigm).

4. They are finished expressing their emotions and are ready to make some decisions and get into action to achieve their goals (shift to the Decision Paradigm and the Action Paradigm).

Decision Paradigm

The Key Question: Which path are you taking?

Making the best choices among alternatives

In this paradigm, you work with your clients so that they can make the best decision for execution. If they are ready, then move forward with them. If they are not ready, don't push them into making a decision as this could result in making hasty and wrong decisions or deciding on things that they are not fully committed to. Both of these will ultimately result in things not getting accomplished.

If your clients are not ready to decide, you need to ask more questions to find out why. Shift to another paradigm as necessary and come back to this paradigm when appropriate. It could very well turn out that your client does not have enough facts and needs to do further research or consult others before making a decision about his future. Under such circumstances, shift to the action paradigm and identify whatever action steps he needs to take in order to help him make a good decision in a later coaching conversation.

If clients are confronted with too many decisions to make, you can ask questions to help them prioritize and make the more important decisions first. Then they can get into action to start producing results around that decision. Each and every win builds confidence. Enabling people to make a good decision and take an action is one of your most important roles of a coach.

Exemplary Coaching Questions for Decision

1. Do you think you have enough good options to choose from?

2. Make a list of your options and categorize them under three groups–top priority, second priority, and third priority. What does that look like?

3. How many criteria do you have to help you make a choice?

4. What would be your main criteria?

5. If you reduce the criteria to three main ones, what would they be?

6. What choices best meet those criteria?

7. In what ways would you need to consult others before making this decision?

8. Does one choice clearly stand out as the best? What are your reasons for that?

9. Is there anything holding you back from making a decision?

10. What's your decision on this matter?

11. If you follow your heart's true desire, what would be your decision on this?

12. Which choice do you think would bring you the best outcome?

13. Which solution would you like to work on first?

14. How do you want to proceed?

15. What's your decision on things that you could keep doing?

16. What's your decision on things that you could start doing?

17. What's your decision on things that you could stop doing?

18. What's your conclusion on the strategies that you must adopt to realize your goal?

19. On a scale of 1 to 10 (10 being the highest) what is your level of commitment toward this decision?

Shift into the Decision Paradigm When

1. Your client mentions that they are ready to decide and take action.

2. They need their coach to help them simplify and prioritize things so that they are able to make better decisions.

3. People require support in making the best choice among all the alternatives.

4. People need to come to conclusions on the direction that they want to take for them to reach their goals.

5. Important decisions need to be made so that your client can move to identify action steps and a timeline for action.

Shift out of the Decision Paradigm When

1. The people you coach are happy and satisfied with their decisions and are ready to plan out their action steps (shift to the Action Paradigm).

2. They cannot decide because their goals are not clear or not compelling enough (shift to the Goals Paradigm).

3. Your clients do not have enough information, lack good ideas, and are not convinced that they have the right solutions (shift to the Exploration Paradigm and the Analysis Paradigm).

4. People are not ready to decide because of worries and emotional concerns (shift to the Releasing Paradigm).

5. People need more time to do further research and get further input from others after the coaching session (shift back to this paradigm during a later session).

6. They are not ready to decide because they need more time to consider and reflect on the decision (shift back to this paradigm during a later session).

Action Paradigm

The Key Questions: What action steps do you need to take? By when?

Developing and committing to an action plan with a timeline

Asking questions to get your client to come up with action plans—specific steps, priorities and a timeline to establish accountability and a commitment for action—is the focus of this paradigm.

Action steps are a crucial outcome of coaching, but a coach should not coerce a client to come up with action steps when the client isn't really ready to do so. There could be many possible reasons for this. Among them are

- Not being clear and committed to the goals set earlier

- Lacking good strategies and solutions

- Encountering roadblocks preventing them from moving forward

- Dealing with hasty and wrong decisions made earlier.

When this is the case, shift to the other appropriate paradigms depending on the situation and then come back to this paradigm.

If, even after you do your best, your client still cannot come up with action plans and time is running out for the session, allow her to go back and reflect and search for more ideas. She can consult others, draft the action steps, and send them to you for review before your next session. This, in itself, can constitute an action plan. There will be another time when you and your client can make further progress, so keep the attention on that. It will only be a matter of time before this challenge will turn into opportunities for breakthroughs.

When action plans have been worked out, you can still take your client further by helping him establish accountability and commitment. You can do this by helping him prepare to obtain accountability partners, resources, and support structures that will maximize his chances of succeeding with his action plans.

Always ask for a progress report to be submitted by the next coaching session. In this way you hold your clients accountable to taking the necessary steps to creating their desired futures. It's also good practice to end a session in which the client commits to action steps on a high note by acknowledging his commitment and sharing some inspiring words before concluding the session.

Exemplary Coaching Questions for Action

1. What are the most important action steps that you could take?

2. What action steps will you take?

3. What are the five most important things that you will do every day to follow through on your decision and achieve your goal?

4. What are your next steps, and by when will you complete them?

5. So far you have identified the main action steps. If you think it's necessary to state the substeps for any of the main steps, what might those be?

6. On a scale of 1 to 10, how important is each of the action steps?

7. When will you start doing that first action step, how often, and for how long?

8. When do you aim to complete each of the action steps?

9. How will you include the action steps into your schedule?

10. What other items might you want to add to the action steps?

11. What items might you want to exclude from the action steps?

12. Is there anything that might prevent you from completing them?

13. Is there anything you can do to overcome these barriers?

14. On a scale of 1 to 10, what is the likelihood that each of the action steps will be completed on time?

15. How can we make the score higher to increase your chances of getting them done?

16. What kind of support do you think you need to complete this goal?

17. What kind of support structure could you put in place to make sure you take these steps?

18. Would you like to include creating this support structure as one of your action steps? By when? How often? For how long?

19. Who are the people who can help you ensure that your action steps are accomplished on time?

20. What resources will you need?

21. What might you need to give up to make this happen?

22. What's your level of ownership and commitment toward completing each action step on time?

23. Do you feel accountable?

24. How would you like to be held accountable?

25. Who could be an effective accountability partner for you?

26. What do you need your accountability partner to do for you? How often? For how long?

27. What accountability question would you like this person to ask you?

28. Would you like to include getting an accountability partner as one of your action steps? By when?

29. How will these action steps lead you to achieving your goal?

30. What benefits will you enjoy?

31. Can you imagine having completed all the action steps on time? How do you think you will feel?

32. Can you give me a progress report on your action steps when we meet next time?

Shift into the Action Paradigm When

1. Your clients have decided on what direction to take and are eager to move into action to realize their goals.

2. Clients need to come up with clear and specific action steps and a timeline for implementing them.

3. Clients have spent sufficient time exploring, analyzing, and deciding on their strategies, and they need techniques to help in their execution.

4. You need to ascertain your clients' levels of motivation and commitment to implement their action plans on time.

5. Clients want to be held accountable to take action to achieve their goals.

6. They need to establish ways for you and for them to know how they are progressing with their action steps.

7. It's time for you to help your clients establish support structures to increase their chances of succeeding with their action steps.

8. The coaching conversation is coming to an end and you need to summarize the main action steps to be accomplished by the next coaching conversation or by a specific date.

Shift out of the Action Paradigm When

1. Your client has clear and specific action steps with a timeline and has completed a good action plan that he or she is strongly accountable to and committed to put into action.

2. People are working on the action steps and they suddenly realize that it is important for them to review and revise their original goals (shift to the Goals Paradigm).

3. Your clients are really lacking good ideas and feel that they need much better solutions (shift to the Exploration Paradigm and the Analysis Paradigm).

4. Clients are seriously burdened with worries and negative emotions that are blocking them from working effectively on action steps (shift to the Releasing Paradigm).

5. People have been working on the action steps for decisions made earlier, and they come to a realization that they really need to reevaluate and change their decisions (shift to the Decision Paradigm).

Using the Situational Coaching Model

We created the situational coaching paradigm to meet the challenge of coaching in the real world after we had tried many other existing models and over time found them to be less and less useful. Other existing coaching models tend to prescribe a simplistic step-by-step process of how to structure a coaching conversation. This makes them suitable only for beginners who are first learning about coaching. These models tend to make a coaching conversation rigid, boring, and mechanistic, and they usually do not work effectively in practice. That is why experienced coaches tend not to use such basic models.

The Situational Coaching Model (SCM) is a contemporary conversational model that is designed to be flexible enough to be effectively applied to any coaching challenge. Even though there seems to be a logical sequence to the flow of the six paradigms of situational coaching, in reality coaching conversations are more complex than many people imagine.

No one best configuration fits all coaching conversations. Effective coaches know how to navigate through a coaching conversation by shifting smoothly from one paradigm to another. They know when to go back and forth between paradigms, when to skip certain models, and how to use the paradigms according to a different sequence depending on the needs of the clients, and according to how the situation unfolds during a session.

To help you to quickly remember the six paradigms so you can use the right one at the right time, we created an acronym called GEARDA which represents the first letter of the first word of the six paradigms—Goals, Exploration, Analysis, Releasing, Decision, and Action. This acronym expresses the main objective of coaching, which is to help people **GEAR** up for Decision and Action. This should make it easy for you to remember the six crucial paradigms of situational coaching.

Here are some examples of how the different paradigms of situational coaching are applied under different circumstances.

SITUATIONAL COACHING 1
(DURATION OF CONVERSATION: 80 MINUTES)

THE FLOW OF PARADIGMS:
RELEASING–GOALS–RELEASING–DECISION–RELEASING–ACTION

Description:

One of our coaches worked with Lorenzo, an entrepreneur who runs a chain of retail lighting outlets. Before coaching commenced, he stated that he wanted to work with his coach on work–life balance. In the first conversation, his coach built rapport with him and showed that she really cared by asking questions about how he was doing. She was fully present to listen to him. As a result Lorenzo opened up very quickly and started expressing the many problems he was experiencing connected to his work and his family. Sensing the situation well, the coach shifted right into the Releasing Paradigm and allowed Lorenzo to express the worries that had been building up inside him for years.

After 40 minutes of empathic listening by his coach, Lorenzo felt much better. Then his coach asked a question that got Lorenzo to focus back on his coaching goals and how they were connected with his problems. He realized that the problem in his workplace had been affecting the well-being of his family. He and his coach agreed on his goals: He would focus on improving the relationship with his family members by scheduling more quality time with them and solving his key problems at work.

As it turned out, after agreeing on the coaching goal during the Goals Paradigm, they had to shift back to the Releasing Paradigm as Lorenzo discovered he had even more difficult issues to articulate. He started to talk about his childhood, explaining that his father was a workaholic. The father became verbally abusive when he returned home late and drunk after entertaining customers. As he expressed the pain he felt inside, Lorenzo suddenly realized that one of the things he had unconsciously picked up from his father was the belief that a man's career was his life and would determine his self-worth, happiness, and the well-being of his family. By asking powerful questions, his coach helped him become aware of the limitations of this belief. They then shifted to the Decision Paradigm where Lorenzo made certain concrete decisions and a commitment to take back control of his life and not let his work become the "boss of his life."

Time was running out for the first coaching session, and the coach felt the need to shift to the Action Paradigm. However, before they could get there, Lorenzo had to release even more of his pent-up tension regarding his wife and the serious problems they were facing together. That was when Lorenzo burst into tears. Even though it was time to conclude the coaching session, the coach stayed with Lorenzo for another 15 minutes before shifting to the Action Paradigm where they worked out a few key action steps to be accomplished before their next session.

SITUATIONAL COACHING 2
(DURATION OF CONVERSATION: 60 MINUTES)

THE FLOW OF PARADIGMS: DECISION–ACTION

Description:

One of our coaches had the opportunity to work with Vladimir, engineering director of a nuclear fuel facility. In this particular coaching conversation, Vladimir and his coach worked together to make critical decisions and create a strong action plan. In previous sessions they had already identified goals and spent time engaging in the Exploration and Analysis Paradigms. Therefore, for this session they went straight into the Decision Paradigm.

Based on the analysis done in the last session, Vladimir worked with his coach to decide on three of the most important strategies to enhance the safety of the employees working in the facility. The coach never made any decisions, nor did she attempt to influence Vladimir into making any. She merely asked great questions to facilitate the process for him, to help him make the best possible decisions for his organization. Vladimir even had to make a quick call to his CEO and chairman to get their support on the decisions before moving forward to the final part of the coaching conversation.

By the time the session concluded, Vladimir and the coach had spent almost 30 minutes coming up with a detailed action plan with clear priorities and timelines for the execution of each strategy and task before their next coaching session, scheduled for three weeks later. There was neither time nor need to engage in any other situational coaching paradigm on this occasion.

SITUATIONAL COACHING 3 (DURATION OF CONVERSATION: 45 MINUTES)

THE FLOW OF PARADIGMS: ACTION–RELEASE–ACTION

Description:

The third coaching session with Muzaffar, a research and development manager of a power company in the Middle East, focused initially on the Action Paradigm. In the first two sessions, he had worked with his coach to identify clear coaching goals, explored and analyzed the possible solutions, made key decisions on moving forward, and worked out some action steps. The first two sessions were not long enough to complete an extensive action plan, so the coach had asked that Muzaffar continue to fine-tune his plan for further discussion in the third session.

In this third coaching session, the coach shifted straight into the Action Paradigm to review the action plan with him. After 25 minutes, Muzaffar had crafted an extensive action plan along with a chart showing the proposed completion of each of the different tasks during his six-month project. At that point, his coach asked about his levels of commitment and accountability to carry out all the plans. It was then that Muzaffar started to express all his worries and anxieties. To deal with this, the coach shifted back to the Releasing Paradigm.

After spending 15 minutes in the Releasing Paradigm, the coach asked if Muzaffar wanted to revise any of his action steps. In order to consider this, they shifted back to the Action Paradigm, removing 20 items from the plan and adding three new ones. The Releasing Paradigm had succeeded in creating the needed awareness that led Muzaffar to commit to an action plan, one that he felt much more confident about completing and to which he was willing to hold himself accountable.

SITUATIONAL COACHING 4
(DURATION OF CONVERSATION: 40 MINUTES)

THE FLOW OF PARADIGMS: EXPLORE-ACTION

Description:

Ming Wei was a learning and development director of a multinational learning corporation in Sydney, Australia. She had a very clear objective: work with her coach to develop a cutting-edge leadership development program for her client. Since she was certain that she wanted to focus on this very specific goal first, her coach shifted straight into the Exploration Paradigm.

They spent a good 30 minutes exploring all the possible innovative ways of creating a world-class leadership program for Ming Wei's client. The coach asked if Ming Wei wanted to draw a one-page mind map to show how all her ideas were connected. She agreed and proceeded to draw the map. After receiving some feedback and suggestions from her coach, she added colors and pictures. The process turned out to be extremely useful for her, and she came up with quite a few innovative ideas.

Ten minutes before the end of the session, the coach asked if they could shift into the Action Paradigm. Ming Wei agreed and worked with her coach on a six-point action process to analyze her ideas with her coach and a few other experts. She planned to bring the results back to the next coaching session for further analysis and decision.

SITUATIONAL COACHING 5
(DURATION OF CONVERSATION: 120 MINUTES)

THE FLOW OF PARADIGM: GOALS–EXPLORATION–ANALYSIS–GOALS–EXPLORATION–ANALYSIS–DECISION–ACTION

Description:

Orlando was a movie production director based in Madrid, Spain, when he engaged us to coach him on new business start-ups. We started discussing with him his goals in coaching. They centered mainly on his business goals. He had a large amount of capital on hand, and he wanted to make the best use of it. He mentioned that he wanted to open three traditional Spanish fine dining restaurants and a spa near his home.

Once his goals were established, we shifted into the Exploration Paradigm to help him generate as many creative ideas as possible. When we asked several questions that, from our experience, normally spark some creative solutions, we found that Orlando was not highly creative in his ideas. We decided to shift into the Analysis Paradigm. It was only after looking deeper and evaluating the pros and cons of his goal and his values, that Orlando realized that the restaurant and spa businesses were not his true passion and priority. The goal had been influenced by his mother's dreams and not his own.

Realizing this, we shifted seamlessly back to the Goals Paradigm to ask him about *his* true passion and strengths and how he could use those to set truly inspiring goals for himself. It turned out that what he really wanted was to get into the fashion industry. This was a good match with his talent and love for design, art, and fashion. We shifted into the Exploration Paradigm again and this time managed to draw out many creative solutions and ideas from him on pursuing his new goal. After that, we moved into the Analysis Paradigm and then on to the Decision Paradigm to help him narrow down his options and decide on the best strategies to adopt in starting his new business. We then used the Action Paradigm to move him into an action plan through which he could realize his dream.

As a result, Orlando subsequently pursued his dream and apart from continuing to produce movies, became well known in the fashion industry.

The movie stars in his shows were also known to be among the most fashionably dressed people in the film industry in Europe.

SITUATIONAL COACHING 6
(DURATION OF CONVERSATION: 90 MINUTES)
THE FLOW OF PARADIGMS:
GOALS–EXPLORE–ANALYSIS–RELEASING–DECISION–ACTION

Description:

Allan was working as a leader of the Scouting movement when he asked his coach to work with him to help him discover and focus on his life purpose. His coach shifted into the Goals Paradigm and spent a good amount of time helping him clarify what he really wanted to achieve from discovering and focusing on his life purpose.

Once the goals were clear, the two proceeded to explore Allan's true passion and giftedness. His coach used a multipronged approach to draw out as many ideas as possible. Allan had talked about his real strengths and passion and how he could best use them to serve his community. He drew information from his own experience, his defining moments in his life, and other people's consistent comments about his passion and strengths. As well, he used feedback from an online strengths assessment.

The coach asked Allan if they could shift into the Analysis Paradigm to go deeper into his core strengths. They needed to explore what he really loved to do and how he could use that to best serve the world. Allan agreed, and after working for 30 minutes on this, they shifted into the Decision Paradigm where his coach helped him to make his own decision on the key focus of his life purpose. This, Allan concluded, would be adding value to people by engaging his greatest talent and passion.

With some suggestions from his coach, Allan then crafted his life purpose statement: "To coach and train leaders to be the best they can be with love and gratitude." Once Allan made the decision to focus on this, he and his coach spent the remaining 25 minutes of the coaching conversation coming up with a clear step-by-step action plan on how he could live a purpose-driven life.

As you can see, each of the above conversations has a unique character. During our several decades of coaching experience, we have encountered a countless number of coaching situations. We prefer to see each coaching conversation and relationship as being unique and special, just as each person is unique and different. Instead of trying to control and predetermine the configuration of each coaching conversation, just allow yourself to sense when it is the best time to shift in and out of a particular paradigm and let the coaching conversation flow smoothly until completion, so as to produce the best possible outcome for your client.

The best way to learn how to use the paradigms of situational coaching is by engaging in regular practice and taking the time to reflect after each conversation on how you can keep improving. Eventually, your intuition will develop and you will instinctively know what to do under every different situation to help people get the best results from coaching. If you are willing to continually practice, trust your intuition, and pay attention to what happens, you will eventually master the fine art of coaching.

PART III

ACHIEVERS COACHING TECHNIQUES (ACT)

The Energy of a Coach

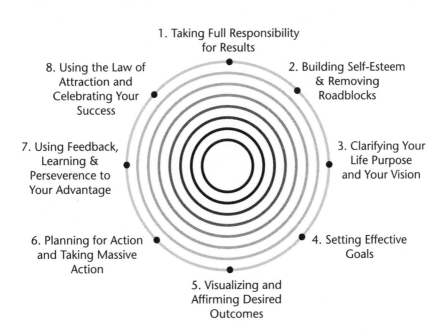

1. Taking Full Responsibility for Results

2. Building Self-Esteem & Removing Roadblocks

3. Clarifying Your Life Purpose and Your Vision

4. Setting Effective Goals

5. Visualizing and Affirming Desired Outcomes

6. Planning for Action and Taking Massive Action

7. Using Feedback, Learning & Perseverence to Your Advantage

8. Using the Law of Attraction and Celebrating Your Success

T HE ACHIEVERS COACHING TECHNIQUES (ACT) is symbolized by the *energy of a coach,* which resonates within eight key themes. We have found these to be some of the most powerful techniques practiced by many of the world's top achievers, and they will facilitate your effectiveness as a coach. The Achievers Coaching Techniques does not operate independently of The Coaching Principles (TCP) and the Situational Coaching Model (SCM). They all work together in synergy, and the "Coaching for Breakthrough Success Meta Model (30-6-8)," shown at the beginning of this book, puts them all together in a holistic manner.

When using the ACT, the core principles of coaching require a coach to disclose the use of these techniques and use them only after gaining consent from the person being coached. As a coach, you provide the structure and process but the contents that fill them should come from your clients as a result of your asking effective questions. For example, when using a technique that enables a person to switch from feeling negative and angry to being positive and happy, rather than telling them something like, "You have a wonderful sense of humor, and this is something that you should love about yourself," you would ask questions such as, "What do you love about yourself?" Bear in mind Coaching Principle 16, which states, "Listen Rather than Tell."

Although the eight themes of the Achievers Coaching Techniques seem to flow in a logical order, you do not necessarily need to apply them in this sequence. You can use the techniques according to the needs of your client. For example, when you shift into the Goals Paradigm, you might use the SMARTEST Goals Technique (as explained in Chapter 13), if that is appropriate to help people set effective goals.

There are many more techniques for accelerating the achievement of success than we can put in one book, but we have decided to focus on what we have found to be a few of the most effective ones in our experience as coaches. We have chosen to share techniques that we know are easy to learn and apply yet are powerful when you put them into practice in the right circumstances. The next eight chapters will provide you with an explanation of why and how these techniques work, along with many sample achievers coaching questions that will get you started.

If you would like to learn even more powerful strategies and techniques for accelerating your clients' journeys to success, we suggest you read *The Success Principles : How to Get from Where You Are to Where You Want to Be* by Jack Canfield and Janet Switzer.

CHAPTER 10

TAKING FULL RESPONSIBILITY FOR RESULTS

Ninety-nine percent of all failures come from people who have a habit of making excuses.
—George Washington Carver

If you observe the behaviors and thought patterns of people who achieve very little in life, you will notice one thing they have in common: They do not take full responsibility for the results that they produce. They frequently blame others as well as outside factors for their lack of progress. They are fond of giving excuses for why things cannot be done and are good at justifying why they are not responsible for their own failures. Does this sound familiar? Unfortunately there are many such people around. No wonder, most people are not high performers.

When we deliver high-impact programs on the Success Principles around the world, the very first principle we coach people on is "Take 100 percent responsibility for your life and your results." If you want to be successful, you have to take 100 percent responsibility for what you experience in your life. This includes the level of your achievements, the results you produce, the quality of your relationships, the state of your health and physical fitness, your income, your debts, your feelings—*everything*! This is not easy, and it's why coaching is so needed in our world.

If you want to create the life of your dreams, then *you* are going to have to take 100 percent responsibility for your life as well. That means giving up all your excuses, all your victim stories, all the reasons why you can't and why you haven't up until now. You have to stop blaming your life on outside circumstances. If something doesn't turn out as planned, ask yourself, "How did I create that? What was I thinking? What were my beliefs? What did I say or not say? What did I do or not do to create that result? How did I get the other person to act that way? What do I need to do differently next time to get the result I want?"

Dr. Robert Resnick, a psychotherapist in Los Angeles, California, talked about a very simple but very important formula that made this idea of 100 percent responsibility even clearer to us. The formula is:

$$E + R = O:$$
(Event + Response = Outcome)

The basic idea is this: Every outcome people experience in life (whether it is success or failure, wealth or poverty, health or illness, intimacy or estrangement, joy or frustration) is the result of how they have responded to an earlier event or events in their life. If people don't like the outcomes they are currently getting, there are two basic choices they can make.

1. They can blame the event (E) for their lack of results (O). In other words, they can blame the economy, the weather, the lack of money, their lack of education, racism, gender bias, the government, their wife or husband, their boss's attitude, the lack of support, the political climate, the system or lack of systems, and so on. If they're a golfer, they've probably even blamed their clubs . . . and the course they played on. No doubt all these factors do exist, but if they were *the* deciding factor, nobody would ever succeed.

Jackie Chan would never have become a world famous movie star, Bill Gates would never have founded Microsoft,

Steve Jobs would never have started Apple Computers, and Nelson Mandela would never have been given the Nobel Peace Prize. For every reason why it's not possible, there are a dozen people who have faced the same circumstances and succeeded.

People stop themselves from achieving! People think limiting thoughts and engage in self-defeating behaviors. They ignore useful feedback, fail to continuously educate themselves and learn new skills, waste time on the trivial aspects of their lives, engage in idle gossip, eat unhealthy food, fail to exercise, spend more money than they make, fail to invest in their future, fail to tell the truth, don't ask for what they want—and then wonder why their lives aren't working out. But this is what most people do. They place the blame for everything that isn't the way they want it on outside events and circumstances. They have an excuse for everything.

2. They can instead simply change their responses (R) to the events (E)—the way things are—until they get the outcomes (O) they want.

People can change their thinking, change their communication, change the pictures they hold in their head (their images of themselves and the world)—and they can change their behavior (the things they do). That is all people really have any control over. Unfortunately, most people are so controlled by their habits that they never change their behavior. They get stuck in their conditioned responses—to their spouses and their children, to their colleagues at work, to their customers and their clients, to their students, and to the world at large. In fact, they are a bundle of conditioned reflexes that operate outside of their control. *To be happy, people have to regain control of their thoughts, their images, their dreams, and their behavior.* The things that they think, say, and do need to become intentional and aligned with their goals, their vision, and their purpose.

Controlling the Three Things

If people don't like their outcomes, they need to change their responses
People have control over three main things in their lives—the thoughts
they think, the images they visualize, and the actions they take (their
behavior). How they use these three things determines the outcomes
they will experience. If they don't like what they are producing and
experiencing, they have to change their response:

- Change their negative thoughts to positive ones

- Change what they daydream about

- Change their habits

- Change what they read

- Change their friends

- Change how they talk

So how do we get people to change? If we try to coerce them, they
will resist. Instead we use the coaching process to empower people to
want to change. Then we support them in order to make the change
happen. We start by listening, observing, using our intuition, and asking
powerful questions, using a simple and yet powerful Reframing Technique according to the E + R = O formula. Here are two scenarios
that demonstrate what happens when people reframe and change to
a different response to create a different outcome that they want with
the help of a coach.

E + R = O Reframing Technique

CASE 1

Event:
Oliver and his colleague worked very hard to get promotions. After
12 months, his colleague got promoted but Oliver did not get a
promotion.

Response:
Oliver felt unfairly treated and jealous of his colleague. He blamed others, felt demoralized, and wanted to quit his job.

Outcome:
His relationship with his boss and colleague deteriorated, and his performance on the job dropped drastically.

Reframe:
Same Event:
Oliver and his colleague worked very hard to get promotions. After 12 months, his colleague got promoted but Oliver did not receive a promotion.

Different Response:
Oliver talked to his coach about how to take responsibility for the results that he wanted. He talked to his colleague to find out what his colleague did to get the promotion. He sought advice from his boss about where he stood and what he needed to do to get his promotion.

Different Outcome:
Oliver obtained useful and positive input from his boss and his colleague about what actions to take. With support from his coach, Oliver continued to improve until he received his promotion six months later.

———————

CASE 2

Event:
Dastan's wife was not happy that he had not been spending time with his family and his attention always seemed to be elsewhere. She expressed her frustration and feelings to Dastan.

Response:
Dastan felt hurt and concluded that he was not being appreciated for having worked hard for his family's well-being. He got angry and shouted at his wife and blamed his boss for his difficult schedule.

Outcome:
Dastan and his wife got into a heated argument and shouted at each other. Their relationship suffered, and their kids were also negatively impacted.

Reframe:
Same **E**vent:
Dastan's wife was not happy that he had not been spending time with his family, and his attention had always seemed to be elsewhere. She expressed her frustration and feelings to Dastan.

Different **R**esponse:
Dastan brainstormed with his coach for solutions on how to create more free time, which was the outcome he wanted. He listened to his wife and assured her that he loved her and the family and that he was working very hard to provide for them. He comforted her with love and scheduled more time with his family.

Different **O**utcome:
His wife and kids felt more secure and appreciated him more. Dastan began to enjoy a more balanced life, and his relationship with his wife improved tremendously.

As you have just seen from the cases of Oliver and Dastan, this Reframing Technique is very useful in enabling people to take responsibility for changing their thoughts, imagery, and behavior to produce the outcome that they really want. Initially with the help of a coach, most clients are able to be reactive in changing their response only when faced with an undesired outcome, obtained as a result of undesired responses to an undesired event. Over time, once they begin to use the habit of Reframing, their lives are so changed that they can proactively and consistently Reframe in order to get the right solutions. They can then continue to creatively respond to any event until they produce the outcome that they are happy with.

Reframing helps people to change their mindsets and enables them to redirect their energies to focus on the positive things and opportunities. These become available when they replace their self-defeating reactions with empowering reactions to achieve their desired state. Use the Reframing Technique at the appropriate time when you pick up red flags such as limiting and self-defeating thoughts and interpretations, poor attitude, and assumptions that are creating problems and preventing people from achieving their goals. The Reframing Technique will help people move from being stuck to becoming resourceful, from being preoccupied with doom stories to focusing on creating success stories.

Here are a series of questions that will help when preparing to help people use the E + R = O Reframing Technique

Achievers Coaching Questions for Reframing

1. What happened? How did the situation unfold?

2. What was the sequence of events?

3. What's your view about this issue?

4. Who and what was involved in this matter?

5. How do you feel about what happened?

6. What were your thoughts when this happened?

7. What images did you visualize in your head at that time?

8. Was there any gut reaction to this incident? Please tell me more.

9. What was your instinctive inclination in responding to this issue?

10. How did you respond? What did you do?

11. What outcome did you get from what you did?

12. How do you feel about the results you got?

13. What is it that you don't want out of this situation?

14. Step out of that situation and look at the bigger picture. How is this connected with your goals and your future?

15. Is this an important issue? How would it affect you?

16. What outcome would you prefer?

17. Is there something else that you wish for? Please elaborate on that.

18. If you could change your response to produce the outcome that you wanted, what would it be?

19. How can you look at this issue in a different way that gives you a positively energizing feeling?

20. In what way can you think, imagine, or act differently to get the happy outcome that you want?

21. What would be a different reaction to this event that could give you a more positive outcome?

22. Assuming you are not able to change others, what could you do to make the situation better?

23. If you had the power to change your own destiny, how would you respond?

24. If you were to take full responsibility to create the results you want, what would you do?

25. As a very able and resourceful person, how would you solve this issue?

26. Since you can be in full control of your responses, what choices could you make?

27. What is the next course of action you could decide on that would give you the results you want?

28. What benefits would you be likely to enjoy as a result of that choice?

29. What's your level of commitment to implementing your decision?

30. When and how often will you do the action steps?

31. In what way would you want to be held accountable for your decision so as to be sure to achieve your desired results?

In the context of a coaching conversation, you can employ the Reframing Technique under any of the six paradigms of situational coaching that were explained in the previous chapter. In practice however we have found that this technique is used most often during the Releasing Paradigm. This is because when people have articulated their problems, worries, and negative emotions, they feel much better and are more ready to face change. This is usually also the time when people become more aware of their own issues and circumstances and need help to change their responses in order to create the different outcomes that they want.

Reframing helps people find solutions and break free from the problems and emotions that are blocking their progress. The E + R = O Reframing Technique is a simple yet powerful process. When this technique is applied consistently, people's imaginations, thought patterns, behaviors, achievements, and lives are transformed. That's when people take full responsibility for their lives and the results they produce.

You must take personal responsibility. You cannot change the circumstances, the seasons, or the wind, but you can change yourself.
—Jim Rohn

CHAPTER 11

BUILDING SELF-ESTEEM AND REMOVING ROADBLOCKS

Outstanding leaders go out of their way to boost the self-esteem of their personnel. If people believe in themselves, it's amazing what they can accomplish.
—Sam Walton

Self-Esteem and Acknowledgment

Why are we making such a big deal about acknowledging our past successes? Because of its impact on our self-esteem. Research has shown over and over again that the more you acknowledge your past successes, the more confident you become in taking on and successfully accomplishing new challenges.

One of the best boosters of self-esteem is getting things done well. Have you ever felt terrible about yourself because of all the things that you had not done or the long list of things that you did not do well? On the other hand, how about when you managed to accomplish a lot and did it well—what did that do for your self-worth and self-esteem? Acknowledging that you have had successes in the past will give you the self-confidence that you can have more such victories in the future. So let's look at some simple but powerful ways to build and maintain a high level of self-confidence and self-esteem.

Create a Victory Log

A powerful way to keep building your self-esteem is to keep a written record of your successes. It can be as simple as a running list in a spiral-bound notebook or a document on your computer, or it can be as elaborate as a leather-bound journal. By recalling and writing down your successes each day or week, you log them into your long-term memory. This enhances your self-esteem and builds your self-confidence. Later, if you need a boost of self-confidence, you can reread what you have written.

Peter Thigpen, a former vice president at Levi Strauss & Co., kept such a victory log on his desk. When he was about to do something scary, such as negotiate for a multimillion dollar bank loan or make a speech to the board of directors, he would read his victory log to build up his self-confidence. His list included diverse entries such as "I opened up China as a market," "I got my teenage son to clean up his room," and "I got the board to approve the new expansion plan."

When most people are about to embark on some frightening task, they tend to focus on all the times they tried before and didn't succeed. This undermines their self-confidence and feeds their fear that they will fail again. Referring to your victory log keeps you focused on your successes.

Start your own victory log as soon as possible. If you want, you can also embellish it like a scrapbook with photos, certificates, memos, and other reminders of your success. This will help you become a better coach. Talk to the people you coach about this and encourage them to keep a victory log to enhance their capacity to perform even better.

Dealing with Roadblocks and Negative Issues

Aside from building healthy self-esteem for yourself and the people whom you coach, another crucial area of concern is helping people overcome the roadblocks and negative issues that prevent them from achieving the results that they want. The remaining part of this chapter will focus on providing you with questioning techniques and processes that you can use to help yourself and the people you coach to overcome the negative issues they may be facing.

It's important to bear in mind that, as a coach, *your job is to champion your client's agenda, not yours.* You only apply techniques when people have expressed a desire to overcome the problems that are getting in the way of their progress. As a coach it is a good practice to get buy-in from your client before using any of these techniques.

Flip Switching Technique

This is a simple yet powerful technique that can help you and the people you coach to overcome recurring negative feelings, fears, and self-sabotage such as the habit of scolding people whenever you are angry or not being able to control your negative emotional outbursts.

The Steps for Flip Switching:

1. Make a list of things you really love about yourself.

2. Choose one item from step 1 that gives you the strongest positive emotion and feeling of love.

3. Visualize it clearly and feel the strongest emotion of love in your heart. Develop a physical anchor such as tightening your right hand into a fist or clasping your two hands together in a prayer gesture that can help you remember how to bring back this feeling anytime you want it. Make the physical gesture every time you create or recall the feeling, and soon you will only have to make the physical gesture and it will immediately evoke the feeling. They will become anchored together.

4. Whenever a particular negative thought, feeling, fear, or self-sabotage is about to emerge, replace this by switching immediately to step 3.

5. Over time you can choose to use different items from step 1 to deal with different issues as long as they create a very strong feeling of love in your heart.

Achievers Coaching Questions for Flip Switching

1. What do you love most about yourself? Make a list.

2. From the list, which items are able to bring the greatest feeling of love in your heart when you imagine them?

3. Could you visualize this feeling as clearly as you can and then make a unique gesture that can help you recall it in the future? What does it feel like?

4. In what way do you feel a very strong impulse in your heart?

5. What are instances in your life when any recurring undesired thought, behavior, or response emerges almost automatically?

6. Can you choose one that you would like to deal with first?

7. Is this something that you want to replace?

8. How would you feel if you succeeded in overcoming this?

9. Every time this problem is about to emerge, could you replace it by visualizing and focusing on what you love most about yourself?

10. Could you evoke a very strong feeling of love in your heart by doing this?

11. How committed are you to doing this and to winning this challenge?

12. When will you start to implement this technique?

13. For how long will you do it?

14. How often will you do it?

15. What support structures will you need to put in place to remind yourself to do this?

16. How will you celebrate your success in winning this battle?

Anchoring technique

This is a very helpful technique that will enable you and your client to overcome negative feelings and stress much more easily and solve any problems that come up.

The steps for Anchoring:

1. List three things about which you have built up stress or negative feelings and say how they affect you.

2. List three things that you easily appreciate, care about, and love most in your life. They can be people, places or things, including animals.

3. Close your eyes and focus on the area around your heart.

4. Keep breathing in and out. Count from one to six when breathing in and count from one to six when breathing out. Imagine the breath is coming in and out through your heart.

5. Think of one of the things identified in step 2 that you love and appreciate. Visualize it clearly in all dimensions and feel it bringing forth the strongest feeling of appreciation in your heart.

6. Put your hand on your heart and feel the rise and fall of your chest as you breathe in and out. Make this a gesture that reminds you of this strongest feeling of love and appreciation.

7. As you are in this state, ask yourself what would be a more effective response to one of the stressful and negative situations you identified in step 1.

8. Repeat steps 5 and 6 for one of the other stressful situations or feelings in your life.

9. Repeat step 7.

10. Quietly sense the change in your perception and feeling and see what solutions to the problems you can come up with now.

11. Repeat this process whenever you are faced with a situation causing you negative feelings, stress, or problems.

Achievers Coaching Questions for Anchoring

1. What are the negative feelings, stress, and problems affecting you? List at least three items.

2. What do you easily appreciate, care about, and love most? List at least three items?

3. Would you please clear your mind of all thoughts, relax, and focus on the area around your heart. Would you like some soft relaxing music?

4. Would you please count from one to six when breathing in and count from one to six when breathing out, and maintain that breathing rhythm?

5. Could you please close your eyes and visualize as clearly as you can the one thing that brings the strongest feeling of love to you.

6. Could you please put your hand on your heart and feel your chest rise and fall and continue to feel the greatest feeling of love flowing into your heart and throughout your body.

7. Could you now recall one instance of a negative feeling, something that is stressing you out, or a problem that you are currrently facing.

8. Once again could you please visualize as clearly as you can the same thing that brings the strongest feeling of love to you.

9. Once again could you now recall the same instance of a negative feeling, a cause of stress, or a problem that you are currently dealing with.

10. Could you now quietly sense the change in your perception and feeling and see what solutions to your problem you can come up with now.

11. Take your time to relax for a while. What was your experience like?

12. How do you feel about your problem now?

13. How would you feel if you succeeded in overcoming this?

14. Every time you face a problem that you want to solve, would you like to practice this technique?

15. When will you start to do this?

16. For how long will you do it?

17. How often will you do this?

18. What support structures will you need to remind yourself to do this?

Overcoming Limiting Beliefs

Many of us have beliefs that limit our success—whether they are beliefs about our own capabilities, beliefs about what it takes to succeed, beliefs about how we should relate with other people, or even common myths that modern-day science or studies have long since refuted. Moving beyond your limiting beliefs is a critical first step toward becoming successful. You can learn how to identify those beliefs that are limiting you and then replace them with positive ones that support your success.

One of the most common limiting beliefs is that somehow we are not capable of accomplishing our goals. Despite the best educational materials available, and despite decades of recorded knowledge about how to accomplish any task, we somehow choose to say, "I can't do that. I don't know how. There's no one to show me. I'm not smart enough." And on and on.

Some typical limiting beliefs are derived from personal perceptions:

- "I am bad with figures."

- "I am a slow learner."

- "I'm so stupid."

- "I don't know how to talk properly."

Some of these beliefs derive from negative past experiences:

- "People are dishonest and cannot be trusted."

- "Things never work out the way I hope."

- "There are always more problems than I anticipate."

Others stem from failed relationships:

- "I will always have problems with my love life."

- "I can't find anyone who really likes me."

- "I'll always be on the outside looking in."

When not addressed, these limitations can lead to self-sabotage and recurring negative consequences.

Where do they come from? For most people, it's our early childhood programming. Whether we knew it or not, our parents, grandparents, and other adult role models told us things like, "No, no, honey. That's too much for you to handle. Let me do that for you. Maybe next year you can try that. You should follow my footsteps and believe that people cannot be trusted; otherwise you'll regret it."

We take this sense of inability or negative belief into adulthood, where it is reinforced through workplace mistakes and other so-called "failures." But what if, instead, you decided to say, "I can do this. I am capable. I can change my belief. Other people have accomplished this. If I don't have the knowledge, there's someone out there who can teach me."

You make the shift to positive belief, competence, and mastery. This shift in thinking can mean the difference between a lifetime of "could haves" and instead accomplishing what you really want in life.

Here are the steps for overcoming limiting beliefs:

1. Write down your limiting belief.

2. Identify the ways that it is limiting you.

3. Imagine the worst-case scenario and feel the extreme pain this will cause you if you continue to believe in it.

4. Identify how you would prefer to act and feel.

5. Imagine the benefits of changing this belief. Visualize the best possible outcome.

6. Make a turnaround statement that affirms what you want.

7. Use your turnaround statement as an affirmation until you have a new empowering belief in place.

8. Repeat it many times a day without allowing any doubts to disrupt your thinking for a minimum of 30 days.*

9. Visualize the new you and the benefits you will be enjoying with this new empowering belief.

10. Repeat this process with all other limiting beliefs you become aware of.

Examples of Achievers Coaching Questions and Answers for Overcoming Limiting Beliefs

What's your limiting belief?

People are dishonest and cannot be trusted.

In what way is this belief limiting you?

It negatively affects my relationship with people, and I avoid partnering with people. I miss out on a lot of good business opportunities.

What would be the worst-case scenario if you keep believing this?

I can't sustain competitiveness, my business fails, and my family and I suffer severe consequences.

How would you prefer to be, act, and feel?

---

*If you continue to have negative critical internal self-talk in response to your affirmations, you can use the Little Voice Tapping Technique outlined in *Tapping into Ultimate Success: How to Overcome Any Obstacle and Skyrocket Your Results* by Jack Canfield and Pamela Bruner. Tapping is a new breakthrough technology that we recommend all coaches eventually learn and master.

I want to feel good about others, have trusting and strong relationships with many people, and attract good people who want to partner and work with me.

What would be the best-case scenario and the benefits that you want?
I have many successful strategic partnerships, and as a result my business flourishes and my family and I enjoy the many rewards.

What would your turnaround statement sound like?
There are many people who are honest and ethical.

How will you use this as your affirmation?
I will repeat it many times daily without allowing any doubts to disrupt my thinking and I will visualize the benefit that I would enjoy with this change.

In what way does this reflect what you really want?
I really want to make this change. I need it badly.

When will you start using the affirmation? For how long? How frequently?
I will start today itself. I will do it every day as a ritual after my prayers and before meals and continue doing so until the limiting belief stops limiting me.

Could you visualize the benefits you will enjoy with a new empowering belief?
Yes, I would like to do that right now. Just give me three minutes.

How do you feel?
I am feeling great, and I am confident that I can create the new belief that I want. I am fully motivated to make this turnaround.

If you don't see yourself as a winner, then you cannot perform as a winner.
—Zig Ziglar

CHAPTER 12

CLARIFYING YOUR LIFE PURPOSE AND VISION

*Living your life to the fullest becomes possible when
you know your life purpose.*
—Jack Canfield and Peter Chee

You are not living to your fullest potential, or contributing to your fullest abilities unless you are living a life of purpose. You have been given clues to your purpose throughout your life. One set of clues is your own completely unique gifts, talents, interests, strengths, and qualities—and you are meant to use them.

The things that bring you the greatest joy in life and make you feel really alive provide another clue to your purpose. So what it boils down to is that you are *meant* to do what brings you joy. Your gifts and talents are *meant* to be your contribution to the world. A life lived with purpose and intention is one that will honor and nourish your spirit on a deep level while simultaneously contributing to the world around you.

Working with clients on discovering and living their life purpose is one of the most fulfilling jobs of a coach. When people are clear about their purpose of being in this world, their life takes on a higher meaning. They can see more clearly the overall direction that they are taking and can align their vision and goals to their purpose.

The process of discovering your life purpose means identifying your talents and strengths, then figuring out the best ways you can use them to add value and serve your family, community, and the world. What we have found is that most schools and business organizations focus on finding and improving people's weaknesses. Very few organizations do an effective job in placing people in the jobs that engage their strengths and talent.

To help your clients identify and utilize their strengths and talents, and to help them eventually discover their life purpose, use the following questions to prepare for a coaching conversation:

Achievers Coaching Questions on Talent

Talent Assessment

1. What do most people say are your greatest strength and greatest talent?

2. What do you think are your greatest strengths and talents?

3. What types of activities make you feel most happy and fulfilled when you do them over and over again? Please list them.

For each of the items listed above, please rate the accuracy of the following 10 statements. Give a score based on a 1 to 5 scale (1 strongly disagree, 5 strongly agree).

1. Other people often tell me that I am gifted, based on how I do this activity.

2. I have won prizes or awards for engaging in this type of activity.

3. I have been very successful at this type of activity.

4. I volunteer for this type of activity.

5. I'm instinctively attracted to this type of activity.

6. I perform this type of activity on a daily basis.

7. I learn very quickly how to perform this type of activity.

8. I look forward to learning more ways of doing this activity better.

9. I constantly look forward to engaging in this type of activity.

10. I feel happy and strong when I do this type of activity.

Talent Confirmation and Engagement

1. Among all of the items assessed above, after adding up the scores for all 10 questions, which ones have the highest total scores that are above 40?

2. Which ones among them would you consider to be your greatest gifts?

3. In what way can you engage more in using these gifts?

4. How can you best develop these talents so you can become one of the best at performing this type of activity?

5. What might be some new ways you can use your talents to create high performance?

6. Is there a unique way you can combine your gifts and talents to create a synergy for producing the best results?

Achievers Coaching Questions for Talent and Life Purpose Discovery

1. When are the times when you feel most alive and joyful?

2. What are your natural gifts?

3. What are your skills and talents?

4. What do you love to do?

5. What are you passionate about?

6. What brings you the greatest joy in life?

7. When do you feel best about yourself?

8. What are your personal strengths and characteristics?

9. What do you enjoy most when interacting with other people?

10. What have others always said that you are good at?

11. What would you change in the world if you could?

12. If you could, how would you use your strengths, talents, and passion to change the world?

13. What difference could you make in your community?

14. What are the common characteristics from all your answers to the above questions? Your life purpose is to use your natural talents to do things that bring you the greatest joy in the service of others.

15. What do you most want to accomplish before you come to the end of your life?

16. Think of a situation when you did something that you really felt you were born to do. How would you describe it?

17. What's stopping you from pursuing your dream in life? What could you do about it?

18. What kind of work would make you jump out of bed every morning and look forward to each day with great eagerness? What most makes you come alive?

19. What have you experienced in your life that brought you great joy and fulfillment, something you'd like to experience more of?

20. From all of the answers generated so far, can you briefly describe how you can best use your talents to serve your community and the world?

21. If you were to put it all together into one sentence, what would the most important part of your life purpose be?

Vision and Work–Life Balance

Many professionals are so caught up with their careers that they find themselves almost totally engrossed in the pursuit of job-related goals. Their work continues to demand more and more of their time— they become workaholics, and their career ends up consuming other important areas of their lives. Weeks and years pass by; one morning, they wake up to a life filled with regrets. We know many well-accomplished executives with big titles, big offices, and big bank accounts who consider themselves bankrupt in life.

In our experience, work–life balance is one of the greatest needs that people have. To avoid regrets, people need to plan and pursue goals in several different and important areas of their lives rather than focusing only their job-related goals.

This presents a great opportunity for you to work with people as they map out a vision that involves key goals in different aspects of life, ensuring work–life balance. Begin by identifying areas in which people are progressing well and areas where they need improvement. Then come up with action steps and schedules to put these steps into practice. Keep your clients accountable for doing the things that are important in their life that for some reason they keep procrastinating.

Achievers Coaching Questions for Vision and Work–Life Balance

1. What's your ideal vision of what you want to achieve in all the different areas of your life? (Work, financial, relationships, health, fun, personal and service.)

2. Considering your desire for work–life balance, what would you most like to experience or achieve in all the different areas of your life? Please write them down as specific goals for each area.

3. On a scale of 1 to 10, how satisfied are you with what you are achieving with each of the goals you listed?

4. Can you elaborate further on each of your scores?

5. What areas of your life are you most satisfied with?

6. What areas of your life are you least satisfied with?

7. What would you like to do about them?

8. What are the goals in your life that are not related to work that you would like to focus on first?

9. What actions will you take to improve your work–life balance? By when will you take them?

> *If you are working on something exciting that you*
> *really care about, you don't have to be pushed.*
> *The vision pulls you.*
> —Steve Jobs

CHAPTER 13

SETTING EFFECTIVE GOALS

A goal properly set is halfway reached.
—Abraham Lincoln

Create an "I Want" List

During the initial process of goal-setting it is fine to have many different possible goals so that you will be able to choose from a range of options the goals that you most want to pursue. You can start by making an "I Want" list. One of the easiest ways to begin clarifying what you truly want is to make a list of 30 things you want to *do*, 30 things you want to *have*, and 30 things you want to *be* before you die. This is a great way to get the ball rolling.

Repeating Questions for a Purpose

Similarly, a powerful technique to unearth your client's wants is to use the following repeating question technique. Ask your client (without making any suggestions), "What do you want?" As soon as he answers, write down his answer and again ask, "What do you want?" Repeat this for five to ten minutes, and continue to jot down his answers. People can find this repetitive questioning technique to be rather humorous (and occasionally, annoying). You'll find the first wants aren't all that profound. In fact, most people usually say, "I want a Mercedes," "I want a big house by the ocean," and so on. However, by the end of the exercise, the deeper, more authentic person begins to speak: "I want people to love me," "I want to express myself," "I want to make a difference," "I want to feel powerful"revealing wants that are true expressions of their core needs and values.

Goal Setting

After articulating their wants and choosing the goals that they most want to work on, it's time to take the goal-setting process further by making sure that their goals are effectively set. A powerful way of more effectively setting goals is to use the SMARTEST mnemonic criteria. These are goals that are:

- Specific
- Measurable
- Attainable
- Relevant
- Time-bound
- Engaging
- Satisfying
- Team-based

Use the following examples to guide you in asking questions that make the goal-setting process more effective.

Achievers Coaching Questions for SMARTEST Goals

Specific

1. How can you define more clearly what you want to accomplish?
2. How can you state your goal in one simple, specific sentence?
3. What exactly do you want to accomplish?
4. Be more specific: What is the final outcome you want?

Measurable

1. How will you and others know when you have reached this goal?

2. How can you quantify and measure the outcome?

3. How can you evaluate the progress you are making toward the goal?

4. Can you state this objective in a way that your progress can be measured?

Attainable

1. To what extent do you have control over the attainment of this goal?

2. Who else might you need to depend on to meet this goal?

3. How certain are you that they will deliver?

5. What other options and backup plans do you have so that you can still achieve the goal if other people don't deliver?

5. Is there anything that could prevent you from reaching this goal?

6. What can you do about it?

7. In what way might you want to revise your goal so that it would depend more on you and less on others to achieve it?

8. Is this goal within your reach? Is it really possible?

Relevant

1. Why is this goal important to you? How is it relevant to you?

2. How is this goal related to the attainment of your other goals?

3. How is this goal relevant to your vision and your life?

4. In what way is this goal aligned with your life purpose?

Time-bound

1. What is the date and time by which you will commit to reaching this goal?

2. When will you start on this project?

3. By when will you finish it?

4. How long will you continue to do this? How frequently?

Engaging

1. Do you feel like you really own this goal, like it's your own "baby"?

2. On a scale of 1 to 10, how motivated are you by this goal?

3. Is this truly your heart's desire?

4. Does your dream compel you to follow it?

Satisfying

1. In what way would attaining this goal bring you satisfaction and joy?

2. How would achieving this goal fulfill your heart's longing?

3. What lasting benefit and satisfaction would you derive from attaining your objective?

4. How will your life be different after attaining this goal?

Team-based

1. Who are the people who could work with you on this dream?

2. How are other people supporting your dream?

3. To what extent is your team capable of helping you to achieve your goal?

As a coach, you may choose to take this SMARTEST process of setting goals a step further by drawing an imaginary line in front of the person being coached. Ask her to take deep breaths and visualize her goal and action plans. Only when she truly is ready to commit does she step across the line. This is a strong symbolic exercise that stays in a person's memory and will impact her commitment toward realizing her goal.

Once effective and clear goals are set, the person is in a better position to visualize, create affirmations and develop concrete action plans. This process also makes it easier to ascertain whether or not tangible progress is being made, and people tend to be much more accountable to achieve their goals.

Create a Breakthrough Goal

In addition to turning every aspect of a client's vision into a measurable goal, and all the quarterly, weekly, and daily goals that he routinely sets, encourage him to set what we call a "breakthrough goal" that would represent a quantum leap for him and his career. Most goals represent incremental improvements in our lives. They are like plays that gain you four yards in the game of football. But what if the client could come out on the first play of the game and throw a 50-yard pass? That would be a quantum leap in his progress. Just as there are plays in football that move you far up the field in one move, there are plays in life that will do the same thing.

They include things such as:

- Losing 60 pounds

- Writing a book

- Publishing an article in *Fortune* magazine

- Getting on *Oprah*

- Winning a gold medal at the Olympics

- Successfully setting up your company in another country

- Getting your masters or doctoral degree

- Getting certified as a professional coach

- Opening your own spa

- Getting elected president of your union or professional association

- Hosting your own radio show

The achievement of that one big goal would change everything. Wouldn't that be a goal worth pursuing with passion? Wouldn't that be something to focus on each day until you achieved it?

If you were an independent sales professional and knew you could get a better territory, a substantial bonus commission, and maybe even a promotion once you landed a certain number of customers, wouldn't you work day and night to achieve that goal?

If you were a stay-at-home mom whose entire lifestyle and finances would change if you earned an extra $1,000 a month through participating in a network marketing company, wouldn't you pursue every possible opportunity until you achieved that goal?

That's what we mean by a breakthrough goal—something that changes your life, brings you new opportunities, gets you in front of the right people, and takes every activity, relationship, or group you're involved in to a higher level.

In our coaching programs we also frequently refer to a breakthrough goal as a goal that would stretch you in the process of achieving it, you would become a different person. In other words, you grow tremendously in the process of pursuing a very ambitious goal that greatly challenges you. You can make the biggest difference for the people you coach when you work with them on creating and realizing their breakthrough goals.

You want to set a goal that's big enough that in the process of achieving it, you become someone worth becoming.
—Jim Rohn

CHAPTER 14

VISUALIZING AND AFFIRMING DESIRED OUTCOMES

The significant problems we face cannot be solved
by the same level of thinking that created them.
—Albert Einstein

All too often we get stuck in an endless loop of reinforcing behavior that keeps us stuck in a constant downward spiral. Our limiting thoughts create images in our minds, and those govern our behavior, which in turn reinforces those limiting thoughts. Imagine thinking that you are going to forget your lines when you give a presentation at work. That thought stimulates a picture of you forgetting a key point. The image creates an experience of fear. The fear clouds your clear thinking that makes you forget one of your key points that reinforces your self-talk that you can't speak in front of groups. "See, I knew I would forget what I was going to say. I can't speak in front of groups."

As long as you keep complaining about your present circumstances, your mind will focus on it. By continually talking, thinking, and writing about the way things are, you continually reinforce those same neuro-pathways in your brain that got you to where you are today. To change this cycle, you must focus instead on thinking, talking, and writing about the reality you want to create. You must flood your subconscious mind with thoughts and images of this new reality.

The Power of Affirmations

One way to stretch out of your comfort zone is to bombard your subconscious mind with the new thoughts and images—of a big bank account, a trim and healthy body, exciting work, interesting friends, and memorable vacations. You want to think of all your goals as already complete. A technique you can use to do this is called repeating *affirmations*. An affirmation is a statement that describes a goal in its completed state: for instance, "I am enjoying watching the sunset from the lanai of my beautiful beachfront condo on the Ka'anapali coast of Maui" or "I am celebrating feeling light and alive at my perfect body weight of 125 pounds."

Guidelines for Creating Effective Affirmations

To be effective, your affirmations should be constructed using the following eight guidelines:

1. Start with the words *I am*. The words *I am* are the two most powerful words in the language. The subconscious mind takes any sentence that starts with the words *I am* and interprets it as a command—a directive to make it happen.

2. Use the present tense. Describe what you want as though you already have it, as though it is already accomplished.

   • *Wrong:* I am going to get a new red Porsche 911 Carrera.

   • *Right:* I am enjoying driving my new red Porsche 911 Carrera.

3. State it in the positive. Affirm what you want, not what you don't want. State your affirmations in the positive. The subconscious mind does not hear the word no. This means that the statement "I am no longer afraid of flying" evokes an image of being afraid of flying, while the phrase "I am enjoying the thrill of flying" evokes an image of enjoyment.

- *Wrong:* I am no longer afraid of flying.
- *Right:* I am enjoying the thrill of flying.

4. Keep it brief. Think of your affirmation as an advertising jingle. Act as if each word costs $1,000. It needs to be short enough and memorable enough to be easily remembered.

5. Make it specific. Vague affirmations produce vague results.

   - *Wrong:* I am driving my new red car.
   - *Right:* I am driving my new red Porsche 911 Carrera.

6. Include an action word ending with *-ing.* The active verb adds power to the effect by evoking an image of doing it right now.

   - *Wrong:* I express myself openly and honestly.
   - *Right:* I am confidently expressing myself openly and honestly.

7. Include at least one dynamic emotion or feeling word. Include the emotional state you would be feeling if you had already achieved the goal. Some commonly used words are *enjoying, joyfully, happily, celebrating, proudly, calmly, peacefully, delighted, enthusiastic, lovingly, secure, serenely,* and *triumphant.*

   - *Wrong:* I am maintaining my perfect body weight of 138 pounds.
   - *Right:* I am feeling agile and great at 138! *or* I am proudly looking at my weight of 138 pounds on my scale.

8. Make affirmations for yourself, not others. When you are constructing your affirmations, make them describe your behavior, not the behavior of others.

   - *Wrong:* I am watching Johnny clean up his room.
   - *Right:* I am effectively communicating my needs and desires to Johnny.

A Simple Way to Create Affirmations

1. Visualize what you would like to create. See things just as you would like them to be. Place yourself inside the picture and see things through your eyes. If you want a car, see the world from inside the car as you are driving it.

2. Hear the sounds you would be hearing if you had already achieved your vision.

3. Feel the feeling you want to feel when you have created what you want.

4. Then describe what you are experiencing in a brief statement, including what you are feeling. Start the sentence with the words I am so happy and grateful that I now. ... Make sure it is stated in the present.

5. If necessary, edit your affirmation to make it meet all of the above guidelines.

Work with the people you coach to create their own affirmations and help them put in place support structures that will ensure that they use their affirmations on a regular and consistent basis.

The Power of Visualization

Here are the reasons why it is highly beneficial for you and your clients to use visualization:

1. Visualization activates the creative powers of your subconscious mind.

2. Visualization focuses your brain by programming its reticular activating system (RAS) to notice available resources that were always there but were previously unnoticed.

3. Visualization magnetizes and attracts to you the people, resources, and opportunities you need to achieve your goal.

When you perform any task in real life, researchers have found, your brain uses the same identical processes it would use if you were only vividly visualizing that activity. In other words, your brain sees no difference whatsoever between visualizing something and actually doing it, and in this way you can effectively program your subconscious mind for success.

This principle also applies to learning anything new. Harvard University researchers found that students who visualized in advance performed tasks with nearly 100 percent accuracy, whereas students who didn't visualize achieved only 55 percent accuracy.

Visualization simply makes the brain achieve more. And though none of us were ever taught this in school, sports psychologists and peak performance experts have been popularizing the power of visualization since the 1980s. Many Olympic and professional athletes now employ the power of visualization.

Jack Nicklaus, the legendary golfer with more than 100 tournament victories and over $5.7 million in winnings, once said, "I never hit a shot, not even in practice, without having a very sharp, in-focus picture of it in my head. It's like a color movie. First I 'see' where I want it to finish, nice and white and sitting high on the bright green grass. Then the scene quickly changes, and I 'see' the ball going there: its path, trajectory, and shape, even its behavior on landing. Then there's sort of a fade-out, and the next scene shows me making the kind of swing that will turn the previous images into reality."

How Visualization Works to Enhance Performance

When you visualize your goals as already complete each and every day, for at least 30 days in a row without fail, it creates a conflict in your subconscious mind between what you are visualizing and what you are currently experiencing as your reality. Your subconscious mind then tries to resolve that conflict by turning your current reality into the new, more exciting vision.

This structural conflict, when intensified over time through constant visualization, actually causes three things to happen:

1. It programs your brain's RAS to start letting into your awareness anything that will help you achieve your goals.

2. It activates your subconscious mind to create solutions for getting the goals you want. You'll start waking up in the morning with new ideas. You'll find yourself having ideas in the shower, while you are taking long walks, and while you are driving to work.

3. It creates new levels of motivation. You'll start to notice you are unexpectedly doing things that take you to your goal. All of a sudden, you are raising your hand in class, volunteering to take on new assignments at work, speaking out at staff meetings, asking more directly for what you want, saving money for the things that you want, paying off a credit card debt, or taking more risks in your personal life.

Let's take a closer look at how the RAS works. At any one time, there are about eight million bits of information streaming into your brain—most of which you cannot attend to, nor do you need to. So your brain's RAS filters most of them out, letting into your awareness only those signals that can help you survive and achieve your most important goals.

So how does your RAS know what to let in and what to filter out? It lets in anything that will help you achieve the goals you set and *constantly* visualize and affirm. It also lets in anything that matches your beliefs and images about yourself, others, and the world. That's why it's so important to work on your beliefs.

The RAS is a powerful tool, but it can only look for ways to achieve the exact pictures you give it. Your creative subconscious doesn't think in words—it thinks in pictures. So how does this help your effort to become successful and achieve the life of your dreams?

When you give your brain specific, colorful, and vividly compelling pictures to manifest, it will seek out and capture all the information necessary to bring that picture into reality for you. If you give your mind a $10,000 problem, it will come up with a $10,000 solution. If you give your mind a $1 million problem, it will eventually come up with $1 million solutions.

If you give it pictures of a beautiful home, an adoring spouse, an exciting career and exotic vacations, it will go to work on manifesting those. By contrast, if you are constantly feeding it negative, fearful, and anxious pictures—guess what?—it will manifest those too.

Adding Sounds and Feelings to the Pictures

To multiply the effect many times over, add sound, smells, tastes, and feelings to your pictures. What sounds would you be hearing, what smells would you be smelling, what tastes would you be tasting, and—most importantly—what emotions and bodily sensations would you be feeling if you had already achieved your goal?

If you were imagining your dream house on the beach, you might add in the sound of the surf lapping at the shore outside your home, the sound of your kids playing on the sand, and the sound of your spouse's voice thanking you for being such a good provider.

Then add in the feelings of pride of ownership, satisfaction at having achieved your goal, and the feeling of the sun on your face as you sit on your deck looking out over the ocean at a beautiful sunset.

By far, these emotions are what propel your vision forward. Neuroscientists know that when accompanied by intense emotions, an image of a scene can stay locked in the memory forever.

Backcasting Technique (Ideal Future Technique)

This technique asks your client to visualize their ideal future as if their dream is already realized, and then work backward step by step to where they stand in the present. They would visualize how things were accomplished each step of the way until they arrive back to the present.

When people look at their current reality versus their dream, they often get stuck in the present due to many perceived limitations and roadblocks. This technique helps them to break free from the present inertia so that they can conceptualize effective solutions more fluently and increases their motivation to take action.

The Steps for Backcasting

1. Go to the destination and experience it as fully as possible.

2. Visualize each step of the journey backward. Identify what happened and how things were done each step of the way.

3. Come back to the present moment and discuss practical steps you can take to move forward.

Achievers Coaching Questions for Backcasting

Step 1

1. Relax and continue taking deep breaths. Could you please close your eyes and take yourself into the future? Imagine that you have already achieved your goal. What date and time is it exactly?

2. What do you see? What images come to your mind? Capture it clearly.

3. Can you imagine using all your senses to touch, smell, taste, see, and hear what it is like now that you have achieved your goal?

4. How do you feel now that you have achieved your goal?

Step 2

1. Now that you have experienced what it's like to achieve your goal, can you travel back one step in time, just one month before you achieved your goal? What happened? What did you do?

2. Now take another step back closer to the present. What happened? What did you do?

3. Now imagine clearly using all your senses, each step of the way back to the present. What happened? What did you do?

Step 3

1. Would you like to come back to the present and open your eyes?

2. What did you experience during the whole journey from where you want to be to where you are now?

3. What did you learn from this? What creative steps can you take to get to your goal?

4. Which of these ways are practical and realistic?

5. What will you do? By when?

> *You've got to get up every morning with*
> *determination if you're going to go to bed*
> *with satisfaction.*
> —George Horace Lorimer

CHAPTER 15

PLANNING FOR ACTION AND TAKING MASSIVE ACTION

There is never enough time to do everything, but there is always enough time to do the most important thing.
—Brian Tracy

First Things First

The goal is to stay on schedule and complete the most important item first. In his excellent book *Eat That Frog! 21 Great Ways to Stop Procrastinating and Get More Done in Less Time*, Brian Tracy reveals not just how to conquer procrastination but also how to prioritize and complete all of your action items.

In his unique system, Brian advises goal setters to identify one to five things you must accomplish on any given day. Then pick the one you absolutely must do first. This becomes your biggest and ugliest frog. He then suggests you accomplish that task first—in essence, eat that frog first—and, by so doing, make the rest of your day much, much easier. It's a great strategy.

Unfortunately, most of us leave the biggest and ugliest frog for last, hoping it will go away or somehow become easier. It never does. However, when you accomplish your toughest task early in the day, it sets the tone for the rest of your day. It creates momentum and builds your confidence, both of which will move you nearer and faster to your goal. Help your clients eat their ugliest frogs first so they will tackle the most important things first and make a quick win. In this way they'll gain momentum to reach their dreams sooner.

Plan Your Day the Night Before

One of the most powerful tools high achievers use for breaking down tasks, gaining control over their life, and increasing their productivity is to plan their next day the night before. There are two major reasons why this is such a powerful strategy for success:

1. If you plan your day the night before—making a to-do list and spending a few minutes visualizing exactly how you want the day to go—your subconscious mind will work on these tasks all night long. It will think of creative ways to solve any problem, overcome any obstacle, and achieve your desired outcomes. And, if we can believe some of the newer theories of quantum physics, it will also send out waves of energy that will attract the people and resources to you that you need to help accomplish your goals.

2. By creating your to-do list the night before, you can start your day running. You know exactly what you're going to do and in what order, and you've already pulled together any materials you need. If you have five telephone calls to make, you'll have had them written down in the order you plan to make them, with each phone number next to the person's name and all the support materials at hand. By mid-morning, you'll be way ahead of most people, who waste the first half hour of the day clearing their desk, making lists, finding necessary paperwork—in short, just getting *ready* to work.

Breaking Down Your Goals Using the Mind-Mapping Technique

No matter what kind of goals an individual has, the strategies to achieve them are important. A valuable technique for creating an action plan for the goals is the mind-mapping process. Mind mapping helps people visualize their plans. It starts with a central theme, then branches out to encompass ideas, notes, images, tasks—even hyperlinks and attachments. By presenting ideas in a radial, graphic, nonlinear manner, mind maps encourage a creative approach to planning for action.

The elements of a given mind map are arranged creatively according to the importance of the concepts and are classified into groupings. As a coach, using mind maps can help you to quickly identify and understand the structure of the client's goal, and the way pieces of information fit together to form the action plan. They help us organize and visualize all the information into a big picture, while still capturing the essential details. What is more, they are very easy to review; you can often refresh information in your mind just by glancing at them.

If the person you coach is familiar with and believes in the value of mind mapping, encourage him to draw a mind map of his key goal. It will show, on one landscape sheet of paper, the big picture plus all the essential steps he needs to take to achieve his target. It serves as an effective memory aid and unleashes creative thinking while also using drawings, pictures and colors.

Creative Action Planning Using the Sticky Note Technique

This technique uses sticky notes (example: 3M Post-it notes) to micromap from bigger goals to the smaller parts. The process entails the following steps:

1. Have the client write her main goals on large color-coded sticky notes.

2. Give her smaller sticky notes and ask her, "What will it take to attain your goal?" She will then start to list all of the tasks that she needs to do under each goal. The process continues, and you repeat the question until the two of you have drilled down to the smallest of essential details. Your objective is to make sure that all important things have been considered.

3. Once the list of all the tasks is completed, ask the client to set a deadline to achieve her goal and commit to a goal achievement schedule. Use a different colored ink to mark the time it will take to complete each task on the small sticky notes. The sticky notes are then arranged in sequential order.

The Sticky Note Technique uses a similar strategy to mind mapping in that it helps clients visualize their big picture plans. It starts with a central theme, then branches out to encompass the different tasks needed to accomplish the goals.

This method of presenting ideas will encourage people to approach their task planning in a more innovative manner. Using the sticky notes also gives flexibility when the client needs to update or move certain tasks around as she progresses with her plans. When a task is completed, the notes can also be easily removed. This kind of big-picture-to-detail planning is essential in helping us to organize and visualize all the information and track every important aspect of achieving a goal. You can also do the "sticky note" format on a whiteboard, where clients can see and visualize their goals, or even in their personal notebooks.

Practice the Rule of 5

Ron Scolastico, a wonderful teacher, once told us, "If you would go every day to a very large tree and take five swings at it with a very sharp axe, eventually, no matter how large the tree, it would have to come down." How very simple and how very true! Out of that we developed what we call the Rule of 5. This simply means that every day, we do five specific things that will move our goal toward completion.

Ask questions to assist your clients to come up with the five most important things that they would like to focus on daily to realize their dreams. Then find ways to motivate them to put that into action. Help them stay accountable to establish a habit of disciplined execution.

In closing this chapter we want to provide you with some potentially great questions relating to planning for action and taking massive action.

Achievers Coaching Questions for Getting to Action

First Things First

1. Which is the most important thing that you need to get done first?

2. What are your top three priorities in order to achieve your goals?

3. Which is the most challenging task that you need to do first?

4. Which of these tasks would give you the greatest satisfaction when you complete it?

Action Planning and Breaking Down Bigger Goals

1. What are the necessary action steps you need to take to achieve this objective?

2. How would you break down this big goal into smaller parts so you can start tackling each key task?

3. Could you map out a one-page sketch of the main things that you need to do to achieve your goal and how they are connected to each other?

Rule of 5

What are the five most important things that you need to focus on every day to get you to your goal?

1. What are five action steps you could take tomorrow to move the goal forward?

2. What results would you get if you focused on these five things? Anything else?

3. Is this something you would like to commit to doing? When would you like to start? For how long will you keep up your focus on these five things?

Keeping Score of Progress

1. How will you keep track of your progress toward your goal each step of the way?
2. What would be a good way to keep score of your progress?

3. If you had a scoreboard that would show where you are at any point in time and how far you are from your goal, what would that look like?

4. What value could you gain from having such a scoreboard?

Success is the sum of small consistent efforts,
repeated day in and day out.
—Robert Collier

CHAPTER 16

USING FEEDBACK, LEARNING, AND PERSEVERANCE TO YOUR ADVANTAGE

Winners Never Quit and Quitters Never Win.
—Napoleon Hill

This is the most valuable question you may ever learn.

It's a question that can radically change the quality of your life; a question that can improve the quality of every relationship you are in, every product you produce, every service you deliver, every meeting you conduct, every class you teach, and every transaction you enter into. Here it is:

On a scale of 1 to 10, how would you rate the quality of my/our (performance relationship/service/product) during the last week (two weeks/month/quarter/semester/season)?

Simple, isn't it? But incredibly powerful. It's a question that sooner or later every coach should put to every client they work with.

There are a number of variations on the same question that have served us well over the years. For instance:

On a scale of 1 to 10, how would you rate the meeting we just had? How would you rate me as a manager? Me as a parent? Me as a teacher? This class? This meal? My cooking? Our sex life? This deal? This book?

Any answer less than a 10 gets the follow-up question: What would it take to make it a 10?

The answers to this question and its variations are what provide you with the valuable information you need to help your client determine effective action steps in meeting her or his goals. Knowing that someone is dissatisfied is not enough. Knowing in detail *what will satisfy them* gives you the information needed to create a winning product, service, or relationship. Make it a habit to constantly ask this question of your clients and other people who are important to you. And teach your clients to ask it of their managers, clients, customers, direct reports and so on.

Be Willing to Ask

Most people don't ask for corrective feedback because they are afraid of what they are going to hear. In fact, this is a false fear. The truth is the truth. You are better off knowing it than remaining ignorant of it. Once you know the truth, you can do something about it; you cannot fix what you don't know is broken. You cannot improve your life, your relationships, your game, or your performance without feedback.

The worst part of this avoidance approach to life is that you are the only one who is not in on the secret. Other people who are affected by your problem have usually already told their spouses, their friends, their parents, their business associates, and other potential customers what they are dissatisfied with. Most people would rather complain than take constructive action to solve their problems. In fact, complaining—or at least discussing the problem—can, in itself, be a constructive action. The only problem, of course, is that the critics are complaining to the wrong person. They should be telling you, but they are unwilling to for fear of your reaction. As a result, you are being deprived of the very thing you need to improve your performance, your relationship, your product, your service, your teaching, or your parenting: information about what's gone wrong.

To remedy this you must do two things.

1. First, you must intentionally and actively solicit feedback. Ask your partner, your friends, your colleagues, your boss, your

employees, your clients and other important people. Use the question frequently. Make it a habit to always ask for feedback. "What can I/we do to make this better? What would it take to make it a 10 for you?"

2. Second, you must show appreciation for the feedback. Do not get defensive. Just say, "Thank you for caring enough to share that with me!" If you are truly grateful for the fact that someone took the trouble to talk to you about you and the impact you're making on those around you, you will get a reputation for being open to feedback. Constructive feedback is a gift that helps you and your client to be more effective.

As you read this book, we hope you are beginning to see the value of asking questions—both of yourself and of others. You'll be surprised at how much feedback and information is available to you if you'll just ask.

She Asked Her Way to Success in Three Short Months

One of the best selling weight-loss books ever published was *Thin Thighs in 30 Days* by Wendy Stehling. What's so interesting about it, though, is that it was developed solely using feedback. Stehling worked in an advertising agency but hated her job. She wanted to start her own agency but didn't have the money to do so. She knew she would need about $100,000, so she began asking, "What's the quickest way to raise $100,000?" Sell a book, said the feedback.

She decided if she wrote a book that could sell 100,000 copies in 90 days—and she made $1 per book—she would raise the $100,000 she needed. But what kind of book would 100,000 people want? "Well, what are the best-selling books in America?" she asked. Weight-loss books, said the feedback.

"Yes, but how would I distinguish myself as an expert?" she asked. Ask other women, said the feedback. So she went out to the marketplace and asked, "If you could lose weight in only one part of your body, which part would you choose?" The overwhelming response from women was "my thighs." "When would you want to lose it?" she asked. Around April or May, in time for swimsuit season, said the feedback.

So what did she do? She wrote a book called *Thin Thighs in 30 Days* and released it on April 15. By June, she had her $100,000—all because she asked people what they wanted and responded to the feedback by giving it to them.

Look for Patterns

When you study the feedback you get, you'll start to see a series of patterns. As our friend and consultant Jack Rosenblum likes to say, "If one person tells you you're a horse, they're crazy. If three people tell you you're a horse, there's a conspiracy afoot. If 10 people tell you you're a horse, it's time to buy a saddle." The point is that if several people are telling you the same thing, there is probably some truth in it. Why resist it? You may think you get to be right, but the question you have to ask yourself is *Would I rather be right or be happy? Would I rather be right or be successful?*

We have a friend who would rather be right than be happy and successful. He got angry with anyone who tried to give him feedback. "Don't you talk to me that way, young lady!" "Don't tell me how to run my business." "This is my business and I'll run it the way I want to." "I don't give a hoot what you think." He was a "my way or the highway" person. He wasn't interested in anyone else's opinion or feedback. In the process, he alienated his wife, his two daughters, his clients, and all of his employees. He ended up with two divorces, kids who didn't want to speak to him, and two bankrupt businesses. But he was "right." So be it, but was it really worth it? Don't let yourself or your clients get caught in this trap. It is a dead-end street.

What feedback have you been receiving from your clients, family, friends, coworkers, boss, partners, vendors, and your body that you need to pay more attention to? Are there any patterns that stand out? Make a list, and next to each item, write an action step you can take to get back on course. Recommend this same method to the people you coach to help them thrive on feedback.

Learning

One of the most valuable ways that you can support your clients for their long-term well-being is to help them establish a habit of continuous learning and constant, never-ending improvement. As you progress in your coaching journey with them, you want to ensure that they capture the learning derived from the coaching experience so that by the time the coaching journey has ended, they will be much more capable and empowered to lead and help themselves in the future. Ask them great questions that enable them to enhance their learning and also to seek out people that they can learn from to keep getting better.

Achievers Coaching Questions on Learning

1. What are the key things that you have learned from today's coaching session?

2. What was the most important point that you picked up from the feedback you received?

3. How can you do better next time based on what you have learned from this experience?

4. What's the main teaching you picked up from here that you would like to share with others?

5. Anthony Robbins once said that success leaves clues. How can you use this idea by seeking out and learning from people who have already succeeded in doing what you aim to do?

6. Who could you seek to learn from so that you can make a quantum leap in your progress? When will you do that?

7. Make a summary of your key insights from our coaching so you can use it to your advantage in the future. What would this look like? What learning discoveries have you made so far?

8. Moving forward, after we complete our coaching sessions, how can you make use of what you have learned here to manage yourself even better?

Perseverance

Thomas Edison, one of the world's greatest inventors, believed that "many of life's failures are people who did not realize how close they were to success when they gave up." When people asked him how he managed to invent a workable lightbulb, he pointed to his more than 2,000 failures. When they asked for the connection between those failures and his eventual success, his reply was that each of the 2,000 failed attempts was a step on his road to success.

Many people tend to give up on their dream when the going gets tough; this is when they need support from a great coach. You provide tremendous value to the people you coach when you are able to help them sustain their efforts and enable them to stay committed to their dreams.

Achievers Coaching Questions on Perseverance

1. If this dream is very important and means a lot to you, what will you do to ensure that you persevere to the end?

2. What makes it worthwhile for you to maintain your efforts until you fulfill your objective?

3. You have tried many times and have yet to accomplish this task and complete this goal. Is this something that you are still committed to? How important is it for you?

4. How can other people help you to sustain this journey until your goal is accomplished?

5. What would it take for you to press on until this dream is fulfilled?

6. Napoleon Hill once said that winners never quit and quitters never win. In what way is this statement relevant to you?

Effort only fully releases its reward after
a person refuses to quit.
—Napoleon Hill

CHAPTER 17

USING THE LAW OF ATTRACTION AND CELEBRATING SUCCESS

The person who sends positive thoughts activates the world around him positively and draws back to him positive results.
—Norman Vincent Peale

Activating the Law of Attraction

The essence of applying the Law of Attraction is to think, imagine, feel, act, and focus on what you want, and attract more of that into your life.

Here's how it works; like attracts like. If you are feeling excited, enthusiastic, passionate, happy, joyful, appreciative, or abundant, then you are sending out positive energy. On the other hand, if you are feeling bored, anxious, stressed out, angry, ungrateful, or resentful, you are sending out negative energy. The universe through the Law of Attraction will respond to both these vibrations. It responds to whatever energy you are creating, and gives you more of the same. You get back more of what you put out there. Whatever you are thinking and feeling at any given time is your request to the universe for the same kind of energy.

Because your energy vibrations will attract energy back to you of the same frequencies you're emitting, you need to make sure that you are continually sending out energy, thoughts, and feelings that resonate with what you want to be, do, and experience. Your energy frequencies need to be in tune with what you want to attract in your life. If love and joy are what you want to attract, then the emotional energy of love and joy are what you want to create.

It's like transmitting and receiving radio waves. Your frequency has to match the frequency of what you want to receive. You can't close your eyes, spin your FM dial, and expect to land on the station you're looking for. It just won't happen. Your energy has to synchronize with, or match the energy frequency of the sender. So you have to keep your vibration tuned to a positive frequency in order to attract positive energy back to you.

You are like a living magnet; you literally attract the things, people, ideas, and circumstances that vibrate and resonate at the same frequency as you do. Your energy field changes constantly, based on your thoughts and feelings. The universe acts like a mirror, reflecting the energy that you are projecting. The stronger and more intense your thoughts and emotions are, the greater the magnetic pull becomes.

Language and Thought

When Mother Teresa was asked if she would go to an antiwar rally, she replied, "No, but when you have a rally for peace, I will gladly attend." She was applying the Law of Attraction. She knew that if what we want is peace, then we should use the language of peace and focus on that. Focusing on fighting against war would attract more war, and that was not what she wanted. Mother Teresa was able to impact the world with her gift of love and compassion, and she attracted a lot of that into her life.

As a coach you need to be constantly aware that language is the vehicle of thought. Many people use language that reflects things that they don't want; over time it becomes a habit, and their thought processes follow suit. What people think about constantly ultimately translates to their emotions. Later, people wonder why their actions seem to also take the same undesired direction.

When we coach people we also want to ask the right questions to attract what people want and constantly encourage them to use language and thought patterns that activate the Law of Attraction. We can all consciously make a choice to either use language that attracts what we don't want or language that attracts what we do want.

Language that attracts what you don't want	Language that attracts what you do want
1. Don't slam the door; it's very rude when you to do that.	1. Would you please close the door quietly and gently.
2. I don't like feeling revengeful and unhappy.	2. I would love to be in a forgiving and joyful state.
3. Don't be late.	3. See you on time.
4. I hate it when you are so ungrateful.	4. I love it when you show your gratitude.
5. Why were you so unkind to her?	5. How could you be more kind to her?
6. I don't want to get hurt.	6. I want to stay safe and healthy.
7. I detest being in debt.	7. I want financial freedom.

Table 17-1 **The Power of Language**

Mantra Technique

Another simple but effective way of igniting the Law of Attraction is to help your clients create a mantra. Let them repeat that continuously until they create a new habit of focusing on what they want. They can also create a mantra from their favorite song, recited during certain times of the day or recorded on their mobile phone so it plays continuously when their phone rings.

Coaches help people find their own creative ways of how they want to be reminded and supported to ensure that they use their mantra continuously until new habits are established.

We are pleased to share with you some of the mantras that have been used effectively by the people that we had the opportunity of coaching. The positive results that we see from helping people change their thought patterns and focus on what they want continue to amaze us.

1. Opportunities always come to me and I give thanks.

2. I love myself, I love others, I love what I do, and I love Life!

3. I am living a healthy, happy, and successful life.

4. I am always joyful and loving.

5. I am a magnet to wealth and abundance, and I share that with others.

6. I am so grateful for my loving family and team members.

It would be highly beneficial for you to practice using various questioning techniques that help your clients utilize the powerful Law of Attraction more effectively.

Achievers Coaching Questions for The Law Of Attraction

1. I believe you know about the Law of Attraction—focusing on what you want and attracting more of that. How could you rephrase your statement to take advantage of this law?

2. If you reword this in a way so that it focuses on what you want rather that what you don't want, how would that sound?

3. Instead of using the words "I don't want to get hurt," which is what you don't want, how can you replace this with positive words that reflect what you want?

4. What kind of thoughts, imagery, feelings, and actions can you focus on to get you what you really want?

5. Would you write down and then share with me three things you feel most grateful for in your life?

6. What are you thankful for?

7. What kind of people and opportunities would you like to attract? What thoughts and actions are needed for you to do that?

8. What can you focus on in your life that would evoke feelings of gratitude and joy?

9. You mentioned that you don't want to get hurt. How can you rephrase this to reflect what you want? (Note: you can ask many variations of this question using different words.)

10. I heard you describe how terrible things have been; how about describing what you would really prefer?

11. Andrew Matthews once said, "Look for reasons to be unhappy and you will find them, look for reasons to be happy and you will find them. You find what you look for." What reasons do you have in your life (at work) to be happy?

12. What could you do to create more positive thoughts and happy feelings?

13. What things will you do to create more good feelings for yourself?

14. What can you do to establish the habit of focusing your thoughts, feelings, and actions on what you want instead of on what you don't want?

15. An example of a mantra you could use could be "Opportunities always come to me, and I give thanks." What might your affirmation or mantra sound like?

16. How would you like to use this affirmation or mantra to activate the Law of Attraction?

Your Ego States

Inside all of us are three distinct and totally separate ego states that work in concert to make up our unique personality. We have an adult ego, a parentlike ego, and a childlike ego that act much the same way adults, parents and children do in real life.

Your adult ego state is the rational part of yourself. It gathers data and makes logical decisions devoid of emotion. It plans your schedule, balances your checkbook, figures out your taxes, and determines when to rotate your tires. Your parentlike ego tells you to tie your shoes, brush your teeth, eat your vegetables, do your homework, exercise, meet your deadlines and finish your projects. It is also your inner critic—the part that judges you when you don't live up to its standards. But it's also the nurturing part of you that makes sure you're protected, taken care of, and provided for. It is also the part that validates, appreciates, and acknowledges you for doing a good job.

Your childlike ego, on the other hand, does what all children do—it whines, begs for attention, craves, hugs, and acts out when it doesn't get its needs met. As we go through life, it's almost as if we have a three-year old holding on to us who's constantly asking, "Why are we sitting at this desk? Why aren't we having more fun? Why am I still up at three in the morning? Why am I reading this boring report?"

The Importance of Rewards

As the parent of this "inner child," one of your most important tasks is to engage it and reward it for behaving itself while you get your work done. If you had a three-year old in real life, you might say, "Mommy has to finish this proposal in the next 20 minutes. But after Mommy's done, we'll go for an ice cream or play a video game." Your real-life three-year old might answer, "Okay; I'll be good because I know I'm going to get something good at the end of it."

Well, not surprisingly, your inner child is no different. When you ask it to be still, let you finish your work, stay up late, and so on, it will behave as long as it knows there's a reward at the end of the behaving. At some point, it needs to know it will get to read a novel, go to the movies, play with a friend, listen to music, go dancing, let loose, eat out, get a new "toy," or take a vacation.

A big part of creating more success in your life is rewarding yourself when you succeed. In reality, rewarding yourself for your successes keeps your inner child happy and compliant the next time it must behave. It knows it can trust you to eventually deliver on your promises. Whatever works for you also applies to other human beings and the people whom you coach, so help your clients plan and take action on different ways to reward themselves when they achieve something worthwhile.

A Sense of Accomplishment

Another reason to celebrate your successes is because you don't feel complete until you've been acknowledged. Recognition gives you a sense of accomplishment. If you spend weeks producing a report and your boss doesn't acknowledge it, you feel incomplete. If you send someone a gift and get no acknowledgment, there's this little feeling taking up attention units inside of your mind. Your mind needs to complete the cycle.

Of course, even more important than feeling complete is that the simple, enjoyable act of acknowledging and rewarding our successes causes our subconscious mind to say, "Hey, succeeding is cool! Everytime we produce a success, we get to do something fun, buy ourselves something we want, or go some place nice. Let's have more of these successes, so we can go out to play."

Rewarding yourself for your wins powerfully reinforces your subconscious mind's desire to want to work harder for you. It's just basic human nature.

As coaches we need to constantly encourage our clients to celebrate their success and rejoice with them when they make significant progress toward their goals. The following questions provide you with some useful examples of what to ask.

Achievers Coaching Questions for Celebrating Success

1. How and when do you plan to reward yourself?

2. What would be a really happy and fun thing to do when you achieve this?

3. What are some of the best ways of motivating yourself so that you can accomplish even more?

4. As you complete each significant step of the goal how could you reward your "inner child"? When would you do that?

5. How will you celebrate your achievements?

6. Who are the people that will celebrate with you?

7. What would be some of your most meaningful achievements so far?

8. Congratulations! How would you like to celebrate your success?

9. With all the achievements made so far, how do you feel?

10. What benefits have you enjoyed since achieving the goals?

11. How do you intend to appreciate yourself and the people who have helped you realize this dream?

Success is a journey and there are moments when we stop along the way to "refuel" before going farther. For example, if your client is writing a book over 10 months and the book has four parts, help your client to decide how to celebrate when each of the four parts of the book are completed. She'll probably want to have an even bigger celebration when the book is published.

When people have big goals to achieve, we work with them to break down their goals to smaller parts. When significant subgoals are achieved, we encourage them to celebrate, reward themselves, and show gratitude to the people who have supported them. This helps them build up momentum to achieve even more success. When we fully experience the positive power of gratitude we are working in alignment with and harnessing the incredible power of the Law of Attraction.

The essence of the Law of Attraction is to think,
imagine, feel, act and focus on what you want
positively and attract more of that into your life.
—Jack Canfield and Peter Chee

CHAPTER 18

MAKING THE IMPOSSIBLE DREAM POSSIBLE

To dream the impossible dream and to make the impossible dream possible is to experience the ultimate greatness of coaching.
—Jack Canfield and Peter Chee

People have dreams they want to fulfill in their lives, but for many, their dreams remain just dreams. For some people, their dreams seem like an illusion because they keep going around in circles, not knowing clearly enough what they really want and what they need to do to fulfill those dreams. Some people lack the self-confidence and drive to achieve their dreams, and they face external roadblocks that make them doubt they will ever realize their dreams.

This is where you as a coach can make a huge difference in people's lives. Their dreams don't have to remain just visions. When they have a great coach to work with them, those dreams can become reality. Coaching works best by focusing people on the positive emotional attractors of goals and dreams rather than on negative emotional attractors such as correcting what is wrong in people.

In the process of focusing on goals and dreams as the main theme in coaching, people are more willing to deal with the roadblocks and problems that stand in the way of achieving their passionate goals. People will change when they are ready and willing and when they have a strong enough motivation to do so. Remember that effective coaching takes place in the domain of achievement, not in the domain of therapy. The people whom you coach do not need to be fixed or coerced to change. They simply need to reconnect with their most heartfelt dreams and passions and align their daily actions with them.

A CEO of a multinational corporation once asked us to coach one of his senior managers in order to "deal with her mistakes and short-comings." When she discovered these had been our instructions, she became extremely resistant to coaching. However, when we shifted the focus of the coaching to the goals and dreams that she wanted to achieve, she opened up and became excited about coaching. Focusing on her strengths and her dreams rather than her mistakes and her shortcomings, she began to flourish, and her problems began to clear up. In fact, after only 18 months of coaching she was able to realize her dream of becoming the vice president of marketing.

Through our many years of experience in coaching, we have seen countless lives change for the better. People who were once unhappy became joyful, poor leaders turned into great leaders, destructive habits were replaced with empowering habits, lives of emptiness transformed into lives of fulfillment, and much, much more.

We have also witnessed whole organizations turn around, creating a culture of coaching and leadership excellence. Leaders who are effective coaches are able to fulfill their three key responsibilities, which are to establish good relationships, ensure performance, and grow their people to enable sustainable growth. In addition to transforming people and organizations, we believe that with coaching we can also impact our community at large and make the world a much better place.

Coaching is the ultimate self-development and growth experience. It's about helping people to grow and develop as human beings and experience greater fulfillment. It's about expanding people's capacity to produce extraordinary results and to make their impossible dreams possible. We wish you much joy, love, and abundance in your exciting journey to becoming the best coach you can possibly be.

INDEX

value of, 70–71

why type questions in, 73

work-life balance through, 223–224

Attainable goals, 227

Authentic rapport, 39–43, 39

Avoidance approach, 248

Awareness, xviii, 99–112

B

Backcasting, 237–239

Balance, work-life, 222–224

Baruch, Bernard, 78

Behavior, changing to change outcomes, 200–207

Being present, xviii, 83–86

Believing in human potential, 3–8

Bell, Alexander G., 54

Benefits derived from coaching, 29–32

Big picture thinking, 166

Blanchard, Ken, 14, 99

Blink (Gladwell), 96

Bombarding questions, 75

Bottom-lining, 120–122

Boyatzis, Richard, 9

Breakdowns, 144

Breakthrough goals, 229–230, 229

Breakthroughs, 122, 144, 229–230

Bringing out the best in others, xviii, 13–17

Broad-based questions, 68

Bruner, Pamela, 217

Buffet, Warren, 122

Burley-Allen, Madelyn, 93

Buscaglia, Leo, 44

Buy-in, xviii, 118

questions that build, 56–60, 56

C

Calling in life, 8. See also Fulfillment

Canfield, Jack, xiii–xiv, xv, 17, 21, 29, 33, 34, 38, 56, 60, 64, 89, 107, 112, 113, 118, 123, 127, 131, 132, 137, 142, 150, 159, 198, 217, 219, 260, 261

Caring, xviii, 44–46

Carnegie, Dale, 41

Carver, George Washington, 199

Celebrating success, xix, 195, 253–260

Ceran, C. W., 119

Chace, Jonathon, 90–91

Chaleff, Ira, 95

Challenges, xviii, 22–28

Chan, Jackie, 200

Change, resistance to, 14

Changing behavior to change outcomes, 200–207

Chee, Peter, xiv–xv, 17, 21, 29, 33, 34, 38, 56, 60, 64, 82, 89, 107, 112, 113, 118, 123, 127, 131, 132, 137, 142, 150, 159, 219, 260, 261

Chee, Thomas, xiv–xv

Cheong, Angelina, 127

Chicken Soup for the Soul (Canfield/ Hansen), xiv, 86

Childre, Doc, 44

Churchill, Winston, 79

Clarifying purpose and vision, xix, 195, 219–224

Clarity in questioning, 68–69

Client, xv–xvi

Close-ended questions, 67, 72

ABOUT THE AUTHORS

Jack Canfield

As the beloved originator of the Chicken Soup for the Soul series, Jack Canfield fostered the emergence of inspirational anthologies as a genre, and watched it grow to a billion dollar market. As the driving force behind the development and delivery of over 500 million books in print through the Chicken Soup for the Soul franchise, Jack Canfield is uniquely qualified to talk about success. Behind the empire *Time Magazine* called the "publishing phenomenon of the decade" is America's leading expert in creating peak performance for entrepreneurs, corporate leaders, managers, sales professionals, corporate employees and educators. He is a compelling, empowering and compassionate coach who for the past 30 years has helped hundreds of thousands of individuals achieve their dreams.

Affectionately known as "America's #1 Success Coach", Jack has studied and reported on what makes successful people different. He knows what motivates them, what drives them, and what inspires them. He brings this critical insight to countless audiences internationally—sharing his success strategies in the media, with companies, universities and professional associations in more than 30 countries around the world.

Jack is a Harvard graduate with a master's degree in psychological education and one of the earliest champions of peak-performance, developing the specific methodology and results-oriented activities to help people take on greater challenges and produce breakthrough results. He's personally taught millions of individuals his unique and modernized formulas for success and has packaged them in his latest book *The Success Principles™: How to Get From Where You Are to Where You Want to Be*. This new self-improvement standard contains 64 powerful principles of success utilized by top achievers from all walks of life and all areas of commerce. *The Success Principles*—and the entire empire of "Principles" books, products, coaching programs and branded retail merchandise—is Mr. Canfield's next offering to the more than 100 million readers he currently reaches worldwide.

Mr. Canfield's other best-selling books *The Power of Focus, The Aladdin Factor, and Dare to Win*, have generated millions of bookstore and Internet sales, and have launched complementary products such as audio programs, video programs, corporate training programs and syndicated columns to enthusiastic corporate buyers. He is founder and chairman of the Canfield Training Group in Santa Barbara, California, which trains entrepreneurs, educators, corporate leaders and motivated individuals how to accelerate the achievement of their personal and professional goals.

Jack is also the former CEO of Chicken Soup for the Soul Enterprises, a billion dollar empire that encompasses licensing, merchandising and publishing activities around the globe. Jack's nationally syndicated newspaper column is read in 150 papers worldwide, and the *Chicken Soup for the Soul* radio shows are syndicated throughout North America. Jack is also a syndicated columnist through King Features Syndicate and is a popular news subject featured not only in major trade publications, but in most major metro newspapers across America and in hundreds more around the globe.

Jack's background includes a BA from Harvard University and he also holds a master's degree in Psychological Education from the University of Massachusetts and a Honorary Doctorate from the University of Santa Monica, Parker College of Chiropractic and St. Ambrose University. Over the past 30 years, he has been a psychotherapist, an educational consultant, trainer, and a leading authority in the areas of self-esteem, achievement motivation and peak performance.

Jack Canfield holds the Guinness World Records for having seven books simultaneously on the *New York Times* Bestseller List—beating out Stephen King. He even holds the Guinness World Records for the largest book signing ever for *Chicken Soup for the Kids Soul*. And he's the only author to have won both the ABBY Award and the Southern California Book Publicist Award in the same year—honoring him as both an outstanding writer and a consummate book marketer.

Jack has also been a featured guest on more than 1,000 radio and television programs in nearly every major market worldwide—many of them on a repeat basis. A sample of these shows include *The Oprah Winfrey Show, 20/20, Inside Edition, The Today Show, Larry King Live, Fox and Friends, The CBS Evening News, The NBC Nightly News, Eye to Eye,* CNN's *Talk Back Live!,* PBS, QVC and many others.

For further details on Dr. Jack Canfield please visit
www.jackcanfield.com

Dr. Peter Chee is president and CEO of ITD World (The Institute of Training and Development), a leading multinational corporation for Human Resource Development. With Dr. Chee's leadership contribution for more than 26 years, ITD World has established itself as a global learning solutions expert.

He works in close partnership with best-selling and award-winning author William J. Rothwell, who has written more than 80 books and Jack Canfield, the world's leading success coach and authority on peak performance who holds the Guinness World Records for the most books on *New York Times* bestseller list with 210 books and 125 million copies in print. Dr. Chee and Dr. Jack Canfield are coauthors of *Coaching for Breakthrough Success* whereas Dr. Chee and Dr. William Rothwell are coauthors of the book entitled *Becoming an Effective Mentoring Leader*. Dr. Chee is also the author of *The 12 Disciplines of Leadership Excellence* with Brian Tracy.

Dr. Chee holds a doctor of business administration degree from the University of South Australia (UniSA), an MSc. in Training and HRM from the University of Leicester, UK, and was also a graduate of the Chartered Institute of Marketing, UK. He holds a certificate in Change Management and Performance Consulting from Pennsylvania State University, ranked the number one university in the United States for postgraduate programs in HRD, and a certificate in Human Performance Improvement (HPI) from The American Society of Training and Development (ASTD). Dr. Chee's doctoral research work lies in the area of motivation and performance management.

As a trainer and developer of leaders and senior executives from more than 80 countries, Dr. Chee's training, coaching, consulting, and research experience resonate in the areas of personal excellence; the success principles—techniques for breakthrough results; leadership and team excellence; coaching and mentoring excellence; work, life, and time management; motivation and performance management; strategic management; sales and marketing; human resource development; and creativity and innovation.

Dr. Chee was the creator of the Coaching Principles (TCP), the Situational Coaching Model (SCM), and Achievers Coaching Techniques (ACT). He is a leading certified trainer for Dr. John C. Maxwell programs (the world's number one leadership guru), Zig Ziglar programs (the world's number one motivation guru), and a certified master trainer for Jack Canfield programs. Dr. Chee is the chief coach and developer of the Certified Coaching and Mentoring Professional (CCMP) program's Advance Certificate in Coaching and Certificate in Performance Coaching, which is accredited and recognized by the International Coaching Federation (ICF).

Dr. Chee is a Baden Powell Fellow of the World Scout Foundation, an honor bestowed by the king of Sweden. He was the president of ARTDO International, a nonprofit professional umbrella body that brings together renowned national HRD bodies, governments, and multinational companies active in HRD work globally. With his commitment to a societal-oriented philosophy, the ITD World's "love thy nation" campaigns have channelled sizable funds to support the needy sections of many national societies.

Dr. Chee has fulfilled many of his dreams. His purpose is to transform leaders and change the world with love for God and people. He lives close to the sea and hills of the beautiful island of Penang with his wife Eunice and daughter Adelina.

To invite Dr. Peter Chee to speak at your events or to train and coach your team, please go to www.itdworld.com/speakers.

For further information on Dr. Peter Chee and his organization, please visit:
www.itdworld.com
www.itdworld.com/drpeterchee.php

ABOUT THE CONTRIBUTING AUTHORS

Angelina Cheong is the Group CEO of WIN World Group. She is a global marketing and branding communications expert with over 20 years of experience. She is a mentor coach and expert in marketing and brand-building strategies. As an accomplished entrepreneur who single-handedly grew four flourishing companies and pioneered a first-of-its-kind global creative hub, Angelina Cheong is a staunch believer of lifelong learning in nurturing innovation.

Angelina holds a double degree in Business Administration (Marketing) and Fine Arts (Advertising) and is currently pursuing her doctorate in Advertising and Marketing (specializing in Branding). Spurred by a love for academics, Angelina took on the role of Instructor at the top-ranking Stamford University in the United States for several years. Since then, she has gone on to teach at several other international and local colleges and universities. Today, she also sits on the advisory board of Kolej Damansara Utama, lectures at the Universiti Sains Malaysia and gives talks and workshops to students.

Through the years, Angelina has garnered numerous international industry awards and accolades including the Birmingham American Awards and the ADDY, a prestigious American Advertising award. In 2007, she won the JCI (Junior Chamber International) Creative Young Entrepreneur Award and represented the country in the international leg of the competition, subsequently ranking among the Top 3 winners worldwide.

Serely Alcaraz is the Country Head, Senior Mentor, Executive Coach and Master Trainer of ITD World Manila, Philippines. She was the president of the Philippine Society for Training and Development (PSTD) and Director of People Management Association of the Philippines (PMAP). Ms. Alcaraz is a vice president of ARTDO International and has been in the human resource and organization development profession for more than twenty years. She is a certified master trainer of programs from Thomas Crane and Jack Canfield, and a certified facilitator for John Maxwell, Dr. Leonard Yong, Dale Carnegie and Development Dimensions International (DDI) programs.

Ms. Alcaraz graduated with double degrees in BS Psychology and BS in Commerce Major in Human Resources Development, under the 3-year Honors Program of St. Scholastica's College, Manila. She also pursued her MBA degree, Master in Management program, at the Asian Institute of Management (AIM).

An advocate of lifelong learning, she had the great opportunity to personally learn from many of the world's greatest gurus including Al Ries, Anthony Robbins, Dr. Barry Posner, Dr. David Ulrich, Dr. Denis Waitley, Dr. Donald J. Ford, Hale Dwoskin, Jack Canfield, Jay Conrad Levinson, Jim Rohn, Dr. John Maxwell, Dr. Kenneth Blanchard, Ram Charan, Robert Tucker, Stephen Covey, T. Harv Eker, Thomas Crane, Tony Buzan, Dr. William Byham, and Dr. William Rothwell.

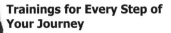

JACKCANFIELD
Maximizing Your Potential

Award Winning Speaker ♦ Master Trainer ♦ Celebrated Thought Leader
Best-selling author of *The Success Principles* and originator
of the beloved *Chicken Soup for the Soul* book series.

Trainings for Every Step of Your Journey

Breakthrough to your next level of success with Jack's help. If you're ready to experience dramatic and permanent changes in your clarity, confidence and ability to achieve your dreams, a live Jack Canfield training is just the ticket!

* **Breakthrough to Success** is a powerful training where you'll master Jack's proven system for success.

* **Train the Trainer** is where Jack personally trains you to become a high-quality, effective success trainer using the *Success Principles*.

* **Private Luxury Retreats** in exotic locations where you work privately with Jack and his team on your vision.

Bring the Power of Jack Canfield to Your Organization

Keynotes ♦ Seminars ♦ Workshops ♦ Customized In-House Training

Topics include:
* *Success Principles*
* *Leadership Principles for Success*
* *7 Ways to Boost Your Business*
* *Training the Trainer*

Self-Study Programs

Jack has a full line of self-study programs, all designed to help you master the *Success Principles* and Law of Attraction to effortlessly create your personal vision of success.

Learn more at: www.JackCanfield.com

"The greatest contribution you can make to the world is to grow in self-awareness, self-realization and the power to manifest your dreams and desires. The next greatest thing you can do is to help others to do the same." —Jack Canfield

---

Join the Success Principles Team!
Get your <u>FREE Training Kit</u> including these powerful tools:

▶ **FREE Success Principles Instructor's Manual:** Complete with reproducible handouts, forms and the actual words to use when facilitating each of the six lessons Jack's created for you!

▶ **FREE Success Principles Chapters:** Discover Jack's #1 principle for taking complete control over your life.

▶ **FREE Audio Coaching:** Teaching Principles of Success

▶ **PLUS**—You'll receive invitations to Jack's live events, complimentary webinars, special offers and more!

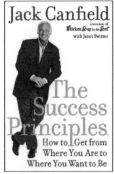

To receive your FREE Success Principles Training Kit
go to: www.JackCanfield.com/CBS

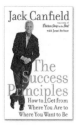

DR. PETER CHEE
Mentor Coach, Speaker, and Trainer

HIGHLIGHTS

- Trained and developed leaders from over 80 countries with over 26 years international experience.
- Author of *Coaching for Breakthrough Success* with Jack Canfield.
- Inventor of the Situational Coaching Model (SCM) The Coaching Principles (TCP) and Achievers Coaching Techniques (ACT).
- Author of *Becoming an Effective Mentoring Leader* with William J. Rothwell who is an award-winning author of over 80 books and professor at Pennsylvania State University.
- Author of *The 12 Disciplines of Leadership Excellence* with Brian Tracy who has written 56 books in 38 languages.
- Doctor of business administration degree from the University of South Australia, MSc. in Training and HRM from the University of Leicester, UK.
- Chief Mentor Coach and developer of the Certified Coaching and Mentoring Professional (CCMP) program.
- President and CEO of ITD World: The Global Learning Solutions Expert.

AREAS OF EXPERTISE

Personal Excellence & The Success Principles-Techniques for Breakthrough Results, Coaching & Mentoring Excellence, Leadership & Team Excellence, Motivation & Performance Management, Work, Life and Time Management

ITD**WORLD**
The Global Learning Solutions Expert

COACHES, MENTORS & SPEAKERS BUREAU
ENRICHING YOU WITH OUTSTANDING RESULTS

AT ITD WORLD WE ENSURE THAT YOUR NEEDS AND OBJECTIVES ARE MATCHED WITH THE BEST RESOURCE PERSON

We have over 238 programs and more than 100 dedicated mega gurus, top international resource persons, trainers, speakers, coaches, mentors and consultants from around the world and many of them are featured on this site:

www.itdworld.com/speakers
www.itdworld.com/coachesmentors

CERTIFIED COACHING & MENTORING PROFESSIONAL (CCMP) PROGRAM

with

Certificate in Performance Coaching
Certificate in Advanced Coaching and Mentoring

" The CCMP is one of the only truly international courses in Asia that is recognized and approved by ICF (International Coach Federation) the world's leading professional non-profit body for coaching. Mentoring, coaching and growing people is one of the most fulfilling and rewarding work of a lifetime

- William J. Rothwell Ph.D "

PROGRAM MAP

THE 3 PHASES

Phase 1
Course 1 & 2: 4 days + Assignments

Phase 2
Course 3 & 4: 5 days + Assignments

Phase 3
Coaching & Mentoring Action Project: 120 days + Conformance to Professional Ethics and Continuous Professional Development (CPD)

THE 3 AWARDS

CERTIFICATE IN PERFORMANCE COACHING

CERTIFICATE IN ADVANCED COACHING AND MENTORING

CERTIFIED COACHING & MENTORING PROFESSIONAL (CCMP)

WHAT MAKES THE CCMP PROGRAM OUTSTANDING?

- ✔ Brings together program intellect and design from the world's top authorities in coaching, mentoring and peak performance: Dr. William Rothwell, Dr. Jack Canfield, Dr. Peter Chee, and Thomas G Crane.
- ✔ The CCMP is recognized and approved by ICF (International Coach Federation), the world's leading professional non-profit professional body for coaching.
- ✔ Uses training, coaching, mentoring, action and experiential learning all in one comprehensive results-based learning solution.

- ✔ Includes cutting-edge tools, learning materials and best-selling books to support effective learning, application, and for ongoing research.
- ✔ A continuous learning intervention over 5 months that leads to professional mastery of coaching and mentoring. Delivered by the most experienced and competent facilitators and trainers.
- ✔ Learning support provided by a mentor coach throughout the action learning project phase.
- ✔ Comprehensive and effective assessment of each participant to demonstrate attainment of bottom-line results from coaching and mentoring.

For full details please go to: http://www.itdworld.com/CCMP.php

ITD WORLD
The Global Learning Solutions Expert

ISO 9001 Registered
Global Provision of Corporate Training and Development
Institute of Training and Development's HQ
Penang, Malaysia

www.itdworld.com

ACSTH
Approved Coach Specific Training Hours
International Coach Federation

ICF
International Coach Federation